W9-AVS-408

Meanings of the Market

EXPLORATIONS IN ANTHROPOLOGY
A University College London Series

Series Editors: Barbara Bender, John Gledhill and Bruce Kapferer

Thomas C. Patterson, *The Inca Empire: The Formation and Disintegration of a Pre-Capitalist State*

Max and Eleanor Rimoldi, *Hahalis and the Labour of Love: A Social Movement on Buka Island*

Pnina Werbner, *The Migration Process: Capital, Gifts and Offerings among Pakistanis in Britain*

Joel S. Kahn, *Constituting the Minangkabau: Peasants, Culture, and Modernity in Colonial Indonesia*

Gisli Pálsson, *Beyond Boundaries: Understanding, Translation and Anthropological Discourse*

Stephen Nugent, *Amazonian Caboclo Society*

Barbara Bender, *Landscape: Politics and Perspectives*

Christopher Tilley (ed.), *Interpretative Archaeology*

Ernest S. Burch Jr and Linda J. Ellanna (eds), *Key Issues in Hunter-Gatherer Research*

Daniel Miller, *Modernity – An Ethnographic Approach: Dualism and Mass Consumption in Trinidad*

Robert Pool, *Dialogue and the Interpretation of Illness: Conversations in a Cameroon Village*

Cécile Barraud, Daniel de Coppet, André Iteanu and Raymond Jamous (eds), *Of Relations and the Dead: Four Societies Viewed from the Angle of their Exchanges*

Christopher Tilley, *A Phenomenology of Landscape: Places, Paths and Monuments*

Victoria Goddard, Josep Llobera and Cris Shore (eds), *The Anthropology of Europe: Identity and Boundaries in Conflict*

Pat Caplan (ed.), *Understanding Disputes: The Politics of Argument*

Daniel de Coppet and André Iteanu (ed.), *Society and Cosmos: Their Interrelations or Their Coalescence in Melanesia*

Alisdair Rogers and Steven Vertovec (eds), *The Urban Context: Ethnicity, Social Networks and situational Analysis*

Saskia Kersenboom, *Word, Sound, Image: The Life of the Tamil Text*

Daniel de Coppet and André Iteanu (eds), *Cosmos and Society in Oceania*

Roy Ellen and Katsuyoshi Fukui, *Redefining Nature: Ecology, Culture and Domestication*

William Washabaugh, *Flamenco: Passion, Politics and Popular Culture*

Bernard Juillerat, *Children of the Blood: Society, Reproduction and Imaginary Representations in New Guinea*

Karsten Paerregaard, *Linking Separate Worlds: Urban Migrants and Rural Lives in Peru*

Nicole Rodriguez Toulis, *Believing Identity: Pentecostalism and the Mediation of Jamaican Ethnicity and Gender in England*

Jerome R. Mintz, *Carnival Song and Society: Gossip, Sexuality and Creativity in Andalusia*

Neil Jarman, *Parading Culture, Parades and Visual Displays in Northern Ireland*

Gary Armstrong and Richard Giulianotti, *Entering the Field: Perspectives on World Football*

Meanings of the Market

The Free Market in Western Culture

**Edited by
James G. Carrier**

Oxford • New York

First published in 1997 by
Berg
Editorial offices:
150 Cowley Road, Oxford, OX4 1JJ, UK
70 Washington Square South, New York, NY 10012, USA

Berg is an imprint of Oxford International Publishers Ltd.

Library of Congress Cataloging-in-Publication Data

A catalogue record for this book is available from the Library of
Congress.

British Library Cataloguing-in-Publication Data

A catalogue record for this book is available from the British Library.

ISBN 1 85973 144 9 (Cloth)
      1 85973 149 X (Paper)

Typeset by JS Typesetting, Wellingborough, Northants.
Printed and bound in Great Britain by
Biddles Ltd, Guildford and King's Lynn

Contents

Preface

The idea of economy is an invention of western civilization
(Hart 1990: 138).

This collection is about economy, but it is not economics; it is about
a phenomenon that is global, but equally rooted in the United
States and Britain; it is by anthropologists, but is not distinctly
anthropological. Its concern is the idea of the Free Market.

Because it is about the Market, it is about economy. However,
'the Market' is not what people do and think and how they interact
when they buy and sell, give and take. Instead, it is a conception
people have about an idealised form of buying and selling. This
conception is important. It is invoked, implicitly or explicitly, when
Americans debate the wisdom of the North American Free Trade
Agreement, the balance of trade with Japan or the General
Agreement on Trade and Tariffs. Likewise, it is invoked when the
British debate selling state-owned industries or the Common
Market or labour legislation. These debates concern many issues
and reflect many interests. However, running through them, on
one side or another, is a claim and a belief that a certain sort of
buying and selling benefits all those involved economically,
politically, socially and even morally. And that that is the sort of
buying and selling associated with the Free Market.

The idea of the Market has many roots, but its most important
historical ones are lodged in British soil, in the writings of political
economists in Edinburgh in the eighteenth century and in Manchester in the nineteenth. However, in popular consciousness the
idea flourishes best in the United States, with its long traditions
of that secular, acquisitive individualism and concern with equality
of process rather than of outcome that form part of the Market.
America is, after all, the land where the streets have been paved
with gold, where the prairies were open to those who would settle
them, where equality of opportunity is a national goal. Louis

Dumont (1977) may be correct when he argues that economy has become central to Western people's conceptions of themselves. But in America, it is a certain kind of economy, the economy of the Free Market, a concept that reverberates in most areas of American life and thought.

But while America may be the land of the Market, with the growth of American power since the Second World War the Market has become more global. One way this has occurred is through the spread of financial institutions that put pressure on governments and firms to conform to the Market model of how they ought to operate. Foreign exchange and international bond markets are obvious examples of these institutions. Less obvious examples are bodies that promulgate international standards for accounting, banking and stock market regulation and the like. Although many of these institutions and the firms that operate in and through them see themselves as global, it is also true that they are oriented toward the United States. Equally, American government policy has helped put pressure on institutions around the world to conform to the Market model. Sometimes this works indirectly, through bodies dominated by the United States. The World Bank is perhaps the most obvious example (Wade 1996). Often, however, there is direct government action. The North American Free Trade Agreement, which I have mentioned already, is one illustration; another is government pressure on Japan and the Common Market to change their internal policies to make them conform to American standards.

Just as the idea of the Market can spread in many ways, so it can be approached in many ways. The concern in this collection is to treat the idea as a part of Western culture, and to tease out its assumptions and contradictions, powers and limitations. The contributors to this collection are anthropologists, commonly they refer to anthropological literature, the word 'culture' is invoked here. Equally, however, this collection is concerned with history, politics and policy, and academic economics. But this breadth is appropriate in a collection that is oriented not inward toward disciplinary concerns, but outward toward an important element of modern life and thought.

This collection reflects my interest in economy, in the broad, substantive sense of the production and circulation of objects and services. I developed this interest when I was trying to understand

Ponam, a small island society in Papua New Guinea (Carrier and Carrier 1989). I carried this interest with me when I returned to the United States in 1986, and began to investigate changes in the social aspects of the economies of Britain and the United States in the early-modern and modern eras (Carrier 1994). I found my interest sharpening when I went to Britain in 1994, and so confronted more directly the intrusion of Market thought in a society that had a much stronger collectivist tradition than did the United States – a tradition I had experienced when I lived in Britain in the 1970s.

During these migrations my initial concerns have become transformed. What had been a fairly straightforward effort to describe different ways that people in different places give and take became an interest in how anthropologists perceive and mis-perceive the nature of the West and its economy (Carrier 1995). This in turn led to a broader set of questions: How do Westerners understand their economy? What are the manifestations of those understandings? What are the consequences? While I am concerned to a degree with the specialist understandings of professional analysis of Western economy, which is to say with economists and economic historians, my main interest is the common understandings that I see expressed, at times obliquely, in newspaper and magazine articles, public debate and everyday thought and action. This collection is part of an attempt to answer some of those questions.

I realise that it is somewhat disingenuous to try to separate understandings of Western economy held popularly from those produced by economists. The two overlap at too many points, particularly in their fundamental assumptions. Some readers are sure to see this collection as an attack on neo-classical economics. To a degree they are justified in doing so, not least because some of the material here directly addresses aspects of academic economics. However, seeing this collection as really being about that discipline is to miss a more profound point: to the degree that the Market has become important in Western culture, we are all neo-classical economists now.

Common understandings of the economy constitute a huge topic that can be approached in many ways. This collection focuses on one particular model of the economy in Western culture, the Market model, which I describe in the Introduction. Like any cultural model, this one is complex, to some degree contradictory, and the subject of debate and disagreement. It is, however, worth investigating as an element of Western culture in its own right, as one common way people represent aspects of their own economic lives.[1] This model is distinct from, is not reducible to and will not to be assessed here in terms of academic economics. In other words, I do not approach it as some economists do, as a muddled version of real economics, to which it is to be subordinated.

Although I distinguish the Market model from formal economics, and especially neo-classical economics, such a distinction is easier to maintain in theory than in practice. This is illustrated by the differing responses I have received to versions of the Introduction to this collection. I have delivered it as a talk to a number of anthropology departmental seminars in Britain, and audiences generally seemed to think that while it was dealing with topics also dealt with by academic economics, it was ultimately about something else: Margaret Thatcher and Conservative politics. Had I delivered those talks in the United States, the general assumption probably would have been that it was ultimately about Ronald Reagan, George Bush and Newt Gingrich. In addition, three people who are economists or with strong economic backgrounds have read versions of the Introduction. Invariably, they read it as a discussion of academic economics.

In their different and restricted ways, both responses are correct. This project is motivated by the political swing to the right in the 1980s, a shift that was accompanied by a surge of talk about the virtues of the Market and consumer choice. Equally, those readers with backgrounds in economics are right because this collection touches on, and considers alternative understandings of, areas that academic economics has claimed as its own. It is almost impossible to separate fully the Market model and neo-classical economics, so that a consideration of the former looks inevitably like a consideration of the latter. The model contains many elements that resemble neo-classical economics, and many academic economists have written for and spoken to popular audiences in what I, but possibly not they, would see as an effort to shape the Market model. Perhaps more important, however, is the fact that academic economics is an expansive discipline – a point I return to in the Introduction. Its practitioners seek to apply its basic assumptions to areas of life well outside its conventional area of concern, the behaviour of market actors. In effect, then, any consideration of how people think about material decisions, any discussion of how they make those decisions and, indeed, almost any discussion of how people make decisions at all, can be seen as a challenge to economics.

This collection can be seen to challenge economics in another way. With the decay of the older political economy late in the nineteenth century, economics turned increasingly to the formal modelling of abstract economic activities. The discipline, in other words, largely abandoned the description of the economic activities that occurred among and between social units, and pursued instead the strategy used by disciplines like physics, concerned with the formal modelling of abstract processes and relationships. Just as physics has its point masses, frictionless surfaces and pure vacuums, so positive economics has its cost-less transactions, rational actors and perfect knowledge. Economists, understandably enough, sought to become scientists and adopted the rhetoric of science, as Donald McCloskey (1986) has observed. This strategy might be called the Power of Positive Thinking, for economists saw themselves as pursuing a positivist scientific approach. However, economics differs from physics in one way that is particularly important to anthropologists: it is about people, us. Hence, economists face a test physicists do not: do their models make sense to the entities being described? Atoms are not notably self-reflective; they do not seem to care very much what you say about them. People are; they do. By addressing how people think about their economic lives, this collection necessarily, if only implicitly, challenges those who would ignore what people think.

To repeat, this collection is concerned not with economy itself, but with popular representations of it. Should justification be thought necessary for a collection that deals with popular Western representations of the Market, it is this: those representations affect how people in the West understand their world, affect the symbols people invoke to persuade each other, affect how people act in the world, and those representations have these effects because people adopt, espouse and respond to them, not because they are true.

Although this collection comes within the ambit of the general and growing scholarly interest in representation, I am made somewhat uneasy by the prospect of being the editor of a collection on 'representations of the Market'. This is because interest in representation carries at times an air of cultural idealism, of the belief that representations and their associated discourses constitute a realm that 'is potentially unrelated to reality and can be left to float off on its own' (Jameson 1991: 264). This idealism has two aspects. One is a sense that cultural representations live only in a world of representations and need not be, perhaps can not be, linked to material factors and social practices, either as cause or consequence. The other is a sense that we can construe, perhaps should or even must construe, these representations without regard for the degree to which they are distortions or partial renderings of the things they are supposed to represent.

Both of these aspects strike me as a failure on the part of cultural idealists that reflects a presumption of a radical separation of culture and society, and thus a failure to keep in mind that ideas have practical social origins, manifestations and consequences. Letting these origins, manifestations and consequences slip from mind is particularly unfortunate when the representations at issue concern the economy. Representations of the economy have become especially salient over the last ten or fifteen years, and their salience has been profoundly political. As I note in the Introduction, models of the economy have been used to guide and justify government actions in liberal capitalist countries and in formerly Communist ones, not to mention in Third World countries whose governments seek to conform to the strictures of national and international granting and lending agencies, bond traders and commercial banks. In the light of these facts, treating assumptions about the economy in terms of cultural idealism seems positively perverse. To illuminate the Market, then, a concern with culture and representation must be complemented by an awareness that it is linked with how people behave in their economic activities and with the social, economic and political consequences of the Market model.

Particularly since around 1980 there has been a flurry of books by anthropologists on markets and market systems. A jaundiced reader may want to know why yet another is necessary. In answering, I want to locate this book in relation to those, a task that also will help explain its conceptual boundaries.

One such collection is Roger Friedland and A. F. Robertson's *Beyond the Marketplace* (1990 b). Several of their contributors address cultural understandings of the economy and economic processes (most notably Marcus 1990). However, the purpose of that collection is not to analyse 'the market' as a cultural entity.

Rather, the market is an empirical entity, and the goal is to understand the relationship between the market and society more adequately, to see how social, political and economic forces interact. As Friedland and Robertson (1990 *a*: 1) themselves put it, their collection revolves around two distinct, albeit related, questions, 'the pursuit of economic meaning in society and the pursuit of social meaning in the economy'.

Another such work is *Markets and Marketing*, a collection edited by Stuart Plattner (1985). Like the Friedland and Robertson collection, this one takes markets and their related processes to be empirical entities to be described, rather than conceptual categories to be analysed. However, Plattner's collection differs from *Beyond the Marketplace* and from this collection because, reflecting its origins in economic anthropology, its contributors overwhelmingly are concerned with economic activities outside the modern West (the primary exception is Acheson 1985). A concern with events outside the West also characterises the work of two writers with very different theoretical orientations, Stephen Gudeman (1986; Gudeman and Rivera 1991) and Michael Taussig (1977, 1980). Both deal with Latin America, and thus fall outside the geographical focus of this collection. However, their scholarly concerns are not at all distant. Although both describe economic activities, these are not topics of analysis in their own right. Instead, Gudeman and Taussig use these to illustrate and expand upon their main concern, the ways that people think about and understand those activities, their models of economic activities.

The work that this volume most closely approaches is Roy Dilley's (1992 *b*) collection *Contesting Markets*. Like Dilley's, the present work is concerned more with analysing how people conceive of market systems than it is with analysing the operation of those systems themselves or the activities of market actors. However, there are important differences between the two sets of papers. One of Dilley's main concerns is 'the articulation of economic discourses' (Dilley 1992 *a*: 1). Pursuing this interest entails attending to the ways that different sets of people, located beyond or on the edge of the modern West, construe economy, and seeing how those constructions interact with dominant Western ones. Such a concern means that Dilley's work is focused less intensely on those dominant Western constructions than is this one.

As my brief attempts to locate this collection in terms of some of the existing anthropological and sociological work indicate, its purpose is to supplement rather than displace that work. It seeks to provide the beginnings of a description of an important Western, public understanding of the economy, and to identify some of the influences of that understanding on public and private life.

Notes

1. While there is little anthropological work on common Western understandings of the economy, there is work on understandings in societies outside the modern West. Perhaps the most noteworthy of these are by Stephen Gudeman (1986; Gudeman and Rivera 1991), Antonius Robben (1989) and Michael Taussig (1977, 1980).

References

Acheson, James M. 1985. The Social Organization of the Maine Lobster Market. Pp. 105–130 in Stuart Plattner (ed.), *Markets and Marketing*. Monographs in Economic Anthropology, No. 4. Lanham, Md: University Press of America.

Carrier, James G. 1994. *Gifts and Commodities: Exchange and Western Capitalism since 1700*. London: Routledge.

Carrier, James G. 1995. Maussian Occidentalism: Gift and Commodity Systems. Pp. 85–108 in J. Carrier (ed.), *Occidentalism: Images of the West*. Oxford: Clarendon Press.

Carrier, James G., and Achsah H. Carrier 1989. *Wage, Trade, and Exchange in Melanesia: A Manus Society in the Modern State*. Los Angeles: University of California Press.

Dilley, Roy 1992 *a*. Contesting Markets. Pp. 1–34 in R. Dilley (ed.), *Contesting Markets: Analyses of Ideology, Discourse and Practice*. Edinburgh: Edinburgh University Press.

Dilley, Roy (ed.) 1992 *b*. *Contesting Markets: Analyses of Ideology, Discourse and Practice*. Edinburgh: Edinburgh University Press.

Dumont, Louis 1977. *From Mandeville to Marx: The Genesis and Triumph of Economic Ideology*. Chicago: University of Chicago Press.

Friedland, Roger, and A. F. Robertson 1990 *a*. Beyond the Market-place. Pp. 1–49 in R. Friedland and A. F. Robertson (eds), *Beyond the Marketplace: Rethinking Economy and Society*. New York: Aldine de Gruyter.

Friedland, Roger, and A. F. Robertson (eds) 1990 *b*. *Beyond the Marketplace: Rethinking Economy and Society*. New York: Aldine de Gruyter.

Gudeman, Stephen 1986. *Economics as Culture: Models and Metaphors of Livelihood*. London: Routledge & Kegan Paul.

Gudeman, Stephen, and Alberto Rivera 1991. *Conversations in Colombia: The Domestic Economy in Life and Text*. New York: Cambridge University Press.

Hart, Keith 1990. The Idea of Economy: Six Modern Dissenters. Pp. 137–160 in Roger Friedland and A. F. Robertson (eds), *Beyond the Marketplace: Rethinking Economy and Society*. New York: Aldine de Gruyter.

Jameson, Fredric 1991. *Postmodernism, or, The Cultural Logic of Late Capitalism*. Durham, N.C.: Duke University Press.

McCloskey, Donald N. 1986. *The Rhetoric of Economics*. Brighton: Wheatsheaf.

Marcus, George E. 1990. Once More into the Breach between Economic and Cultural Analysis. Pp. 331–352 in Roger Friedland and A. F. Robertson (eds), *Beyond the Marketplace: Rethinking Economy and Society*. New York: Aldine de Gruyter.

Plattner, Stuart (ed.) 1985. *Markets and Marketing*. Monographs in Economic Anthropology, No. 4. Lanham, Md: University Press of America.

Robben, Antonius 1989. *Sons of the Sea Goddess: Economic Practice and Discursive Conflict in Brazil*. New York: Columbia University Press.

Taussig, Michael 1977. The Genesis of Capitalism Amongst a South American Peasantry: Devil's Labor and the Baptism of Money. *Comparative Studies in Society and History* 19: 130–155.

Taussig, Michael 1980. *The Devil and Commodity Fetishism in South America*. Chapel Hill: University of North Carolina Press.

Wade, Robert 1996. Japan, the World Bank, and the Art of Paradigm Maintenance: *The East Asian Miracle* in Political Perspective. *New Left Review* 217: 3–36.

Acknowledgement

This volume has benefited from the encouragement of Fred Damon, of the University of Virginia, who was a commentator at the session at the 1995 meeting of the American Anthropological Association that was devoted to this collection. My own attendance at that session was supported in part by the Special Staff Travel Fund of Durham University and in part by the Department of Anthropology of Durham University. I am grateful for their assistance.

Introduction

> Practical men, who believe themselves to be quite exempt from any intellectual influences, are usually the slaves of some defunct economist. Madmen in authority, who hear voices in the air, are distilling their frenzy from some academic scribbler of a few years back.
>
> John Maynard Keynes, *The General Theory*

The long decade of the 1980s was framed by parallel political events. It began in 1979 with the victory of the Conservatives in Britain, marking clearly a shift to the right in Western political regimes. It ended, less sharply, in the early 1990s with the victory of anti-Communists in Eastern Europe, marking clearly a shift to the right in regimes there. These events frame a period during which the concept of the Market solidified its hold in Western culture. The concept has had a long history in the West, and has been particularly important in the United States, with its fascination with free enterprise and starting your own business (Berthoff 1980). However, it is the case that since around the Second World War the Market had existed primarily as a political icon or a formal economic abstraction. The attraction of the Market was, after all, swamped by the Keynesian consensus that markets definitely were *not* best left alone, and by the belief, held by many, that all people were entitled to minimal standards of living (Morgan and Evans 1993). This consensus faded in the 1970s for a number of reasons, arguably including the very success of that older consensus in generating economic security. During the long 1980s the notion of the Market became as important for understanding the West as *ie* is for understanding Japan or *nif* is for understanding the Kabyle.

One purpose that unites the contributors to this collection is making this central concept seem strange. We can not make it as strange to a Western readership as *ie* or *nif*, but we can try to make it seem somewhat less self-evident. I will begin this process by presenting a brief description of the concept. This is cast in terms

1

as simple as those used by an ethnographer giving a first description of a concept important in an exotic culture about which
the reader knows nothing. Like all such introductory ethnographic
renderings, this brief description of *Market* is not only simple, but
necessarily simplistic, a blunt instrument that cracks open a notion
at the cost of rendering practical possibilities as cultural certainties
and replacing the shading and colour of ambiguity and subtlety
with a monochrome cartoon. However, this rendering will provide
a start in investigating this important cultural symbol, and from
this start the associations, nuances and contradictions can be filled
in. Moreover, and unlike many ethnographic simplifications, the
simplicity of my rendering here is warranted to the degree that it
reflects what many who espouse the model see as one of its
advantages. That is the way that, as the British Market advocate
John O'Sullivan put it, the model 'provides clear, consistent and
above all, simple solutions to the problems thrown up by society
and the economy' (quoted in Cockett 1994: 194).

The cultural model of *Market* rests on certain assumptions that
are far-reaching and that I want to present first in their most
pronounced and idealised form. Perhaps the most basic assumption is that the world consists only of free individuals. The belief
that these individuals are free means that they are the only source
and judge of their desires and that these individuals are not subject
to constraints other than those they accept voluntarily, as in the
constraint accepted by an individual who contracts to deliver a
ton of coking coal to a certain place on a certain day. There is,
consequently, no imperative structure beyond the individual, no
definitive moral framework, no general will. Indeed, there is no
'public' except in the statistical sense of the aggregate of individual
choices and actions. As Alan Haworth (1994: 12) summarises this
view, 'the fully developed market economy is "nothing more than"
(or "reducible to") the sum . . . of its discrete components, the
individual bilateral exchanges which actually take place'.

Associated with this individualism is the assumption that the
reasons why people desire this or that thing are irrelevant. All that
matters is that they want it, with the corollary that they should
have it if they can afford it. The other key assumption is that people
are instrumentally rational. In essence this means that they want
more for less, however difficult that may be to achieve in practice.
When confronted with two things in identical settings that are
identical in all regards but *price*, for instance, people will buy the

cheaper. The cultural justification for this assumption is that *buyers* who pay a lower *price* have more money left with which to buy further things they want, which is good. 'Forcing consumers to pay double for . . . their choice or buy something else, hardly makes them better off' (*Economist* 1995).

The model posits a world that consists only of *buyers* and *sellers*. These may be individuals or organisations, and an actor who is a *buyer* at one time may be a *seller* at another. *Buyers* and *sellers* both want more for less, so that there is inevitably conflict between them. All other things being equal, the *buyer* wants to pay the least money for an item and the *seller* wants to charge the most money for it. The resolution of this conflict favours *buyers* over *sellers*, through the mechanism of *buyer choice*. When *buyers* exercise *choice*, they select among the things offered by *sellers* the one that most satisfies their desires, taking *price* into account. In aggregate the *choices* of individual *buyers* provide information to *sellers* about what *buyers* want at what *price*. Thus *Market* functions as a means of communication between consumers and producers.

The model asserts that anything that restricts the *choice* of *buyers* is bad, and that anything that extends that *choice* is good. This assertion rests on two premises. One is that *choice* is a moral good, for it is the way that *buyers* can get what they want most rationally. The second premiss that supports *buyer choice* rests less on the morality of *choice* than on its consequences. It is that *choice* entails *competition* among *sellers*. *Competition* has two consequences. The first is that *sellers* will innovate, will try to offer new things to *buyers* and so increase the range of *buyer choice*. The second consequence is that *sellers* are induced or obliged to try to increase their *efficiency* (Leibenstein 1980: Chap. 3), which will allow them to sell at a lower *price* than other *sellers*. This benefits the *buyers*, who, remember, want more for less. This nexus of *choice*, *competition* and *efficiency* means that monopolies and cartels among firms, and unions among people selling their labour power, are bad, as are tariffs and subsidies for firms and unemployment benefits for workers.

The individualist orientation of the Market model does not just reflect the micro-economics that has influenced it. In addition, it resonates with a strong thread in British and American thought (see Carrier 1994: 157–166; Robbins 1994: 30–37), one that values individual identity and autonomy, celebrated as freely-chosen difference, and that commonly takes a more populist form. This individualistic orientation accounts for some of the popular support the model has received. For instance, in Britain, Paul Johnson switched his allegiance from the Labour Party to the Tory right publicly in the *Sunday Telegraph* in 1977. The imagery he uses in his statement illustrates the nature and strength of the appeal that can be exerted by the model's individualism.

> One reason why I joined the Labour Party was that I believed it stood by the helpless and persecuted, and by the angular non-conformist who – wrong-headedly perhaps – reserved the right to think for himself. Labour's closed shop legislation represented a historic shift in its doctrinal loyalties, from the beleaguered individual to the grinning triumph of the field-grey regiment (quoted in Cockett 1994: 227).

The attraction of the model's individualism, here cast in the populist imagery of the self-directed non-conformist confronting the field-grey regiments of bureaucratic uniformity, seems to account for the switch to the Tory right of several Labour supporters in the 1970s (see Cockett 1994: Chaps 6, 7). While this populist individualism accounts for some of the support for the model in the United States (see Nash 1979: Chap. 1), the migration of influential people from the left to the right in the United States late in the 1960s and early in the 1970s seems to have resonated with other concerns, especially a dismay at the civil disorder of anti-war and other forms of public protest (Nash 1979: 320–327).

The rightward political shift of the long 1980s was not the only event that made the Market especially visible and important. Another was the growing sense that industrial production is of decreasing significance in Western economies, a sense signalled by books with titles like *The Coming of Post-Industrial Society* (Bell 1983), *The Post-Industrial Society* (Touraine 1971) and *Postindustrial Possibilities* (Block 1990). The industrial production on which the West was said to rely was commercial, and so necessarily entailed market transactions. Even so, the primary cultural image of industrial society was of manufacturing activity within an organisation, rather than buying and selling among organisations and individuals; it was of the factory rather than the shop. The spreading popular sense of the relative decline of industrial production, a decline often facilitated by Market-oriented government policies in the 1980s, has led to a search for new dominant images and foci of attention. These revolve around the Market.

For many of those who are more economically inclined, the decline of manufacturing has meant the rise of services. While internal relations and activities in most service industries resemble those in manufacturing, much of the imagery surrounding services refers to the provision of the service rather than its production. In other words, the imagery pertains to the Market. Among those who still see a place for industrial production in the West, it is commonly argued that Fordism is dead, that manufacturing firms can survive only by becoming flexible organisations that can respond quickly to changing demand. In other words, they can survive only by making themselves much more sensitive to the Market, though interestingly, in practice this has often meant the capital market as much as the market for manufactures (see Sassen 1990).

For many of those who are more anthropologically and sociologically inclined, on the other hand, the decline of manufacturing has meant the elevation of consumption as the key to understanding Western life (e.g. Gabriel and Lang 1995; Miller 1995 *a*; Mort 1986). This is striking in the case of Marshall Sahlins's *Culture and Practical Reason* (1976). Sahlins explicitly rejected the contention that the organisation of production is the key to social and cultural order. Instead, he argued that the cultural interpretation of objects, which is embodied in buyers' demand, is autonomous and crucial for explaining production.[1] Here too, though perhaps less clearly than with the popular rhetoric of service industries, the master image is associated with Market processes and transactions. After all, these are the ways that people get what they consume and are important for shaping how people perceive what they consume. Likewise, as Daniel Miller (1995 *b*) argues, these processes and transactions are crucial causes of the sense of the rupture, distance and reflexivity that he says are central elements of modernity. Indeed, and perhaps paradoxically, they also seem to underlie and summarise much of what some describe as post-modernity, 'the consumption of sheer commodification as a process' (Jameson 1991: x).

In this shift, many academics found themselves speaking of 'consumption' and 'the market' to describe what they had previously spoken of in terms of 'classes' and 'capitalism.' As I argue at length later in this Introduction, this shift, though terminological, has been much more than just terminological. One aspect of this change in terminology is, however, worth noting here. The shift from terms and concepts that revolved around capitalism and its processes and structures to those that revolve around the Market appears to have rendered irrelevant the mass of critical scholarly and polemical literature concerned with capitalism, and with production more broadly. It is hardly contentious to observe that the Market is, after all, the *capitalist* Market, that what is at issue is 'a system of private ownership of the means of production, i.e., . . . a market society, or capitalism' (von Mises 1944: 48). Karl Polanyi (1957 *c*) made this point clearly some time ago, and a few others have tried to repeat it more recently (e.g. McNally 1993). Be that as it may, Bruce Kapferer (pers. comm.) is right when he says that 'the Market' is a bleached 'capitalism': the institutions and relations involved remain the same, but the scholarly and polemical overtones have been washed away, the old arguments and analyses forgotten, the old academic literature jettisoned as inapplicable.

I have described political events and changing perceptions that made the Market more salient in public and scholarly thought than it had been previously. At the same time, these events and others made the notion of the Market more accessible and problematic. For one thing, the very political successes of those who advocate the Market made possible a greater critical scrutiny of the concept. This is because their attempts to implement the Market necessarily entailed turning this abstraction into precise practice, entailed dissolving the concept into a set of concrete institutions, actors and forms of behaviour. The economists and politicians, whether in Eastern Europe or the West, who sought economic liberalisation could not, after all, implement the Market any more than anyone can implement Justice, Liberty or any abstract notion. Instead, they had to settle on and impose specific policies. They had to create specific organisations and specific objects and encourage or oblige people to act in appropriate ways, and they have had to confront the specific corollaries and consequences, intended or not, of what they had done. Whether or not these specificities led to the results that these economists and politicians desired, they made the concept of the Market concrete, and hence more accessible and problematic, than it had been before.

The decade that saw the ascendancy of political regimes that espoused the Market saw another event, less sudden and dramatic than electoral results or the destruction of the Berlin Wall – an event that also, ultimately, made the notion of the Market more problematic. That event was the spreading popular perception of Japan as a country with significant economic power, yet with an economic system that, in important ways, deviated from the Market, a perception that ultimately expanded to become 'East Asia' and what the World Bank (1993) called *The East Asian Miracle*.[2] The Japanese were not only producing automobiles, televisions and a host of other products better and cheaper than Western firms, and they were not only becoming richer than people in many Western countries. In addition, they were doing so in the context of cartels, restrictive trade practices, lifelong employment and collaboration between the state and commercial organisations, all of which restricted the nexus of competition and buyer choice that is a central feature of the model.

In the 1980s, even the casual reader of periodicals like *Business Week*, the *Economist*, *Fortune* and the *Harvard Business Review* frequently came across articles that described, analysed and drew lessons from the relative success of 'Japan', a term that subsumes the organisation and operation of Japanese firms, their relationship with the government and that government's policies and practices regarding trade and industry. Such articles would routinely point out ways that Japan departs from the Market model, and use that departure to assess the desirability of different elements of it, often by posing a series of questions: Is Japan becoming more like the West? Less? Ought we to become more like them? Ought they to become more like us? The changing perception of Japan operated in different ways from the rightward political shift that I have mentioned, and it called forth different political responses. However, the concern to understand and the attempt to counter or emulate Japanese success produced a similar result, for it also led people to unpack the abstract notion of the Market into specific sorts of institutions and practices, and subject them to scrutiny and debate.

Finally, the 1980s saw other events that also raised uncertainties about the model's adequacy, in the shape of evidence of the wealth of nations in the two countries where the Market model was espoused most visibly as government policy. I refer to Britain under the Conservative government of Margaret Thatcher and the United States under the Republican presidency of Ronald Reagan. By the early 1980s, Thatcher's policies were associated with the worst economic depression since the 1930s and the disappearance of much of the country's manufacturing industry. Things improved only after a change in government fiscal policy, which led to the Lawson boom of the later 1980s, followed by a further weakening of the economy. In the United States there was severe disruption of manufacturing, and between 1980 and 1990 the real wages of production workers, which had been rising every decade since the Second World War, fell to what they had been in the middle of the 1960s (see Schor 1991: 80–81). Considering changes in income inequality only makes the picture more bleak (see Gilbert and Kahl 1987: 98).

The facts of economic life do not prove the model is wrong as a guide to what governments ought to do and how economies ought to run, any more than does the East Asian Miracle. Some argue that the bad economic state of the 1980s was the inevitable consequence of the profligate and unsustainable policies of earlier governments; some argue that it reflects, not too much of the Market model, but too little. But, like the success of Japan, these events led people to unpack and question the Market model.

Questioning the Market

Debates about the nature of Japan, like those about the concrete policies introduced by right-leaning governments and economic performance under those governments, signal ways that some, at least, are uncertain about the relationship between the model on the one hand, and on the other economic success and what economic actors do. Scholarly studies of market actors buttress this uncertainty. These studies address the degree to which markets and market actors actually resemble the Market and actors in it. The points I draw from these studies remind us of what, in a sense, we already know or suspect, rather than shocking us with something totally unexpected. They indicate that, in the words of E. P. Thompson (1971: 91), the Market model is 'a superstition', a 'self-validating essay in logic'. Like a superstition, the model may be true after all. If it is true, however, it is not so in any self-evident way or for the reasons that the model uses to arrive at its truths.

While the Market model is complex and even internally contradictory, a point I will return to later, an important element is the notion that Market actors are autonomous individuals who deal with each other at arm's length. Such actors are important to the model, because only independence allows the considered, dispassionate judgement that is necessary if purchasers are to get the greatest benefit for the least cost. For firms, rational independence is necessary for the greatest possible profit, which is necessary for survival in competition with other dispassionate, independent market actors. However, the fact is that not all firms conform to this ideal, and those who deviate are not always at a disadvantage relative to those who conform. An illustration of this is the New England fishing fleet. To anticipate a point I will make later in this Introduction, the Market model would predict that the fishing firms that recruited crews and money in the impersonal labour and capital markets would be ascendant over firms that recruited through personal relationships. However, the reverse seems to be the case. Firms that recruit through kin ties have been ascendant for the past few decades, while firms that rely on impersonal markets are going out of business or changing the way they operate (Doeringer, Moss and Terkla 1986). This sort of recruitment, moreover, is fairly widespread in a number of industries. Margaret Grieco (1987) describes how a variety of British firms recruit many of their new workers from among the kin of existing workers. Such recruitment violates the dictates of the Market model; but, as Grieco argues, it has important attractions for both firms and workers.

Ronald Dore and Mark Granovetter have provided what are probably the best-known sociological arguments against the idea that markets are populated by autonomous actors. They describe practices in different countries, Dore dealing with Japan and Britain, Granovetter with the United States. Even so, the patterns they describe are similar. When firms deal with each other over any significant length of time, commonly they abandon the impersonality and autonomy of the Market, and instead establish relatively durable relationships that have a clear moral component (see also Block 1990: 69–73; Macaulay 1963). For Dore (1983: 479), these relationships 'become regulated by criteria of fairness'. For Granovetter (1985: 490), these relationships carry 'strong expectations of trust and abstention from opportunism'. For both, then, these market actors may be autonomous some of the time. Equally, however, many of them abandon that autonomy and the competitiveness that goes with it, and instead develop moral relationships with each other. It is, of course, possible to incorporate this sort of trust into a market model. It is possible to see trustworthiness as a market attribute that makes the actor more attractive (see, for example, Gambetta 1988), just as some consumer-goods firms portray themselves in their advertising as trustworthy and seek to promote durable moral relationships with customers (see Carrier 1990). Such an analytic strategy is likely to produce a model that more closely represents the actual behaviour of firms, as James Acheson (1985) shows in his discussion of the Maine lobster industry. However, to anticipate a point I make later, it marks a retreat from the conception of the impersonal and asocial Market, a retreat from the notion of the disembedded commercial sphere.

I said that another common element of the model of the Market is that actors are clear-headed and economically rational. One could argue that Markets require not rational actors, but only actors who make choices. In practice, however, such an argument reduces the model to the assertion that people want what they want given the circumstances. An example of this, in formal economics, is an assertion of Gary Becker's: 'A person enters the marriage market if he expects his marital income to exceed his single income' (1991: 119; 'market' and 'income' are technical terms). In other words, single people think about getting married when they think getting married might be nicer than staying single. This proposition is a tautology, its truth following automatically from the specialised definitions of 'market' and 'income'. It is only by positing some basis of choice, like rationality (or, for anthropologists, culture), that tautology is avoided, a step that also makes the proposition's truth problematic.[3]

In the Market, clear-headed calculation is an attribute that is forced on firms especially, if only because those who lack it will fail in competition with those who have it. Again, however, not all market actors conform to this expectation, as is apparent in William O'Barr and John Conley's (1992) description of actors at the core of capitalism, Wall Street. They studied the managers of pension funds, who, they found, deviated from the model's standards in important ways. Here I focus on only one aspect of their discussion: the ways that pension fund officials dealt with the outside investment firms that they had contracted to manage some of the pension's funds. O'Barr and Conley found that, once hired, these outside managers were almost never fired because of their objective performance, their rate of return. Outside managers were selected on the basis of their investment strategy, and so long as they maintained that strategy they were effectively exempt from dispassionate scrutiny by fund officials and their position was secure. The reason that fund officials gave for this is that poor performance by an outside manager is likely to reflect only the fact that the manager's investment strategy is ill-suited to the current phase in the cycle of the stock market. The outside manager would do better at the appropriate phase of the cycle.

This argument appears to be rational in Market terms, for it speaks of the rational calculation of material gain. However, that appearance is deceptive. The argument reflects not the calculated financial judgement of fund officers, according to O'Barr and Conley, but the uncertainties that confront any official who wants to assess the objective performance of outside managers. Should they be assessed relative to the performance of the stock market generally? If so, against what measure of the market? There are many measures, such as the Dow–Jones Industrial Average, the Standard and Poor's 100, the Standard and Poor's 500, the Wilshire 1000, the Wilshire 3000, the Wilshire 2000 (which is the Wilshire 3000 minus the Wilshire 1000), the Wilshire 5000 and the New York Stock Exchange index, and they produce different statements about the performance of the stock market – sometimes markedly different. Alternatively, should outside managers be assessed against other managers who followed a similar investment strategy? This would seem reasonable, but information on rates of return of other managers was secret and effectively unavailable, so that this means of assessment is foreclosed. Also there is uncertainty about the period over which the outside manager should be assessed. Ought it to be a short period like three months or a year? Some argue that they should be assessed over a whole market cycle; but this is an ambiguous period defined by an uncertain concept. Some say that the market went through an entire cycle in the 1987 crash; some deny that cycles exist.

This sort of uncertainty pervaded many aspects of the world of fund officials, and in the face of it commonly they retreated to subjective interpersonal evaluations of outside managers: are they pleasant, are they easy to deal with, do they seem sensible? The retreat to these evaluations may be reasonable, given the circumstances in which these officials find themselves. However, they are not rational in Market terms.

These reasonable but not rational officials do not, however, represent a pocket of incompetence at the heart of the American capital market. Instead, they represent a failure of the model of the Market. In asserting that Market actors are rational calculators, the model assumes that actors can foresee the consequences of their actions reasonably well and that they can foresee the actions of others reasonably well. No doubt in some circumstances some actors do have the foresight necessary for most practical purposes. These fund officials do not, however, even though they oversee funds of enormous proportions and have the resources to command extensive market research. One could argue, of course, that the model does not apply here, because the stock market is so imperfect that it is not a true market. But if the New York Stock Exchange is not a market, then what in this world is?

The lesson I draw from O'Barr and Conley's work is simple and hardly surprising. The greater the uncertainty, the less it is possible to be a rational, calculating Market actor. To a degree uncertainty is a function of the length of time between making a decision and being able to assess its outcome; and these fund officials were thinking in relatively long terms. Their situation resembles that of the firms that Dore and Granovetter described. There too, actors were thinking in the relatively long term, and thus confronted the associated uncertainties. And in consequence it makes sense for them to try to build and rely on stable, moral relationships rather than trying to meet each situation anew with fresh dispassionate calculations of the abilities and intentions of other firms.

Deviation from the ideal of the Market is also described in an influential sociological paper by Paul DiMaggio and Walter Powell (1983) that seeks to explain why the structures and practices of firms within an industry resemble each other so much; why, for instance, steel manufacturing firms tend to share similar corporate structures and practices. Based on their analysis of American corporations, they argue that many firms adopt practices and strategies for reasons that do not spring from a dispassionate calculation of their financial costs and benefits. Instead, they adopt them because, to put it crudely, they are in fashion, and anyone who reads the business literature quickly learns that fashions change with speed and regularity. Again, however, this concern with fashion marks a shortcoming in the Market model rather than incompetence in the actors. The firm that conforms to fashion will fit in with the expectations within the industry of what a competent and thoughtful firm ought to be doing. Put in other words, the conforming firm will appear worthy of trust and respect and will appear predictable.[4]

Here too, however, the situation reflects uncertainty. Without extensive and expensive investigation, it is difficult for one market actor to be able to predict the behaviour of another over any significant length of time. In the absence of the evidence such an investigation might produce, it is reasonable to look for clues that the actor in question will conform to expectations about what any competent and sensible actor would do, just as pension officials looked for clues about their outside managers. Conformity to current fashion is one such clue, and, it appears, an important one. The point I am making here is hardly novel. Indeed, it reflects Keynes's view of how economic actors face uncertainty and how their decisions can become self-fulfilling (see Wiley 1983: 43–45), a view that helps show how the Market model can be right for the wrong reasons. If conformity to the current conception of good business practice does help to make a business succeed, there is reason to suspect that it does not do so simply because of the overt reason, that conformity to good practice makes a firm objectively more efficient. Rather, it may facilitate success because conformity to the standards of good business practice is a sign that the firm is a good business, a sign that makes it more likely that other firms will be willing to do business with it. To put this more conservatively, the failure to conform to good business practice is likely to be a sign that the firm is unreliable and unpredictable, one to be avoided and hence one that is likely to fail.

I have described work that indicates that market actors deviate from common elements of the Market model, and I have suggested that assessing the results of their conformity may not be so straightforward as it may appear. As I said, I have done so only to illustrate some of the ways that the model is vulnerable, the subject of debate and uncertainty. Certainly the sorts of things I have described can be, as they have been, accounted for among neo-classical economists by elaborating and extending the model. Perhaps the most noteworthy such extension of recent decades is the new institutional economics (e.g. Williamson 1975; but cf. Buckley and Chapman 1995), associated with notions like transaction costs and information costs. Those who put forward these extensions and elaborations are reformers, for their intent is to improve a model that they see as being fundamentally correct. In this they differ from critics such as Sahlins and, of course, Keynes, who see the model as being fundamentally inadequate.

However, if these reformist elaborations and extensions became incorporated into popular constructs of the Market, that model would begin to change in significant ways. First, these complications would weaken the rhetorical appeal of the model. Its clear, compelling vision would become hedged, qualified and elaborated; its spare and logical clarity and its straightforward predictions and explanations of real firms and real people would be lost. Secondly, and relatedly, these elaborations and qualifications would let in by the back door what some of the model's advocates grandly shoo out by the front, the sociality, morality and cultural values that were denied in the idea that Market actors are and must be autonomous individuals. A prime example of such an advocate is Margaret Thatcher, especially with her notorious claim that there is no such thing as society. This claim, on its face empirical, was a logical and normative expression of the Market model. There can not be society, because actors constrained by it and its pressures are disadvantaged in the Market relatively to those not constrained; there should be no society, which interferes with the Market and so reduces its benefits. But, despite Thatcher, it seems that the social collectivity and its manifestations that are denied by the ideal of the autonomous rational calculator end up having a significant place in what market actors actually do when they find that rational calculation will not serve.

The Market as a Model

Thus far I have sought to make a relatively simple point: the Market model bears a questionable relationship to the world it seems to describe. The debates and empirical studies I have described can not disprove the model, but they can make it seem less secure. Those already sceptical of the model's validity may think it unnecessary to spend time establishing this point; but I think it is important. It makes more plausible the purpose of this collection, analysing the model as an element of Western culture. I want now to return to a consideration of the Market as a cultural model.

That model resembles the model promulgated by economists, and particularly the neo-classical economists who dominate the discipline. As Thurman Arnold observed some time ago (Arnold 1937), economists are a small but influential group, who serve effectively as the priestly keepers of the concept and who strive to render it in a clear and consistent way. Because of this resemblance, the consideration of the Market model in this collection is likely to be seen as a consideration of the discipline of economics itself. While it would be silly to pretend that those involved in this collection never concern themselves with the academic economic model of the Market, it would also be silly to deny that there is an important distinction between the concept in public debate and its place in the discipline. This is more true in principle, however, than in practice. While the discipline of economics is distinct from public debate, a number of economists have engaged in that debate, using their economics to justify their particular political positions. In terms of the Market model, the most noteworthy of such economists are probably F. A. Hayek and Milton Friedman (see Bosanquet 1983: Chaps 2, 3) and, of course, Keynes, whose somewhat hyperbolic passage quoted at the beginning of this Introduction points to the porosity of the boundary between discipline and public. Indeed, given the prominent place of the economy in public debate, and even in Western self-conception (Dumont 1977), it would seem difficult to distinguish clearly between economics and culture, economic analysis and policy prescription.

Economists generally use 'the market' as a model in the technical sense of a simplification of a more complex whole that aids prediction and thus is not concerned with what Weber calls interpretative understanding. So, in a classic defence of the simplified model that economists use, Milton Friedman argued that the issue is not whether the model is so simple as to be an unrecognisable caricature of actual human beings. Rather, the issue is whether the predictions based on that simplified model work for the purposes at hand (Friedman 1953; for description and criticism see Hodgson 1988: 28–35; Leibenstein 1980: Chap. 2; Marsden 1986: Chap. 2). In public debate, on the other hand, the model is assumed to have a clear interpretative element, as a strong link is asserted or assumed between the model and the real world of what motivates people and how they think about what they do. As with any important cultural concept, the link can be descriptive or prescriptive: the model can be taken as a true description of how people really think and act; or it can be taken as a guide to how people should think and act. In practice, of course, the boundary between description and prescription is vague, and people often switch from one to the other unreflectively.

This is most notable when people invoke the laws of the market-place (or, more vaguely, the way the market works) in order to persuade people to think and act in certain ways.

This core economic construction of the market is, by virtue of its abstraction, necessarily distinct from the concrete practices and institutions by which people live their economic lives. These concrete practices and institutions are expressed by more restricted notions, such as 'the housing market', 'the art market' or 'the automobile market'. The distinction between the abstraction of the market and these specific institutions and practices is important for economists. This is because it allows the assertion that specific institutions are not pure manifestations of the market as economists construct it, but contain imperfections, often referred to as 'distortions'. The concept of imperfection serves as a *cordon sanitaire* that protects the discipline's construction of the market from criticisms based on its failure to predict or explain concrete markets. As these markets have imperfections, it is possible to assert that it is the imperfections that cause the failure, not flaws in the model itself, just as it is possible to see the predictive successes of the model as springing from the accuracy of the model itself, rather than from the things that are defined as imperfections (see, for example, Hollis and Nell 1975: Chap. 1; Ormerod 1994).

Economics is not peculiar in having this conservative tendency. It is common to organised and institutionalised systems of thought about the world, being just a local manifestation of the same general process that Thomas Kuhn (1970) describes in his treatment of the way that scientific disciplines handle anomalies. Moreover, its equivalent exists in popular thought about the Market. And there, interestingly, this conservative tendency allows people to engage in practical criticism of the Market; it allows them to adhere to the notion of the Market in the abstract, while having practical reservations about the operation of specific markets or the actions of specific market actors. Gouging, chicanery, inequality and sheer offensive greed seem, to many people, to go with markets, and the ranks of the corrupt and corrupting entrepreneurs are better known than the honest and assiduous. This conceptual separation of individual entrepreneurs and practices from the markets in which they operate is a sign of the way that markets are, in Marx's sense, fetishised. That is, people tend to endow markets with an efficacy and even a life of their own that is not connected clearly to the activities of the individuals who constitute the Market model.

However, these practical criticisms are kept narrow, for the undesirable aspects of real markets tend to be seen as individual failures and aberrations and rarely form the basis of a condemnation of the principle of the Market itself.[5] Thus, Lord Vaizey, defecting to the Tories in 1975, distinguished between the free market and 'those who for purely selfish interests . . . seek to make money for themselves and let the rest go to hell' (quoted in Cockett 1994: 228). Similarly, in the introduction to his description of the Prudential-Bache securities scandal in the United States, Kurt Eichenwald warns against the fraudulent few who betray 'the investor faith that is an essential building block of the American economy' (Eichenwald 1995: 8). Just as undesirable aspects are seen as individual failures, so people who experience undesirable consequences of the operation of markets often do not see this as a failure of the Market to deliver its promised prosperity. Instead, these people tend to manifest (and tend to be exposed to) this same differentiation of the Market from markets. For example, house owners who suffer from falling prices tend to see (and to be told) that the housing market is weak, which does not improve their security or question the virtues of markets as ways of allocating key domestic necessities like shelter. Thus, while popular thought may not contain an articulated notion of imperfections of the sort that exists among professional economists, the practical equivalent seems to exist, and while it allows for practical criticisms of the Market, it shares clear conservative tendencies with its professional cousin.

The distinction between the abstraction and specific institutions creates what is probably the only arena that allows people to debate the desirability and applicability of the Market. Because fundamental criticism of the model effectively lost legitimacy during the 1980s, these debates see the Market as valid in essence, and restrict themselves only to relatively marginal changes in the scope and intensity that the Market should have. By variation in scope I mean that people vary in the range of things that they think ought to be transacted in the Market, ought to be available to be bought and sold. One can be an advocate of the Market but still hold that sex or policing or health care should not be sold. By variation in intensity I mean that people differ in the degree to which they think that people and institutions should be dependent on the

Market and subject to its constraints. One can adhere to the model but hold that workers, the poor or the handicapped, that fledgling or strategic industries, are exceptional cases.

These variations occasionally appear as assertions that the Market model does not apply to certain areas of life. The family is the prime such area, and if David Schneider's (1980) analysis is correct, many Americans see Market relations and values, the world of work, as being not only distinct from but antithetical to the relations and values of the family and household. This distinction is common in economics as well, for many in that discipline construe the family as a seat of altruism that is dia-metrically opposed to the self-regarding individualism of the Market (see England 1993). Of course, some argue that the family also conforms to Market logic (especially Becker 1991). Criticisms are likely to be most articulate when areas of life hitherto outside the Market realm become incorporated within it. Reproduction and natural resources are two notable cases. As the biological technology of human reproduction expands, things previously seen as natural processes or natural impossibilities become possible choices that can be purchased. This has engendered debates about whether they ought to be allowed to be purchased, which are debates about the proper limits of the Market, though these debates also suggest that in practical circumstances people are less sure that choice is an unalloyed good than the Market model suggests (see, for example, Hirsch 1993; for an articulate pro-Market answer to such questions, see Duxbury 1996). Debates about such limits also arise when resources previously un-owned become tradeable commodities, and hence effectively private property, such as legal authority to pollute the common air or water, or the legal authority to fish the common sea (see, for example, Pálsson 1995; Pálsson and Helgason 1995).

One of the reasons the model has the force and appeal that it does is that it roots the Market in what is construed as fundamental human nature. The Market is presented as embodying essential humanity and the ethics that spring from it. It is, in effect, what people would do spontaneously among themselves if left alone, if their propensity to truck, barter and exchange were not con-strained. Consequently, any arrangements and practices that depart from the Market model require the expenditure of energy and resources, which those who adhere to the model are prone to attack as wasteful and inefficient. The converse of this is that anything that extends aspects of the Market to areas of transaction that are not in the Market is good. Thus, hiring business consultants to advise governments on how to organise and run themselves is good. Treating citizens as customers of government services is good. Setting up internal markets is good, whether within firms or governments. And, as recent waves of corporate shrinking seem to attest, buying in the Market things and services that previously had been produced within an organisation is good.[6]

In being rooted in a conception of fundamental human nature, the Market can be used to express a range of values and pre-suppositions, many of which help explain what I have pointed to as the populist appeal of the idea of the Free Market. For example, the Market is said to be a protection against an intrusive state, and hence a guarantor of personal liberty. It is said to allow buyers greater utility and satisfaction than they would otherwise have. It is a source of efficiency, assuring the most rational allocation of resources. It is the surest motor for economic growth and personal prosperity. Underlying these is the link between the Market and the liberal capitalist West, the freest and richest place to be. This moralism exists from one of the earliest elaborations of the concept, in the foundation of Western modern economic writings during the Scottish Enlightenment. According to those writers, 'there existed behind the apparent confusion of events an order which was maintained . . . by the operation of instincts planted in men by Providence. This providence was assumed to be benign and the order so established was favourable to the welfare of men' (Habakkuk 1971: 45; see also Lubasz 1992).

As my invocation of the Scottish Enlightenment indicates, for all that the Market model flourished in the 1980s, it has been a feature of Western cultural debate for some time (Dumont 1977). Consequently, over the centuries people with disparate and even conflicting interests have interpreted it in the light of their divergent concerns and situations, so that it ends up meaning different things to different people – a diversity that was only implicit in my initial ethnographic sketch of the concept *Market*.

This diversity is less apparent among professional economists. They have, of course, criticised their own discipline's constructions of market systems and market actors, as is indicated by books with titles like *The End of Economic Man* (Marsden 1986), *Beyond Economic Man* (used twice, by Leibenstein 1980 and by Ferber and Nelson 1993) and, even more alarming, *The Death of Economics* (Ormerod

1994). The critical economic literature is broad, accessible and beyond the focus of this collection, though it must be said that much of it so assumes basic neo-classical arguments that, from the perspective of those seeking to consider the nature of the Market model, it amounts to little more than internecine squabbles over distinctions that make no apparent difference.

The breadth of that internal criticism is illustrated by some books that are fairly recent and that address different elements of academic and professional economics from different perspectives and with different ends in view. Most conventionally economic, from an outsider's viewpoint at least, is that by Richard Nelson and Sidney Winter (1982: esp. Part I), who seek an economics that is less static or synchronic. Somewhat less conventional is the collection edited by Paul Ekins and Manfred Max-Neef (1992), which illustrates attempts to make economics more sensitive to issues of well-being and welfare. Least conventional, but still thoroughly reformist, is Donald McCloskey's (1986, 1990) criticism of the rhetoric of scientistic modernism in economics. Criticisms such as these are important within economics itself, and to the degree that they are taken up more generally by analysts and critics of the model of the Market they will begin to affect common cultural conceptions.

While diversity may be fairly muted within economics, in public debate and popular culture the Market refers to a range of distinct and even competing attributes, processes and consequences. For example, some invocations of the Market connote particular attributes of individuals, such as constructions of the self (the autonomous actor) and forms of thought (self-interest, instrumental rationality). These attributes seem clear and straightforward aspects of the central model as laid out in my initial description. However, they turn out to be vague and contradictory. Thus, the simple notion that Market actors are 'self-interested' appears, on inspection, to be ambiguous, as is illustrated by debates about the relative merits of and the conflicts between short-term and long-term interest. Likewise, as Albert Hirschman (1986 *b*) recounts, in the past 'interest' has taken on meanings that range from the restricted and precise to the vacuous, all put forward with equal confidence. To complicate matters further, the common modern notion that the Market is a realm of conflict and self-interest stands in contrast to a much earlier notion that Markets have a civilising and pacifying influence (see especially Hirschman 1977).

In addition, there is ambiguity about the status of the attributes ascribed to Market actors. In some cases they are seen to be innate, as in Adam Smith's famous assertion of a human propensity to truck, barter and exchange. In others, however, they are seen as environmental, consequences or functions of the operation of the Market itself, as in the somewhat Darwinian belief that Market actors have to behave in certain ways or go under. Competition is supposed to drive the family firm out of business, for the bonds of kinship can not secure qualified management as well as can reliance on the labour market. The fate of the family firm is a special case of the belief that competition will operate against those who are not instrumentally rational, who let their perceptions and economic judgements be clouded by their sentiments, who succumb to the pressures of social obligation. Alfred Chandler (1977) is an important advocate of this view, arguing that firms with family managers lack the ability to innovate, or at least the drive to do so (see, for example, Fitzgerald 1995; but cf. Kirby and Rose 1994).

This example of the family firm shows another way that the Market is ambiguous: while some invocations refer to individual attributes, others refer to systemic ones. The operation of the Market allows, for instance, the most efficient allocation of resources, and so allows the greatest net human welfare. Here, the individuals who are so prominent in some invocations of the Market are submerged into the larger system that they shape and that shapes them. Their autonomy and interests are replaced by the systemic imperatives and attractions of things like competition and free trade. Here is an important ambiguity within the model, though it is one that is hardly peculiar to it. On the one hand is the set of Market attributes that attracted those concerned with the freedom of ordinary people in the face of over-mighty organisations, whether the state or unions (but, curiously, never corporations). These are the attributes that revolve around freedom of choice, a central element of the Market model and one associated with the political demand for a minimal state.[7] On the other hand are the systemic imperatives of the Market, which are crucial to securing the benefits it is supposed to bring. These imperatives can exert powerful constraints on individuals, and it is only by adopting narrow definitions of 'freedom' that Market advocates can claim that those so constrained are not less free than they were before (see Haworth 1994: Chap. 5; Tomlinson 1990: 128–134).

This list of elements of the Market model could be extended, and the contributors to this collection do extend it (for an interesting discussion, see Dilley 1992). My point here, however, is not to produce an exhaustive catalogue or a table of ambiguities and contradictions in the model, or even to suggest that the Market is notably more ambiguous or contradictory than other powerful symbols in Western culture. Instead, it is to note that the model is fluid and polyvalent, so much so that one would be tempted to speak of models, rather than *the* model, were it not for the fact that these different elements are part of a common orientation and pool of images that are invoked to serve common political-economic goals. While it is important to recognise that there is divergence among advocates of the Market as well as in the ways it has been implemented, it is perhaps more important to attend to their unity. After all, the political changes of the long 1980s, which took place in many countries, shared much rhetoric and imagery, venerated many of the same writers and were often supported by the same individuals and organisations (on the activities of British Market advocates in the United States and in Eastern Europe, see Cockett 1994: 305–308).

Studying the Market

This collection seeks to take advantage of and extend the increasing accessibility of the model of the Market by subjecting it to empirical and critical analysis, to see how it affects the ways people think and act and what it tells us about ourselves. However, the goals of the collection are tentative. First, because the focus of this collection is common representations of market activity, generally its purpose is not to joust with professional economists. Economists certainly have influenced policy, debate and everyday thought, but the representations that are the concern of this collection are public, and hence do not necessarily agree with those found among members of the profession.

Second, the contributors do not seek to oust the Market model and replace it with a different and better understanding of Western market economies. Anyone who sought such an end would, in any event, be constrained by the lack of independent evidence about how firms and those within them, not to mention market actors more generally, operate. This claim may seem to be contradicted by the abundance of statistics, company reports and the like, which would appear to provide just the sort of evidence upon which one could build an adequate model. However, these sources are shaped by the Model itself, and hence tend to reproduce it. (See, for example, criticisms of notions and measures of 'capital' and 'output' in Block 1990: Chaps 5, 6.) Likewise, they ignore many of the mundane practices and beliefs that produce the commercial and economic results that they report.

Instead, this collection treats the Market model as an important element of the culture of Western societies, an element that is a fit subject for scholarly analysis. As Karl Polanyi observed (1957 *b*), people's substantive economic behaviour, whether inside or outside markets, is distinct from the constructs with which people represent aspects of that behaviour. The idea of the Market is such a construct. This collection analyses the Market in a range of different ways. It raises questions about the ways that actors in market settings think and talk about what they do. It describes various manifestations of the model in order to bring to the surface the assumptions built into it. It raises questions about various aspects of the model, such as the autonomous and rational Market actor. To put this all in other terms, if the model of the Market is the way that many people think of Western economy, it is appropriate to ask what are the features of the Market model and what are the consequences of thinking about economic activity in this way.

These questions are timely. Even though the events of the 1980s made the notion of the Market more accessible and more problematic than it had been in previous decades, that notion is still powerful and commonly taken for granted. The rightward shift of governments has not been significantly reversed, and the rhetoric of the Market remains central to much political debate. Many still see the Market as embodying the social and economic genius of the modern West, a genius to be extended and exploited even further. Even among those who would dissent from the political and economic programmes that came to the fore in the 1980s, the Market remains a powerful icon of that genius.

A growing number of anthropologists have been studying and reflecting on the ways that Westerners describe and think about market institutions and the market itself (see especially Dilley 1992). One of the purposes of this collection is to bring some of this work together. Doing so will help to increase its visibility and perhaps encourage its spread. Likewise, this collection will help to make anthropologists more aware of the problematic nature of the image of the West that many seem to have acquired unthinkingly as part of their disciplinary stock of assumptions. Beyond these more parochial intentions is a larger one: to challenge, in however circumscribed a way, the popular understandings of the Market that became especially visible and influential in the 1980s.

Were these understandings mere tales that people tell one another there would be little urgency to such a challenge. However, they are used in many parts of the world to explain and buttress, as they appear to guide, government policies that are intended to implement the Market. These policies have significant social costs, which are justified as being much less than the social and economic benefits the policies are supposed to bring when they are fully implemented and the benefits of the Market begin to accrue. In the face of such policies, and spurred by such costs, it seems reasonable to ask what the assumptions are that underlie the model and its attractions as a goal of policy, and to ask how closely it resembles the ways that market actors think and act. One could, of course, question the Market model by comparing it with the theories and findings of conventional economics. Compared to the broader approach used in this collection, however, such a tactic would seem less likely to reveal the cultural assumptions behind and the social forces that support the Market model.

Treating the Market model as a cultural artefact with an uncertain relationship to what people and firms do in and think about their economic lives is not the same as challenging the empirical facts of the extent and distribution of wealth in Western societies. Likewise, questioning the link between economic and political forms forged in the Market model is not the same as challenging the empirical facts of those societies' political structures and forms of participation. Rather, questioning the model reflects uncertainty about whether the Market, as either description or prescription, is the device that underlies and guarantees these things. This uncertainty is hardly novel. Even such a liberal democrat as Charles Lindblom (1977) appears to have strong reservations, not only about the relationship of the Market to wealth and well-being, but also about the nature of the political systems with which it is associated.

In probing the concept of the Market, this collection joins the body of work that analyses economic models and assumptions from a sociological and particularly an anthropological perspective (see Swedberg 1987). This body of work is growing, and it has roots that run deep. Writers in the nineteenth and twentieth centuries such as Karl Marx, Max Weber, Emile Durkheim, Marcel Mauss and Karl Polanyi traced the historical emergence of market institutions and practices in the West and analysed the social and political foundations, pre-requisites and corollaries of market relations. They described, in other words, the ways that both the market and the Market are social and cultural constructions. These constructions rely on and reflect beliefs, practices and institutions that are found in society at large, such as the Protestant Ethic, as well as those that are common among firms, such as those associated with bookkeeping (see, for example, Carruthers and Espeland 1991).[8]

These concerns continue to animate anthropologists, and much of their work can be placed in one of two broad categories. Each bears on the model of the Market, but does so in a distinct way. One category, echoing the conventional anthropological concern with simpler societies, is based on studies of people who live in areas that are on the fringe of market systems (e.g. Gudeman 1986; Gudeman and Rivera 1991; Taussig 1977, 1980). Such studies describe the understandings of what we would identify as market systems that are expressed by the people being described. These writers then use these understandings to bring to the surface and provide novel perspectives on Western assumptions about the Market that often are unspoken because taken for granted. Such works are useful and provocative, and have been influential. However, from the perspective of the aims of this collection they have one important limitation. Their rhetorical force is weakened because they draw on the perceptions and understandings of people located outside the modern West, people who can be said not really to know how proper markets operate.

The other broad category of anthropological work that bears on the model of the Market, closer to the intents of this volume, springs from a consideration of areas that are well within market systems, especially the modern West. For writers in this second category, then, the analysis is developed internal to market societies, rather than springing from marginal areas. For instance, John Davis (1973) and Keith Hart (1986) have analysed in different ways the social context of market relations and institutions in the West, and especially the way that the market is not so impersonal and independent of social relations as it may appear to those who think in terms of the Market.

Underlying the work of many of the authors who have written on economic activities is a recognition that the Market is something special, a way of thinking about certain sorts of transactions that is rooted in certain places and times, particularly the modern West, more particularly the United States. Because of this distinctiveness, it is wrong to naturalise the notion of the Market, it is wrong to say that it is only a reflection or expression of some pan-human propensity to truck, barter and exchange. People in many times and places have engaged in trade, have given and received objects and services among themselves and with those in neighbouring societies, without necessarily having the notion of the Market. Equally, many people have developed markets, more or less elaborate institutions devoted to facilitating and channelling this trade, without necessarily having the notion of the Market. And again, in many societies people engage in commerce, by which I mean market trade as a significant rather than an incidental part of their economic lives, without thereby developing the notion of the Market. Long after the emergence of extensive and complex commercial activity in Britain and America, there were many who advocated fixed pricing and fair rather than free trade (Carrier 1994: 73–74, 90). The sheer existence of certain types of economic activity, then, does not necessarily lead to the emergence of the notion of the Market.

Just as the Market can not be naturalised by reducing it to a reflection of trade or to the existence of markets or commerce, so it can not be seen as only a reflection of some idea of relative autonomy within an economic sphere. Such an idea is common, though hardly universal. As Jean-Christophe Agnew (1986) and Maurice Bloch and Jonathan Parry (1989) show, in many times and places people have understood trade to occupy a commercial or market realm relatively distinct from the more purely social areas of their lives, and have expected people to be more self-regarding in this realm than elsewhere, relatively free of the social ties and moral obligations that pervade other areas of life. Again, however, people in times and places outside the modern West have these understandings without having the notion of the Market, as Alan Everitt (1967) shows in his description of trade in English markets before the modern era, as J. E. Crowley (1974) shows in American conceptions of economic activities in the eighteenth century, and as the contributors to the collection edited by Caroline Humphrey and Stephen Hugh-Jones (1992) show in their descriptions of barter in various societies.

Put somewhat differently, although the notion of the Market may refer to beliefs and practices and institutions in the world, it is important to remember Polanyi's point that the Market is a conception of the world rather than the world itself. It should not, therefore, unreflectively be conflated with those aspects of the world that it labels, as it should not unreflectively be conflated with other ideas that resemble aspects of it. Thus, it should be distinguished from trade, even markets; it should be distinguished from commerce, from the idea of a relatively distinct market sphere, and from the idea of relative freedom within that sphere. There is more here, then, than just the idea that trade or market relations are relatively 'dis-embedded' (see Granovetter 1985; Parry 1986; Polanyi 1957 a), that they are distinguished to some degree from social relations, an idea that, as I have said, is fairly common. Unlike the more restricted ideas of a market sphere and of market freedom, the Market has, for many people, come to be an expansive notion, the measure against which areas of life beyond markets, trade and commerce are to be assessed and to which they are to be subordinated, as Gary S. Becker (1996) seeks to subordinate religion to Market logic in a popular column published in a weekly news magazine. The Market idea that market logic ought to predominate is contained aphoristically in 'the bottom line'. With this phrase, a host of values and decisions are reduced and subordinated to their effect on cost and profit, whether expressed in terms of money or, as in Becker's treatment of religion, in terms of public support. Like all good aphorisms, this one expresses not just exhortation but also resignation: Not only ought we to keep our eyes on the bottom line, we *must* do so, for those who do not will go under.

Another, related ground for distinguishing the Market from the more general notions of a market realm and market freedom is the assumption and assertion that the sort of person contained in the Market model is the true or valid person, the standard against which other notions of the self are measured, and usually found wanting. The person in the Market model is autonomous, rational and self-reliant. Of course other notions of the self exist in the modern West (see, for example, Schneider 1980; Turner 1976). Although the Market self is only one way people judge themselves, in public debate it is an especially important way. Also, some have argued that the Market self is distinctly male and middle-class (Hartsock 1985), suggesting that 'Economic Man' is more accurate than those who use the phrase may think (see Ferber and Nelson 1993; Seguino, Stevens and Lutz 1996). Here, however, I can do no more than note the gender correlates of both the Market model and the neo-classical economics with which it is associated. In any event, the Market self is free of the immoralities of dependence on others – an immorality signalled by the use of 'dependent' rather than, for example, 'reliant' – subordination, lack of foresight, and the fuzzy or mystical thinking that seeks economic goals through non-economic means (Lindstrom 1993). What Marx said of bourgeois individuals nicely sums up Market selves, distinguished by 'Freedom, Equality, Property and Bentham. Freedom, because . . . [they] are constrained only by their free will . . .. Equality, because . . . they exchange equivalent for equivalent. Property, because each disposes only of what is his own. And Bentham, because each looks only to himself' (from *Capital*, Chap. 6, in Tucker 1978: 343).

Using the Market

There is another and more subtle aspect of the Market model that I also need to address in this Introduction. That is the way that people use the model to make sense of social entities by identifying and explaining differences between them. Although this aspect of the model may seem secondary, it is important because the concept of the Market is itself shaped, even if only indirectly, by the uses to which it is put, as it gains legitimacy from those uses.

One use of the Market is in identifying and explaining winners and losers within the West. Put most simply and provocatively, winners frequently are identified and explained by their conformity to the model of the Market actor. Losers, on the other hand, are unfit deviants. This occurs whether the winners and losers are individuals or organisations.

For individuals, winners are autonomous, rational and calculating; losers are dependent, muddled and can not defer gratification. The distinction between autonomous rationality and muddled immediacy that I draw here resembles the point Pierre Bourdieu (1984) makes, that members of the dominated classes are driven by necessity precisely because they lack the resources that enable members of the dominant classes, the winners, to distance themselves from their immediate situation. Here Bourdieu echoes a similar point made much earlier by Max Weber in his discussion of economic classes (1958).

Such a view not only justifies the success of the winners, it also motivates (or at least legitimates) policies that weaken the position of the individuals who are losers. Such policies include attacks on welfare, which is said to decrease the market fitness of the unemployed, those who have failed to find a buyer for their labour, by encouraging dependency and discouraging initiative, calculation and self-reliance (see, for example, Carrier 1994: 203). These policies do not simply blame the victim and thereby protect the model from criticism. In addition, they put pressure on those who do not adhere to Market logic to conform to it. To the degree that such policies succeed, the Market model becomes self-fulfilling.

For organisations, on the other hand, winners shape themselves to market demand and keep up to date; losers think that all they have to do is build a better mousetrap and wait for the world to beat a path to their door. This is illustrated in a sociological study intended in part to find out why British firms are less successful than American ones. Among other things, the study found that the British tended to place more stress on production, on building better mousetraps; the Americans to place more on marketing, on making sure that the world beats a path to their door (Jamieson 1980: esp. 233). However, recalling Thompson's point that the Market model may be a superstition, a stress on marketing may bring success for the 'wrong' reasons. The success of the firm that stresses marketing may not spring from its greater objective efficiency and market fitness. It may spring instead from the assumption within an industry and among its suppliers and customers that such a stress is efficient, in which case a firm that stresses marketing would appear trustworthy and predictable, a fit organisation with which to do business. Such an organisation will, of course, be more likely to attract custom and hence prosper, thereby validating the misrecognition of the reason for its success.

This way of using the model is also clear in something I have mentioned already, the association of the Market with the West, and particularly the United States. This is most notable in the rhetoric of the Cold War, which arrayed Market-based America, and its subordinate allies in Western Europe, against points East. However, the association has a longer and more interesting history, though that history rarely makes the association in so blunt a way. Instead, the Market is associated with the modern and the Western indirectly by portraying the non-Western and the pre-modern in terms that are distinctly non-Market.

An example of this indirection that is pertinent for this collection is the way that Marx linked a particularly static and oppressive form of social and economic organisation with the non-West in the concept of Oriental Despotism. This concept does not identify the West positively. Instead, it does so negatively, by portraying what it is not. Equally, the example of Oriental Despotism illustrates the pervasive way that Market imagery infects some of the important ways that people identify not just an aspect of Western economy, but of the West itself. This is because the image of the despotic Orient addresses, even if only negatively, attributes that pertain to economy but are not uniquely economic, such as stasis, hence dynamism; oppression, hence freedom. Those attributes are common to constructions of both the West and the Market. Edward Said (1978) is perhaps the most famous of those who have charted this process of defining the non-Western in terms of its difference from the West, whether those differences are real or imagined (see also Pearce 1965; Smith 1985). The non-Western is static, passive, sensuous, constrained. The opposites – dynamic, active, rational, free – apply equally to the Market and the West. In a way, then, the claim of Market rhetoric that market freedom brings civil freedom is not an empirical assertion so much as a logical corollary of the conflation of the Market and the West.

The West that is now identified with the Market is, of course, the modern West. The pre-modern West may serve as a source of signs of nascent attributes of the Market (e.g. Macfarlane 1978), but more commonly it is as much an object lesson in modern Western prowess as is the Orient. Before the great transformation, people may have bought and sold, but their institutions and practices did not spring from the rational calculation of self-regarding individuals (Polanyi 1957 *c*; Thompson 1971). Instead, they sprang from a set of values and identities that are constituted as antithetical to Markets and their actors, such as identification with a particular place and membership in a particular community or set of kin (see Carrier 1994: 63–69). These pre-modern attributes had to be overcome before development could occur and the Market, and its actors, emerge (Weber 1958).[9]

However, just as there is reason to doubt that the Market model is a straightforward description of market actors, so there is reason to doubt the straightforward identification of the West as Market-land or, indeed, even market-land.[10] In fact, identifying Western societies as market systems requires acts of selective perception that border on the heroic. First, such an identification ignores the widely-noted fact that much economic activity in the West occurs outside market institutions and relationships, for it occurs within firms rather than between them (e.g. Williamson 1975). Second, the identification ignores another widely-noted fact, the degree to which Western governments, the antithesis of Market freedom and autonomy, dominate important areas of economic life, whether through defence contracts, transfer payments or health and safety regulations (e.g. Lindblom 1977). Third, such an identification ignores the fact, less widely noted, that many important areas of the production, transformation and circulation of objects and services do not rest on buying and selling, and the fact that many people gain their food, shelter and clothing without themselves entering the market in any significant way. The family and its dependent members are the most obvious examples, though hardly the only ones (e.g. Block 1990: 56–66). Finally, it ignores the fact that many market actors and market transactions do not really resemble the features of the Market model all that much, as I noted in my description of the behaviour of some market actors in the preceding section.[11]

It appears, then, that the Market model is more than just an idealisation of economic activities in particular times and places. It is also an idealisation that itself idealises the modern West, what I call an occidentalism (Carrier 1995). Such idealisations start with differences between what goes on in the modern West and what goes on in non-Western societies or in pre-modern Western societies. These differences, invariably partial and relative attributes of particular times and places, are transformed into absolute and defining essences of types of social life that stride, with their capital letters, across the page and through the mind – the West, the Orient, Communism, Capitalism and so forth. In this process of constructing distinct and opposed types of life, the attributes that differentiated the modern West themselves become purified and exaggerated, become essences. This form of occidentalist essentialism is hardly restricted to the Market model, but is found commonly in Western social science and popular thought. This occidentalism and its attendant orientalism appear in Eleanor Smollett's discussion of understandings of what the introduction of the Market would mean in Bulgaria. Many Bulgarians saw the Market in highly symbolic and almost mystical terms, as indeed it was presented to them by the Western advertising agents working for pro-Market politicians, themselves funded by Western governments, parties and individuals. For these Bulgarians, the Market was not a narrow notion that identified specific forms of transaction or economic institutions. Instead, it had a more complex meaning. It betokened a way of life seen as particularly American, novel social and political organisation, and wealth for all, just as its adoption would show that Bulgarians are 'prosperous and civilized, and not backward . . . descendants of the Ottoman Empire' (Smollett 1993: 10).

To re-cast what I have described in terms of the issues raised in this collection, there is a difference in the visibility of market relations and transactions when the modern West is compared with other times and places. This relative difference in the visibility of social and economic practices becomes elevated to an essential description of types of societies: the market becomes emblematic of the West, which itself becomes reduced to little more than the market. Likewise, within the West relations and transactions in the market are likely to be more impersonal, self-regarding and calculating than relations and transactions in many other areas of social life. This relative difference in areas of Western life is itself made absolute, so that impersonality, self-regard and calculation become blazons of the market, which is, in turn, reduced to little more than them, and so becomes transformed into the Market. (For a discussion of this tendency among economists, see England 1993.)

The model of the Market, then, appears to be a symbolic construct, one that is as much concerned with defining the difference between self and other as it is with its putative purpose of describing a form of socio-economic activity. The Free Market stands in heightened and purified distinction from other areas of Western life; the Free-Market West stands in heightened and purified distinction from other times and places. But as my opening invocation of the long 1980s indicates, these collective self-definitions are not absolute or uniform. Instead, they reflect political interests and processes and exist in the face of dissent and disagreement. Even though the Market model decrees that the market should exist outside politics, the Market model itself does not. It is a self-definition with profound political correlates and consequences.

About the Chapters

In the preceding pages I have sought to sketch some of the ways that we can begin to think about, situate and criticise the set of beliefs that I have called the Market model. This pervasive element of Western scholarly and popular thought is too complex to be addressed adequately in a brief Introduction like this (or, indeed, even in a single collection like this). In the chapters that follow, the contributors flesh out my initial sketch. Their discussions fall into two broad clusters. The first and larger set of chapters is concerned with the general intellectual framework of the model, especially the kinds of assumptions it makes about people and institutions, and the broader historical and intellectual context of those assumptions. The chapters in the second and smaller set are focused more narrowly, for each looks at specific aspects and manifestations of the model. Through these more specific instances, contributors help to show the ways that the model is extended, supported and challenged.

Recurrent in talk about the Market is the invocation of Adam Smith's assertion that we owe our dinner not to the benevolence of the butcher, the brewer and the baker, but to their self-interest. This invocation regularly carries with it a connotation that I have noted already, that Market actors are self-serving rational calculators, unconstrained by communal ties and sentiments. The first three chapters in this collection show some of the ways that this connotation is valued, and some of the unspoken assumptions that people bring to it.

Not surprisingly, the Market view that actors are autonomous and self-serving is associated with the assertion that the Market is a corrosive force, one that undercuts and denies legitimacy to collective moral sentiments that value anything much beyond individual advantage. Joel Kahn traces the history of one such criticism of the Market model in his 'Demons, Commodities and the History of Anthropology'. In this chapter Kahn describes the

development of this critical perspective on the Market among a
set of German writers of the nineteenth century who are called
expressivists, though, as he notes, many elements of expressivist
thought find echoes in modern criticisms of the Market and of the
dominance of commodities. For expressivists, the Market was a
manifestation of the Enlightenment view of human beings as
fundamentally uniform and devoid of any common nature other
than a propensity to avoid pain and seek pleasure. Consequently,
and to repeat a point made earlier in this Introduction, the concept
of the Market was not simply an expression of the view that people
truck, barter and exchange. Rather, it represents a reduction of
humanity to nothing other than instrumental transactions guided
by the Benthamite calculus of private pleasure and pain.

The expressivists objected to this because they saw within the
concept of the Market a denial of any human purpose or frame of
meaning that transcends individuals and their private calculations.
Expressivists did not argue that there is a divine or other source
of purpose that is external to and imposed upon societies. Rather,
they said that transcendent purpose emerges in the course of social
interaction and is shaped by the factors that impinge upon it, in a
way that happens with, for instance, the language that a set of
people speak. For the expressivists, then, the Market model is at
least inaccurate when it portrays a world of uniform and atomistic
autonomous actors with no interests beyond pain and pleasure. It
ignores the ways that people form collectivities generated by their
interactions, as it ignores the ways that people embody and are
guided by the transcendent principles that emerge in those
collectivities.

As Kahn notes, the expressivist critics were not just objecting
to the model of the Market as they understood it. Rather, they saw
the Market as an aspect of, and to a degree took it to be representative of, Western modernity, and especially of some of the themes
associated with the Enlightenment: instrumental rationality, a
denial of fundamental differences between people, the primacy
of the calculus of pain and pleasure. In their criticisms, expressivists contrasted what they saw emerging with what they took to
be an earlier and more communal form of life pervaded by sociality
and morality. In other words, each form of life was defined
dialectically, in contrast to the other. The result was an occidentalist
rendering of the modern West, a rendering in which the Market
loomed large, a rendering that stood in contrast to the expressivist

orientalism of a pre-modern world of community, *gemeinschaft*.

Kahn's discussion of expressivist criticism is appropriate as the first chapter in this collection because of the ways that it illuminates certain assumptions that are part of the Market model, particularly the stress on private interest and the associated denial of collective sentiments and interests, cultural values and social orders. The springs of Market motive are, ultimately, purely internal. As Kahn shows in his chapter, some non-Western thinkers and policy-makers are trying to separate the parts of this model. That is, they are trying to establish the market as an economic institution in their countries, in order to gain what they see as its material advantages. At the same time, they are trying to prevent the spread of Market morality, autonomous and self-seeking individualism, from the market-place to civil life beyond.

Kahn's presentation is also significant because it shows how some of the terms of debate between advocates and opponents of the Market have remained relatively stable for a long time. Indeed, the expressivist construction and criticism of the Market seems to anticipate the thoughts of many modern critics, who see in colonisation and spreading Western capitalist influence the devaluation and destruction of pre-colonial, indigenous orders that contain precisely the institutions of morality and sociality that the intruding West lacks. Similarly, of course, it anticipates many critics of the rightward shift of Western governments, who lament the destruction of the sentiments and institutions that had helped society to cohere. In illustrating this, Kahn argues that the expressivist critique of the Market is not a primordial one, but instead springs from the existence of the Market itself. It is, in other words, an aspect of Western modernity as much as is the Market.

When they see the Market as the denial and corrosion of social and moral institutions and structures, the expressivists are putting in negative terms what can also be put positively, for the absence of cohesion is, by another name, freedom from constraint. Susan Love Brown describes such a positive rendering in her 'The Free Market as Salvation from Government: The Anarcho-Capitalist View.' Anarcho-capitalism is a school of thought, dominated by economists and found predominantly in the United States, that sees in the Market just that freedom from constraint. The freedom that particularly concerns anarcho-capitalists is freedom from those constraining institutions that the expressivists held to be an essential part of human life. Prime among these is government. For the anarcho-capitalists, government is neither an embodiment of transcendent purpose nor an expression of collective judgement, however imperfect. Rather, it is an illegitimate intrusion into natural human exchange and the arrangements that flow from it. What distinguishes anarcho-capitalists from the more common advocates of less government and more market is the extreme stand that they take. They see humanity as endowed not just with the propensity to truck, barter and exchange, but with the ability to do so successfully and naturally, for the anarcho-capitalists reject Durkheim's point (1984) that successful markets require external, collective regulation, which means, in practice, state regulation. Markets must be left to run on their own. Even residual functions like the administration of justice and the national defence are not the legitimate activities of government, but are best left to commercial arrangement in the Market.

The anarcho-capitalists, then, both resemble and depart from the expressivist critics that Kahn describes. They both see the Market as corrosive of collectivity. However, while the expressivists value what they see the Market corroding and lament the consequences, the anarcho-capitalists are all for more and faster corrosion. The anarcho-capitalists resemble and depart from the expressivists in another important way as well. I said that the expressivist critics saw the corrosive Market as a creature of modernity. For them, we have fallen from a more desirable past into a tainted present. The anarcho-capitalists have the same notion of a fall from grace, but their golden age is located much farther in the past. They see the Market that is wholly free as aboriginal. It is the primal state of human affairs that actually existed, but that was destroyed by the growth of collective constraint. Here the anarcho-capitalists treat as historical priority what many Market advocates treat as logical priority. Or, as Oliver Williamson (1975: 20) puts it: 'In the beginning there were markets.'

Kahn's and Brown's chapters describe two differing and opposed intellectual understandings of the nature of the Free Market populated by autonomous, self-interested individuals. Moreover, they point up a geographic and cultural divergence in the meanings of the Market. Powerful institutions are urging and obliging more and more people and organisations to accept and conform to a Market-based view of life, so that the Market is becoming more truly international than it was. However, criticism of the Market has, perhaps, its strongest historical roots in Europe, while much of the advocacy of Market thought still lies in the United States. That country has long been a bastion of belief in the free, Benthamite calculator that underlies the Market model, and institutions based there, like the World Bank, reflect that belief (e.g. Wade 1996: 18). The United States is, after all, the country that declares that all people are endowed with liberty and the pursuit of happiness. It is appropriate, then, that the extremity of Brown's anarcho-capitalists is found there. It is equally appropriate that the rejection or qualification of the model comes from elsewhere: Germany for Kahn's expressivists and, of course, East Asia in modern debate.

To say that the United States is the heartland of Market individualism is not to say that all the individuals imagined there are concerned only with the material gain and loss of Market transaction and calculation. In my own chapter, 'Mr Smith, Meet Mr Hawken', I investigate one portrayal of individuals aimed at the American public that is not notably materialist, however individualist it may be. That portrayal is Paul Hawken's *Growing a Business* (1987). This book, associated with a television series, deals with how to set up and run a small business. Hawken's work is interesting because of the model of Market selves that it contains, the way that he portrays owners, their businesses and the relationship between the two. For Hawken, the successful Market actor and the proper Market self are by no means the rational calculator driven by pecuniary interest that seems to lurk within the butcher, the brewer and the baker, or even a more primal actor's drive to seek pleasure and avoid pain. Hawken's actor is self-regarding to be sure, but hardly the locus of instrumental rationality that the expressivists feared. Instead, the self that the self-regarding Market actor regards is intensely a being of sentiments. Moreover, these sentiments are given naturally, for they are beyond calculation and manipulation. Rather, they spring from a non-rational core being that the actor possesses and, seemingly, can do nothing to affect. Here is the transcendence that the expressivists said the Market model denied, a set of meanings that constrain and motivate Market actors. Crucially, however, this transcendence springs from an inaccessible and unalterable part of the self rather than from collective social interaction.

Such a view of the proper Market self is important for making us aware that the implicit motives connoted by the idea of self-interest and self-regard are more problematic than they seem at first glance, as is the distinction between freedom and constraint. In fact, the non-rationality, the complexity and the intractable nature of motive that are expressed in Hawken's book raise the possibility that Market actors are driven by such a complex and incalculable set of motives that they can not be summarised in any revealing way by labels like 'autonomy' and 'self-interest'. But while the points I draw from Hawken, and from a long line of commentators before him, raise doubts about the utility of some of the rhetoric of the Market model, they also raise doubts about the arguments of some of the critics of the Market. This is because Hawken's Market is not the scene of a battle between rapacities, but is instead the scene of a multitude of moral expressions. In a way, then, Hawken echoes the expressivists and resembles those whom Kahn describes, people who value the market as an institution but reject the calculating individualism associated with it.

Hawken's model of the proper Market self accords nicely with the logic of the anarcho-capitalists. The petty entrepreneurs that Hawken describes are, it seems, both humane and benign, for their moral compulsions are, always, moral. Just as the Market of the Scottish Enlightenment was guided by a Divine Providence, so Hawken's moral entrepreneurs never feel compelled to be professional thugs, slave traders or poison-gas manufacturers. Their humane and benign sentiments should not be hindered lest they be perverted and those who embody them be thwarted. However, Hawken's argument can be turned against the anarcho-capitalist position that it seems at first glance to affirm. The very Market that, by its freedom, permits free moral expression also has systemic properties that can hinder that expression and so pervert it. Like the anarcho-capitalists, Hawken fails to consider the ways that the Market is very close to what the expressivists say that it is not: that is, a collective social enterprise that has properties of its own that emerge through interaction, properties that constrain individuals.

This constraint, however, is perceived only dimly by Market advocates, and its social nature is perceived more dimly still. Although competitive discipline, a form of constraint, is a feature of the Market model, choice and autonomy are stressed more often; except, perhaps, when firms fire large numbers of workers. Even when people like Paul Hawken construe actors in a way that indicates that they are constrained, the source of that constraint is interpreted as being internal, an inescapable part of the self, rather than external, springing from state or society and one's position in it. In this sense, the anarcho-capitalists have the rhetorical upper hand. However, as I have described already in this Introduction, there is one area of debate about the Market model where the stress on autonomy, the rejection of constraint and their relationship with prosperity and economic success are brought into question. That is the debate about East Asian economies, the subject of Alan Smart's 'Oriental Despotism and Sugar-Coated Bullets: Representations of the Market in China'.

East Asia is anomalous in terms of the Market model. In that region, transactors are not autonomous individuals. Notoriously, for example, Japanese employees are not free labour, but are incorporated into the firms that employ them in a range of ways. Likewise, state intervention in and guidance of firms and the economy is much more common than the Market model would allow. The anomaly, of course, is that East Asian economies are successful even though they appear to have separated the 'Free' from the 'Market', appear to have separated market institutions from the autonomous, self-seeking individual. This is not to say that Market advocates can not account for that success. They can. However, their explanations often have a distinct air of explaining it away, of *ad hoc* invocations of special circumstance, telling us how much better these economies would be doing if they conformed to the model and how their deviations mean that they are storing up trouble for the future. This is especially so when advocates consider the Chinese economy, perched between market and plan, the focus of Smart's chapter.

In his discussion of East Asian economies and Western efforts to understand them, Smart raises some important points. The one that is perhaps the most pertinent here is that consideration of those anomalous economies brings to the fore another anomaly, that of the position of constraint in the Market model. As I said, even though constraint is perceived only dimly, it appears to be central. Truly autonomous, self-seeking transactors, after all, would be threats to markets, rather than their motors. They would be Lord Vaizey's anathema, 'those who for purely selfish interests . . . seek to make money for themselves and let the rest go to hell' (quoted in Cockett 1994: 228). Such actors would see no *a priori* reason to be honest in their representations or to honour their agreements; the result would be market insecurity and inefficiency, or massive and costly policing efforts. Similarly, and at a different level, there is no reason why actors should want to express entrepreneurially sentiments of which Hawken would approve. While Scottish Enlightenment thinkers got around this problem by invoking Divine Providence, modern Western societies have tended to trust more in the State than in God, in the form of contract law, trades descriptions acts, child labour laws and the like.

As Smart describes them, then, debates about the nature of East Asian economies recapitulate the dialectic sketched in the preceding chapters. The occidentalised modern West of autonomous individuals that is portrayed in the Market model stands opposed to its antithesis, a realm of social and political constraint and obligation. But while these debates recapitulate that dialectic, they also re-cast it. No longer can the advocates of sociality and polity be dismissed as backward-looking and ineffectual, or portrayed as advocating what looks suspiciously like Oriental Despotism, an enduring image that, Smart argues, colours much of the consideration of East Asia. Instead, in these debates the position of these advocates is one of strength. The occidentalism of the Market model now looks increasingly peripheral, and Oriental Despotism is transmuted into Neo-Confucianism, a cohesive order that is a key to East Asian success. It is these transformations that make East Asia so intriguing to those who seek to understand and unpack the Market model.

These first four chapters analyse polemical statements and debates about the Market and its actors and institutions in a way that lays out and investigates some of the basic features of the Market model. These revolve around notions of individuals and the collectivity, the relationship between the two and the place of the Market in that relationship. Together, these chapters offer a sustained description and analysis of a central aspect of the Market model. That is, the assertion that people in general, and Market actors in particular, are and ought to be autonomous individuals who look to their own best interest. While these chapters consider some of the basic assumptions contained in the Market model and begin to situate that model in its broader context, the two remaining chapters are oriented rather differently. They are concerned less with the general features of the model than with its practical uses and applicability, and especially its extension into novel areas.

The first of these chapters does so through consideration of the link between the Market model and political practice in that centre of Markets and autonomous individuals, the United States. It is Carol MacLennan's 'Democracy under the Influence: Cost–Benefit Analysis in the United States'. The Benthamite calculus of pain and pleasure that the expressivists criticised reduces the range of human experience to a single equation. This is the equation that underlies cost–benefit analysis. Previously a fairly obscure way of assessing certain sorts of decisions, it was introduced as a criterion for government decision-making and the formulation of policy in the United States in the 1970s and spread widely in the 1980s.

MacLennan shows how the spread of cost–benefit analysis, together with related devices such as risk assessment, marks a significant change in American governance. Hitherto, she notes, government policy was shaped by considerations that were more clearly political. While those considerations were influenced by commercial interests, the legitimate role of business was restricted to being an advocate of its own interests and a source of ideas about organisational efficiency that government might emulate so that it could achieve its policy goals more effectively. However, the entrenching of cost–benefit analysis in government gradually, but thoroughly, changed all this.

To begin with, cost–benefit analysis requires reducing all policy goals to Market terms: dollars' worth of pain and pleasure. A view of the Grand Canyon, the risk of accident to a worker in a plant and the consequences of that accident for the worker, the range of species in a wetland and the results of its reduction, all must be assigned a monetary value if they are to be the subject of government regulation. Similarly, the costs of that regulation must be put in dollar terms, though here the costs are those incurred by the corporations that will have to change the way they do things. These corporations stand as surrogates for 'the economy' and, though it, 'the society', and thereby are elevated from being one of the interests expressed in political debate to being a key interest incorporated in the structure of policy formulation. Further, government agencies concerned with such regulation are required to introduce cost–benefit consideration at the very beginning of the process by which they formulate proposals for regulatory policy. One consequence, as MacLennan describes, is the stifling of research by agencies like the Environmental Protection Agency on environmental hazards and novel forms of risk generated by new industrial technologies and products.

In her presentation, MacLennan illustrates what I said earlier is an important feature of the Market model, its expansionism. While many societies have markets and conceptions of market freedom, in most of these the logic of markets is taken to apply only to a restricted sphere. This, after all, is the strategy of Kahn's and Smart's Malaysian and Chinese policy-makers, and Paul Hawken's good entrepreneur. With the Market model, however, the logic of the Market and the attributes of Market actors are not restricted. Instead, they become the standard to which the logics and attributes of other spheres of life are reduced and by which they are judged. Thus, MacLennan's tale of the introduction of cost–benefit analysis into government deliberation in the United States is not a unique event, but an example of the tendency of the model to slip its reins and invade areas of life that hitherto were alien to it. This chapter, then, illustrates an important point: although the Market model springs from and speaks of a conception of economic activity, its scope is much broader. It appears to see economy as the core of human existence, and its advocates seek to make many areas of life and thought conform to its normative conception of that core.

The second of this pair of chapters is the only one to deal directly with the discipline of economics. It is Malcolm Chapman and Peter J. Buckley's 'Markets, Transaction Costs, Economists and Social Anthropologists'. The branch of economics that it describes, transaction cost economics, is one that seeks to apply Market logic to areas outside the realm of Market transactions, and particularly to the behaviour of managers and the organisation of firms. Previously in this Introduction I noted that some economists, confronted with the failure of market actors to behave in ways that conform to the Market model, have developed more complex models to accommodate that behaviour, while still maintaining the central notion of the rational, autonomous actor. I said that transaction cost economics is the development that is most widely known. While it is applied conventionally to firms, Oliver Williamson, probably its most famous advocate, sees in it the basis for a wholesale science of human organisation, one that would please the anarcho-capitalists in the way it denies legitimacy, and even a role, to the collectivity and the state (Hodgson 1988: 154–156). As Chapman and Buckley observe, this is the realm of grand claims for the power of a model based on the concept of rational calculation.

Transaction cost economics begins with the observation that transactions in the market carry costs beyond the direct price of the objects or services involved. These include the cost of information searches, of the risk of betrayal and so on, and they are covered under the general label of transaction costs. This branch of economics argues that when the direct costs together with the transaction costs of acquiring things in the market are higher than the costs of producing them within the firm, actors will elect to avoid these costs by expanding the firm and producing those things internally. Alternatively, when the direct and transaction costs of acquiring something in the market are lower than the costs of internal production, actors will elect to shrink the firm, to buy on the market what had hitherto been produced internally. The accounting of transaction costs, then, is central to predicting the size and shape of the firm, and hence the boundary between the firm and the market. This explanation is consonant with one important element of the Market model, for it assumes that economic actors measure and calculate the costs and benefits of different courses of action.

However, as was the case with the pension fund managers described by O'Barr and Conley, Chapman and Buckley found that the decisions made by the pharmaceutical and precision-instrument firms that they studied were not so simple. Commonly they were not made in terms of the monetary measurement and calculation of costs. Instead, more subjective judgements occur, based on sense and intuition, on being comfortable with a particular course of action, on repute or industry fashion. Their findings do not mean that the managers they studied are behaving unreasonably, any more than O'Barr and Conley's pension fund managers are behaving unreasonably. These findings do indicate, however, that these managers are not behaving rationally, in that they are not acting in accord with the assumptions of conventional economics and the Market model. Transaction cost economics, then, is an inadequate representation of how managers decide.

The reason for this, Chapman and Buckley conclude, is that transaction cost economics makes unreasonable assumptions about the context in which managers make their practical decisions. To begin with, managers face a great deal of uncertainty about how to measure direct costs within the firm: different measurement techniques produce different results, and procedures for measuring costs are as much subject to the tides of fashion as any other area of business. Further, managers are even more uncertain about how to calculate the transaction costs associated with different strategies, and few made any sustained effort to do so. Finally, and echoing MacLennan's criticism of cost–benefit analysis, transaction cost economics errs in assuming that definitive monetary costs of the sort required exist in principle, much less in practice. Rather, these costs are indeterminate and thus can not be quantified, and therefore they can not form the basis for rational (as distinct from reasonable) management decisions.

As economists develop more complex models, like those found in transaction cost economics and cost–benefit analysis, they move further away from the confident realm of empirical measurement and quantitative calculation of cost and benefit, pain and pleasure, a realm that is necessary if their discipline is to be the determinant, predictive science of human behaviour that many claim it to be. Chapman and Buckley's study shows that the decisions that transaction cost economics seeks to explain exist in an altogether different and more hesitant realm of subjective assessment, judgement and the like. This is the realm of perceived costs rather than real costs, of assessments based on experience, intuition and argument, rather than the direct comparison of monetary costs. It is, in short, a realm of subjective and perhaps inevitably uncertain assessment rather than objective measurement.

As Chapman and Buckley note, when economists begin to move into this realm, they begin to move toward the second boundary that concerns them in this chapter, the boundary that has conventionally separated economics and anthropology. While both disciplines are concerned with human choice, the former has elected to represent its subject-matter through idealised constructions and simplifying assumptions that reflect and help justify its self-representation as an objective and predictive science based on categories, measurements, variables and rules produced within economics itself (McCloskey 1986). Alternatively, one enduring concern of anthropology is the study of practical action in an imperfect world, the interpretative study of why people do what they do in their own terms and in the terms of their social groups, rather than in terms of objective criteria imposed by the analyst. When transaction cost economists represent the firm and organisational relations within it, they move beyond the modelling of relatively impersonal markets that is the conventional purview of neo-classical economics. In moving into a realm that anthropologists conventionally inhabit, Chapman and Buckley argue, they may provide an opening for anthropologists to begin to unpack and rewrite the assumptions that underlie neo-classical economics, and through it the Market model.

Chapman and Buckley's is appropriate as the final substantive chapter for this collection, for it summarises in terms of an engagement with formal economics a theme that runs through the collection. That theme is the limits of the Market model and hence the boundary of the Market. Their chapter shows that Market logic, at least as reflected in institutional economics, is bounded empirically, a point ignored by those who imposed cost–benefit analysis on government regulatory agencies. In the firm, managers do not, indeed can not, conform to it, any more than can the pension fund managers that O'Barr and Conley describe. This empirical bounding echoes a point made in my own chapter. At least some Market actors see themselves and their work as being the antithesis of the instrumental rationality that is part of the Market model. While Paul Hawken's entrepreneur may be an individualist of the sort supposed by the Market model, that individual is not so Benthamite as the model indicates.

While some chapters indicate ways that the Market model has empirical limits, other suggest that those limits ought to be tightened. As Alan Smart notes, deviation from the model is taken by many to be an important contributor to the East Asian Economic Miracle, where Adam Smith is replaced not by Paul Hawken but by Confucius. In his chapter, Smart repeats a point that has been made before, and is made by Susan Love Brown with regard to the anarcho-capitalists: the Market appears to exist only if it is a sphere of life rather than the whole of life, regardless of the Market visions of the anarcho-capitalists and extremist economists like Gary Becker. The desire to restrict the scope of the Market motivates the Malay policy-makers that Joel Kahn describes, who seek, like many Islamic commentators, to gain the advantages of the Market while restricting its scope to the formal economic sphere. Market advocates may see this desire as wrong-headed and backward; but equally it can be seen as an effort to emulate the economic success of Japan and several other East Asian countries.

As Carol MacLennan shows, however, marking a boundary around the Market may be more difficult than it seems. Market rhetoric is pre-eminently the rhetoric of worldly success, and it is not purely coincidence that the rise of cost–benefit analysis occurred in the United States at the time when that country was experiencing an unusually prolonged period of economic stagnation and inflation, coupled with the political uncertainty that surrounded its defeat in Vietnam. The United States may be unusual in the strength of its adherence to individualism and the notion of the Market. However, MacLennan's picture, of the power of commercial interests to define the very basis of government regulatory policy under presidents Reagan and Bush, applies more generally, for it helps us to unbleach the rhetoric of the Market and see the ways in which it is linked with powerful economic and social interests that usually seek its expansion and resist attempts to restrict it.

The desire to unbleach the Market model, to recall that the Market is, after all, a capitalist Market, makes it clear that the questions raised and arguments put forward in this Introduction and in the chapters of this collection are hardly novel. Rather, they echo the historical concern by social scientists to describe and analyse the nature of Western capitalism. In his Afterword, William Roseberry helps point out some of the ways that this older description and debate anticipates what we say here.

I said at the beginning of this Introduction that one purpose of this collection is to make the familiar, the Market, seem strange, and so to gain that mental distance that allows intellectual reflection. As Roseberry observes, Karl Marx, Max Weber and Karl Polanyi had much the same goal, desired the same critical distance. In doing so they sought a way to take a complex and taken-for-granted set of socio-economic relations and practices and unpack them, showing their cultural and social underpinnings. As Roseberry notes, this collection shares an important concern of theirs, the concern to investigate the ways that this institution that seems so asocial, capitalist Market economy, relies not upon the autonomous and calculating actor surrounded by impersonal objects and impersonal actors, but instead upon the very social relationships and values that the model denies. Roseberry, then, provides us with the salutary lesson, that in our effort to understand the Market we need to go back to our intellectual forebears, for they have much to offer us.

Conclusions

> What we can not speak about, we must pass over in silence.
>
> Ludwig Wittgenstein, *Tractatus Logico-philosophicus*

In their discussions of the different areas of Western life and thought that they present, the contributors to this collection illustrate and extend a number of the general points laid out in this Introduction. Most generally, they show the complexity of the Market model and they show how uncertain is its relationship to the ways that people think about and act in their economic lives.

This complexity is to be expected, for a framework espoused and invoked so widely has to accommodate a range of interests and perspectives. The price is internal contradiction. This is most apparent when we compare the aspects of the model that speak of individual autonomy and choice with those that speak of structural imperatives, imperatives that are important for lending the model its air of inevitability and for linking its operation to the achievement of the greatest good for the greatest number. Of course, this collection is not the first work to note the problematic empirical and conceptual relationship between the model and the way people live their economic lives.

To say that the model is conceptually and empirically dubious and internally inconsistent is to judge it against a certain set of standards: those that apply to statements about the way the world is, or ought to be. In fact, those who espouse the model invite such standards, for they are making empirical and normative claims. However, it may be more appropriate and more interesting to think of it differently, as being like a lingua franca, a linguistic and communicative analogy that echoes Adam Smith's own notion (1976: 17) that the propensity to truck, barter and exchange may derive from speech and communication. I want to consider some of the implications of this analogy.[12]

The Market model is expressed in language, and languages model our experiences. To say this is to say that 'language' and 'model' overlap to some degree. To say that the Market model is like a lingua franca is to suggest a somewhat different point, that the model is a creature of public discourse between groups, though groups defined by the different places they occupy in society rather than the different languages they speak. People in commerce, education, medicine and the like each have their own specialist terms and their own ways of using ordinary words. Often these are of little use when those in one group are speaking to those in another or, more pertinent to my point here, are speaking to a larger audience. Not only do such local usages embody a distinct, local set of practices and experiences, they also serve an exclusionary function. Knowledge and use of the special language define the existence of a specific group, as they identify and distinguish between occupational insiders and outsiders (see, for example, Salaman 1986). Local languages being unsuited for public communication, a lingua franca or public language is useful and probably necessary.

Daniel Defoe describes a similar view of the nature of local occupational languages. In his *Complete English Tradesman*, Defoe is concerned with an aspect of this exclusionary aspect of local languages. That is, the way that they facilitate what Defoe considered deceit in dealing with outsiders, and particularly those in different trades, the tradesmen for whom Defoe was writing. According to Vivienne Brown (1994: 80), Defoe advocated 'a universal trading language', though interestingly what Defoe seems to have envisioned was that commerce itself would become a universal language. Brown quotes Defoe (1987: 25): 'every tradesman would so study the terms of art of other trades, that he might be able to speak to every manufacturer or artist in his own language, and understand them when they talked to one another; this would make trade be a kind of universal language'.

To see the Market model as being like a language suggests that the empirical accuracy of the model is not the point, at least for explaining why it is so common. While a language may have a vocabulary that is rich in certain areas and impoverished in others, we would not normally assess it in terms of whether it is right or wrong, internally consistent or inconsistent. Rather, a language provides the tools by which its speakers communicate with each other about the world. Moreover, the analogy with a lingua franca, a particular type of language, suggests that there is no particular reason to think that the model will reflect most people's practical experiences all that well. As with a lingua franca, people do not choose the Market model voluntarily because it reflects their world; in speaking in its terms, people are not necessarily endorsing it or deceiving themselves or others about its accuracy. Rather, people, even those who may be sceptical about the model, confront it as they confront a lingua franca, as an external reality that they have to adopt if they are to communicate with others.

This imagery of groups and their languages is a socio-linguistic parallel to one of Durkheim's (1984) observations about societies of organic solidarity. People in such societies who occupy different positions in the division of labour have relatively little in common with each other, have relatively little shared experience. For Durkheim, this is manifest as a weak *conscience collective*. Equally, and in terms of my point here, it is manifest as the relative absence of a shared language, in the broad sense in which I am using the term. In such a situation, we could expect a public language to emerge to facilitate communication, and we would expect that such a language would almost necessarily be only a weak reflection of the knowledge and orientation of the separate groups in society.

To say that the Market model is like a public language is not to say that it is a neutral vehicle for communication. Rather, as a language it can be expected to have an influence on those who use it. Many years ago, Kenneth Burke (1973 [1941]) argued that the words of a language do not simply identify objects and actions in the external world. In addition, they necessarily evaluate and motivate. They do not just describe an object, they express an attitude toward it and so suggest actions appropriate to it. This is also true of the more localised languages of different groups in society, though these localised languages do so less obviously because those within such groups are likely already to have a relatively high degree of common experience and orientation (see, for example, Bernstein 1971). To complicate matters, those who are exposed to a lingua franca are shaped by it, learn the ways of thinking and acting associated with it, of the sort that Burke describes. When thus absorbed, the language and the knowledge and orientation can converge. This is, I imagine, one of the things that motivates those who seek to impose public languages of the sort I describe here.

In addition to this motivational structure embedded in it, the Market model as a public language also shapes the discourse in which it is used. Fredric Jameson (1991: 263) points to this power of the Market as a language when he says that 'the rhetoric of the market has been a fundamental and central component of . . . [the] struggle for the legitimation of left discourse'. The language of the Market model, for Jameson, looks like the only acceptable public language.

> Everyone is now willing to mumble, as though it were an inconse-
> quential concession in passing to public opinion and current received
> wisdom (*or shared communication presuppositions*) that no society can
> function effectively without the market and that planning is obviously
> impossible (Jameson 1991: 263, emphasis added).

There is an intriguing irony here. The shift of scholarly concern
from capitalism and production to the Market and consumption,
noted previously in this Introduction, is part of the shift from the
modern, with its master narratives, to the post-modern, with its
multiplicity of voices. The Market, explicitly concerned with choice
and individual difference and explicitly refraining from passing
judgement on those choices and differences, would seem particularly suited to be the liberating mechanism to usher in the post-
modern era. But then, as a post-modernist like Jameson notes, and
as Francis Fukuyama (1992) illustrates, the Market becomes its
own master narrative.

I want to stress that when I write that it may be fruitful to treat
the Market model as a language, I do not mean that we can treat it
only as a language, if one means by 'language' either a neutral
means of communication or an expressive but otherwise inconsequential addendum to what people think and do in their real lives.
In treating the model as being like a public language I am asserting
that there is truth in the point that Jameson (1991: 264) draws from
Stuart Hall, that 'the fundamental level on which political struggle
is waged is that of the legitimacy of concepts like . . . *the market* –
at least *right now*'. But the reason that this public language is
important right now is that it is more than just a way of speaking
to each other. This should be obvious from the very fact that the
language often is a point of conflict and is introduced into
particular areas of people's lives through an exercise of power. I
do not, then, mean that this public language can be treated in a
Geertzian manner as a web of meaning, as just 'an ensemble of
texts' (Geertz 1973: 5, 452).

The separation of what things mean from what they do (which
is implied in treating the Market model as only an ensemble of
texts), the separation of the cultural from the social, ignores the
way that the terminology and the forms of thought expressed by
the Market model (or any public language) are a form of power,
in the way that Steven Lukes (1974) described. For Lukes, the most
subtle form of power is that which shapes what can be debated

and how it can be debated. As a public language, the Market model provides the vocabulary and conceptual equipment that make it relatively easy to define certain sorts of things as problems and relatively hard to define other sorts of things that way. Just as it influences the sorts of problems that can be addressed, so it influences what is likely to appear as an acceptable, plausible solution.

In making an analogy between the Market model and public language, I am drawing a parallel with what Richard Wilk (1995) says in his discussion of beauty pageants in Belize. He notes that the structure of such pageants is relatively uniform through much of the world, which is to say across a range of divergent local groups. This over-arching uniformity is a mechanism through which people in different places express their own values, such as conceptions of beauty and talent, just as the language of the Market model is a mechanism through which people express themselves. However, the structure itself constrains and shapes that expression. In the case of Belize, the desire to succeed in the international field of beauty pageants leads those in charge of national pageants to run them in ways that enhance their international standing. As a consequence, in the progression of pageants in Belize from the local to the national, standards change, as tastes and values that are local give way to those that are more international.

Local diversity, thus, is contained within a common frame, which itself motivates those who participate in such a way that diversity is reduced or, perhaps better said, qualified. Wilk says that the common frame of international beauty pageants produces what he calls 'structures of common difference'. With this he refers to the ways that a system '*promotes difference* instead of suppressing it, but difference of a particular kind' (Wilk 1995: 118). And the 'difference of a particular kind' is the difference that is recognised and rewarded by the governing structure, whether of beauty pageants or consumer capitalism.[13] To continue the parallel with the Market model, Market rhetoric promotes difference because it encourages people to see themselves and their organisations as competitive sellers and buyers of different sorts of goods and services. At the same time, it channels and even suppresses difference, because it encourages people to see themselves and their organisations as Market actors rather than in other ways.

I have related what Wilk says of Belizean beauty pageants not simply because it seems on its face to be so distant from the Market

model. I have related it also because it makes an important point
about the structures through which people act and address their
audience, whether through donning a swimsuit or through talk
of the sanctity of consumer choice. These structures embody social
causes and social power and have concrete social consequences –
aspects which are less visible in the bleached world of the Market
than they had been previously.

A simple example will illustrate the sort of power and consequences I mean. The spread of the language of the Market model
encourages casting people in terms of their market transactions,
and especially as consumers. In doing so, it highlights just one
aspect of their existence, even of their economic existence, by
ignoring the fact that people commonly are also workers or
producers, and that even those who are not workers generally are
dependent upon a worker for their consumption (a parallel point
is in Tomlinson 1990: 136). As the chairman of Unilever put it:
'The old, rigid barriers are disappearing – class and rank; blue
collar and white collar; council tenant and home owner; employee
and housewife. More and more we are simply consumers' (Perry
1994: 4, quoted in Gabriel and Lang 1995: 36). The interests of
people-as-consumers, however, are presented as more uniform,
universal and just than the interests of people-as-workers, which
often are presented as unjust, sectional self-interest. As one writer
casually puts it, the workforce has 'the primary interest of
preserving . . . its jobs, rather than . . . serving the public' (Ormerod
1994: 65).

Thus, 'everyone', which is to say people-as-consumers, is in
favour of lower prices for electricity, for example. The only people
who might be opposed are those with a special, sectional interest.
In practice, this means those who depend upon the electricity
industry for their income, particularly those who work in it. These
are the people whose control over production, wages and levels
of employment are likely to be reduced by the changes that lead
to the reduced prices that benefit 'everyone'. Any rhetoric that
stresses people's identity as consumers to the exclusion of their
identity as producers (or as those who depend on producers)
makes it easier to construe electricity workers, to continue the
example, as a special interest that must bow to the common
interest. The result, as is shown in the history of labour relations
in Britain and the United States since 1980, is that sets of workers,
isolated in particular industries and firms, can be overridden in

the name of the common interest, one at a time, and their interests as people (as both producers and consumers) seriously damaged. A public rhetoric that construed people as producers or as dependent upon them would make this process of serial immiseration much harder.

The Market model, or any candidate for the status of public language, is likely to become powerful when it is adopted by institutions that are central to public debate, particularly governments. Consequently, those who can shape the discourse of government, the sort of language that government understands, can help determine what becomes the leading public language. I do not mean by this that government is a neutral set of machinery that, like a public address system, is unaffected by the message it transmits. Rather, public languages can have implications for the size, shape and duties of government, as Carol MacLennan shows in her chapter, and many who sought to control government in the name of the Market model espoused the goal of reducing it to a minimal function.[14]

In the case of the Market model, an important factor in this shaping of the discourse of government is the movement of senior corporate figures into senior government positions. This movement reflects the increasing size and scope of large corporations and their increasing power relative to governments, as well as reflecting the relatively weak power of other candidates for the status of leading public language. An example of the rising ability of senior managers to influence government in this way is Robert McNamara. President of Ford Motor Company, he was appointed United States Secretary of Defense by John F. Kennedy in 1961, explicitly in order to introduce modern corporate mechanisms of control in the American military. With the translation of people like McNamara, followed by the growing use of firms of corporate consultants to advise governments and shape their policy, the rhetoric of senior management is likely to become important in public debate, is likely to become the dominant public language. To complicate still further, however, a tale already complex, the logic of efficiency and rationality with which corporations and their senior staff explain their decisions frequently may be little more than a translation into Market terms of a set of decisions and actions that are based on rather different and more parochial concerns. This, at least, is one implication of Alexandra Ouroussoff's (1993, 1995) studies of British corporate managers, and of Malcolm Chapman and Peter J. Buckley's chapter in this collection.

Once the model of the Market becomes established, it is maintained in part for the same reasons that any common realm of discourse is maintained, the power of fashion and repute. Everyone is under pressure to adopt it, if only in order to be seen as trustworthy in the manner described previously in this Introduction. Failure to do so is to risk being treated as parochial, and hence of not being taken seriously. As Jane Nadel-Klein (1991) argues, for many powerful groups in the West, localism and the failure to display the signs of a more global orientation are the signs of inadequacy that place one in the ranks of those about whom decisions are made, rather than those who make decisions.

I have drawn the analogy between the Market model and a lingua franca in part because I think it is revealing. I have made it also, however, because it offers a way of approaching the Market model that may turn out to be more fruitful than the empirical investigation of the model's adequacy. Investigating and understanding the model's adequacy is important, not least because it allows an interrogation of its claims to scientific validity and hence of one element of its rhetorical power. However, the problematic nature of the model's relationship both with people's daily lives and with the wealth of nations suggests that much of its strength lies elsewhere, in the social and cultural forces that sustain it. To begin to get at these, however, we need to have a way to approach the Market model, a way to begin to think about it. Doing so requires a way of speaking about what the Market describes, and developing that way of speaking may be easier if we recognise that the Market is also a way of speaking. But to say this is only to repeat a point I made earlier, that the Market model is a fit topic for scholarly analysis. If this collection furthers that analysis, it will have served its purpose.

Acknowledgements

As ever, my writing reflects the clarifying influence of Achsah Carrier. I thank Stephan Carrier, Neil Duxbury, Stephen Gudeman, Eric Hirsch, Donald McCloskey, Avner Offer, Gísli Pálsson and Richard Wilk for their comments on drafts of this Introduction. For their interest and helpful comments at presentations of different parts and versions of this Introduction I thank also participants in anthropology department seminars at University College London, the London School of Economics, Queen's University Belfast, and the Universities of Durham, Edinburgh, Manchester and St Andrews, and a psychology department seminar at the University of Exeter. Finally, the audience at the session of the American Anthropological Association meeting of 1995 were much more enthusiastic and their questions more insightful than anyone would expect early on a Sunday morning. The notion of the Market model as a way of speaking, put forward in the concluding section of this Introduction, draws from the published work of Alexandra Ouroussoff (1993) and on conversations with her. While she was part of the AAA session on the Market model, she was unable to participate in this collection, which is poorer as a result.

Notes

1. Mary Douglas and Baron Isherwood (1978) also stress the cultural interpretation of objects. However, while Sahlins was attacking Marxist anthropology, they were attacking conventional economics, and particularly its truncated conception of 'taste' as a rendering of buyer demand. For an illustration of this use of taste, see Marsden (1986: Chap. 3). A criticism of the economic treatment of demand that begins closer to conventional economics is in Hirschman (1986 *a*).
2. The origin and production of this report illustrates the power of the Market model in World Bank thinking, the place of economists trained in the US and the UK in defending and extending that model, and the threat to it posed by Japan. The history of the report is described in a lucid and revealing way by Robert Wade (1996).
3. This is hardly a novel observation. In 1829, T. B. Macaulay (quoted in Haskell 1993: 448 *n* 7) lodged a parallel criticism against a parallel assumption in utilitarianism, a lineal ancestor of the modern Market model, saying that it reduced to the assertion 'that men, if they can, will do as they choose'.
4. My presentation of conformity, appearing trustworthy and

predictable, draws on a similar argument made by Rosabeth Moss Kanter (1977) in her analysis of relations among managers within a single firm. For a discussion of the importance of trustworthiness and predictability between market transactors, see Kollock (1994: 313–321).

5. Some parts of the environmental movement also contain a practical criticism of the Market, though these tend to be overwhelmed by concerns that bear less directly on the Market (Gabriel and Lang 1995: 181–185). Those engaged in marginal forms of commerce like garage sales (in the US) or car boot sales (in the UK) occasionally produce fairly articulate and thoroughgoing criticisms of the Market (Herrmann 1996; Soiffer and Herrmann 1987). These criticisms do not, however, seem to have attracted much popular following.

6. The belief that the Market reflects what is natural authorises government policies that alter the existing organisation of society and that disrupt people's lives. These government interventions are intended to change existing social relations and practices to bring them into accord with a state of affairs said to be natural. This is just the sort of government action that, when undertaken by governments of the left, outraged those who espouse the Market model.

7. While choice is a central element in the Market model, Paul Alexander (1992) suggests that, in working market systems, choice is in fact restricted in many ways. It might be better to say that in market systems buyers choose among choices that they do not themselves choose. I return to this point near the end of this Introduction.

8. For a critical analysis of some of the mental habits that underlie the Market, see Gorz (1989). Norbert Wiley (1983) draws provocative parallels between Weber and Keynes, parallels that suggest how Keynes was concerned with this issue as well.

9. This emergence is not complete even in the West, where pockets of pre-modernity are seen to linger (e.g. Nadel-Klein 1991, 1995). The struggle is especially apparent in government policies toward farming. These are often shaped by a desire to protect, or be seen to protect, the family farm. This is an institution cloaked in pre-modern values of place, kinship and proximity to nature. The popular appeal of the image of the family farm shows, of course, public ambivalence toward the Market and the modern.

10. Pnina Werbner (pers. comm.) observes that, in at least one of their guises, markets are, in fact, strongly Oriental, for the Orient is the location of the famous souks and bazaars of Western imagination. In accord with Werbner's observation, Caroline Humphrey (1995: 62–63) notes that when, following the collapse of the Soviet Union, the Market came to Moscow, the street markets that had led a healthy if semi-clandestine existence faced increased repression by state authorities. It is worth noting that a similar process seems to have occurred in the West. With the rise of capitalism in the eighteenth century in Britain, towns moved their markets out of the public places they had occupied into enclosed market buildings (Borsay 1989: 107, 294).

11. This conflation of the Market with the modern West is influential in modern anthropology, where invocations of markets and market actors frequently stand for the West in a contrast with non-Western social and cultural systems, in spite of the fact that some important economic anthropologists earlier in this century sought to undercut the equation of markets and the West (e.g. Pospisil 1963; Tax 1953). This tendency is apparent in work on many ethnographic regions, as in the writings on South Asia of Louis Dumont (1970, 1977; see Fuller 1989; Macfarlane 1992/93) and McKim Marriott (e.g. Marriott and Inden 1977; see Spencer 1995). However, it is probably most notable in the anthropology of Melanesia, to a degree in the work of C. A. Gregory (1980, 1982), and particularly in the work of Marilyn Strathern (1988), for whom the West of autonomous actors possessing and transacting private property stands opposed to the Melanesia of people and things defined and even generated by their relationships with others (see Carrier 1995).

12. One could substitute 'hegemonic discourse' for 'lingua franca', as Elizabeth Tonkin (pers. comm.) has suggested. While it presents its own difficulties, especially the tendency to a sort of linguistic determinism, I stick to 'lingua franca' to avoid imposing at the outset the socio-political judgements implicit in Tonkin's preferred phrase.

13. This seems to be implicit in Paul Alexander's (1992) point that consumer choice in existing market systems is in fact limited in important ways. The choices that are available, then, look like Wilk's difference: choice is there but it is 'of a

particular kind'. To pursue this point would entail approaching more closely than is appropriate in this Introduction the boundary between the concept of the Market and consumption studies.

14. Here I want to touch on another contradiction in the Market, though an empirical rather than a conceptual one. For Britain at least, the election of a party espousing a populist version of the Market model led to a pronounced centralisation of many areas of government activity, so strengthening government in the sense of reducing the ability of citizens to affect its operations. Local government power was reduced sharply in the 1980s, most visibly in the way that many aspects of the control of police, education, local taxation and local spending were removed from local bodies and placed in the hands of the national government. Though less pronounced, this happened to a degree in the United States during the 1980s as well. An analogous point could be made about the frequently-renamed Common Market. Its rhetoric of a free internal Market has been associated with extensive legislation that aims to impose through an exercise of government power the uniformity that is said to be a pre-requisite of a free market in goods and services.

References

Acheson, James M. 1985. The Social Organization of the Maine Lobster Market. Pp. 105–130 in Stuart Plattner (ed.), *Markets and Marketing*. Monographs in Economic Anthropology, No. 4. Lanham, Md: University Press of America.

Agnew, Jean-Christophe 1986. *Worlds Apart: The Market and the Theater in Anglo-American Thought, 1550–1750*. New York: Cambridge University Press.

Alexander, Paul 1992. What's in a Price? Trading Practices in Peasant (and Other) Markets. Pp. 79–96 in Roy Dilley (ed.), *Contesting Markets: Analyses of Ideology, Discourse and Practice*. Edinburgh: Edinburgh University Press.

Arnold, Thurman 1937. *The Folklore of Capitalism*. New Haven: Yale University Press.

Becker, Gary S. 1991. *A Treatise on the Family*. Enlarged edition. Cambridge, Mass.: Harvard University Press.

Becker, Gary S. 1996. Religions Thrive in a Free Market, Too. *Business Week* (15 January): 7.

Bell, Daniel 1983. *The Coming of Post-Industrial Society: A Venture in Social Forecasting*. New York: Basic Books.

Bernstein, Basil 1971. A Sociolinguistic Approach to Socialization. Pp. 143–169 in B. Bernstein, *Class, Codes and Control*, Vol. 1. London: Routledge & Kegan Paul.

Berthoff, Rowland 1980. Independence and Enterprise: Small Business in the American Dream. Pp. 28–48 in Stuart W. Bruchey (ed.), *Small Business in American Life*. New York: Columbia University Press.

Bloch, Maurice, and Jonathan Parry 1989. Introduction: Money and the Morality of Exchange. Pp. 1–32 in J. Parry and M. Bloch (eds), *Money and the Morality of Exchange*. Cambridge: Cambridge University Press.

Block, Fred 1990. *Postindustrial Possibilities: A Critique of Economic Discourse*. Berkeley: University of California Press.

Borsay, Peter 1989. *The English Urban Renaissance: Culture and Society in the Provincial Town, 1660–1770*. Oxford: Clarendon Press.

Bosanquet, Nick 1983. *After the New Right*. London: Heinemann.

Bourdieu, Pierre 1984. *Distinction: A Social Critique of the Judgement of Taste*. London: Routledge & Kegan Paul.

Brown, Vivienne 1994. Higgling: The Language of Markets in Economic Discourse. Pp. 66–93 in Neil de Marchi and Mary S. Morgan (eds), *Higgling: Transactors and their Markets in the History of Economics*. (Annual supplement to volume 26 of *History of Political Economy*.) Durham, NC: Duke University Press.

Buckley, Peter J., and Malcolm Chapman 1995. The Perception and Measurement of Transaction Costs. MS.

Burke, Kenneth 1973 (1941). *The Philosophy of Literary Form*. Berkeley: University of California Press.

Carrier, James G. 1990. The Symbolism of Possession in Commodity Advertising. *Man* 25: 190–207.

Carrier, James G. 1994. *Gifts and Commodities: Exchange and Western Capitalism since 1700*. London: Routledge.

Carrier, James G. 1995. Maussian Occidentalism: Gift and Commodity Systems. In J. Carrier (ed.), *Occidentalism: Images of the West*. Oxford: Clarendon Press.

Carruthers, Bruce G., and Wendy Nelson Espeland 1991. Accounting for Rationality: Double-Entry Bookkeeping and the

Rhetoric of Economic Rationality. *American Journal of Sociology* 97: 31–69.

Chandler, Alfred D. 1977. *The Visible Hand: The Managerial Revolution in American Business.* Cambridge, Mass.: Belknap Press.

Cockett, Richard 1994. *Thinking the Unthinkable: Think-Tanks and the Economic Counter-Revolution, 1931–83.* London: Harper Collins.

Crowley, J. E. 1974. *This Sheba, Self: The Conceptualization of Economic Life in Eighteenth Century America.* Baltimore: Johns Hopkins University Press.

Davis, John 1973. Forms and Norms: The Economy of Social Relations. *Man* 18: 159–176.

Defoe, Daniel 1987 (1726). *The Complete English Tradesman.* Gloucester: Alan Sutton.

Dilley, Roy 1992. Contesting Markets. Pp. 1–34 in R. Dilley (ed.), *Contesting Markets: Analyses of Ideology, Discourse and Practice.* Edinburgh: Edinburgh University Press.

DiMaggio, Paul, and Walter Powell 1983. The Iron Cage Revisited: Institutional Isomorphism and Collective Rationality in Organizational Fields. *American Sociological Review* 48: 147–160.

Doeringer, Peter B., Philip I. Moss and David G. Terkla 1986. Capitalism and Kinship: Do Institutions Matter in the Labor Market? *Industrial and Labor Relations Review* 40: 48–60.

Dore, Ronald 1983. Goodwill and the Spirit of Market Capitalism. *British Journal of Sociology* 34: 459–482.

Douglas, Mary, and Baron Isherwood 1978. *The World of Goods.* Harmondsworth: Penguin.

Dumont, Louis 1970. *Homo Hierarchicus: The Caste System and its Implications.* London: Weidenfeld and Nicolson.

Dumont, Louis 1977. *From Mandeville to Marx: The Genesis and Triumph of Economic Ideology.* Chicago: University of Chicago Press.

Durkheim, Emile 1984. *The Division of Labour in Society.* London: Routledge & Kegan Paul.

Duxbury, Neil 1996. Do Markets Degrade? *Modern Law Review* 59: 331–348.

Economist 1995. Car Wars: Mr Kanter's Outrageous Gamble. *The Economist* (20 May): 81.

Eichenwald, Kurt 1995. *Serpent on the Rock.* New York: Harper Collins.

Ekins, Paul, and Manfred Max-Neef (eds) 1992. *Real-Life Economics:*

Understanding Wealth Creation. London: Routledge.

England, Paula 1993. The Separative Self: Androcentric Bias in Neoclassical Assumptions. Pp. 37–53 in Marianne A. Ferber and Julie A. Nelson (eds), *Beyond Economic Man: Feminist Theory and Economics*. Chicago: University of Chicago Press.

Everitt, Alan 1967. The Marketing of Agricultural Produce. Pp. 466–592 in Joan Thirsk (ed.), *The Agrarian History of England and Wales, Vol. IV, 1500–1640*. Cambridge: Cambridge University Press.

Ferber, Marianne A., and Julie A. Nelson (eds) 1993. *Beyond Economic Man: Feminist Theory and Economics*. Chicago: The University of Chicago Press.

Fitzgerald, Robert 1995. *Rowntree and the Marketing Revolution, 1862–1969*. Cambridge: Cambridge University Press.

Friedman, Milton 1953. The Methodology of Positive Economics. Pp. 3–43 in M. Friedman, *Essays in Positive Economics*. Chicago: University of Chicago Press.

Fukuyama, Francis 1992. *The End of History and the Last Man*. New York: The Free Press.

Fuller, Chris J. 1989. Misconceiving the Grain Heap: A Critique of the Concept of the Indian Jajmani System. Pp. 33–63 in Jonathan Parry and Maurice Bloch (eds), *Money and the Morality of Exchange*. Cambridge: Cambridge University Press.

Gabriel, Yiannis, and Tim Lang 1995. *The Unmanageable Consumer: Contemporary Consumption and its Fragmentation*. London: Sage.

Gambetta, Diego (ed.) 1988. *Trust: Making and Breaking Cooperative Relationships*. Oxford: Basil Blackwell.

Geertz, Clifford 1973. *The Interpretation of Cultures*. New York: Basic Books.

Gilbert, Dennis, and Joseph A. Kahl 1987. *The American Class Structure: A New Synthesis*. Belmont, Cal.: Wadsworth.

Gorz, André 1989. *Critique of Economic Reason*. London: Verso.

Granovetter, Mark 1985. Economic Action and Social Structure: The Problem of Embeddedness. *American Journal of Sociology* 91: 481–510.

Gregory, C. A. 1980. Gifts to Men and Gifts to God: Gift Exchange and Capital Accumulation in Contemporary Papua. *Man* 15: 626–652.

Gregory, C. A. 1982. *Gifts and Commodities*. London: Academic Press.

Grieco, Margaret 1987. *Keeping it in the Family: Social Networks and Employment Chance*. London: Tavistock.

Gudeman, Stephen 1986. *Economics as Culture: Models and Metaphors of Livelihood*. London: Routledge & Kegan Paul.

Gudeman, Stephen, and Alberto Rivera 1991. *Conversations in Colombia: The Domestic Economy in Life and Text*. New York: Cambridge University Press.

Habakkuk, H. J. 1971. Population, Commerce and Economic Ideas. Pp. 25–54 in A. Goodwin (ed.), *The New Cambridge Modern History VIII: The American and French Revolutions, 1763–93*. Cambridge: Cambridge University Press.

Hart, Keith 1986. Heads or Tails? Two Sides of the Coin. *Man* 21: 637–656.

Hartsock, Nancy C. N. 1985. Exchange Theory: Critique from a Feminist Standpoint. Pp. 57–70 in S. G. McNall (ed.), *Current Perspectives in Social Theory*, Vol. 6. Greenwich, Conn.: JAI Press.

Haskell, Thomas L. 1993. Persons as Uncaused Causes: John Stuart Mill, the Spirit of Capitalism, and the 'Invention' of Formalism. Pp. 441–502 in T. L. Haskell and Richard F. Teichgraeber III (eds), *The Culture of the Market: Historical Essays*. New York: Cambridge University Press.

Hawken, Paul 1987. *Growing a Business*. New York: Simon & Schuster.

Haworth, Alan 1994. *Anti-Libertarianism: Markets, Philosophy and Myth*. London: Routledge.

Herrmann, Gretchen 1996. Gift or Commodity: What Changes Hands in the U.S. Garage Sale? MS. (Forthcoming in *American Ethnologist*).

Hirsch, Eric 1993. Negotiated Limits: Interviews in South-East England. Pp. 67–95 in Jeanette Edwards, Sarah Franklin, E. Hirsch, Frances Price and Marilyn Strathern, *Technologies of Procreation: Kinship in the Age of Assisted Conception*. Manchester: Manchester University Press.

Hirschman, Albert O. 1977. *The Passions and the Interests*. Princeton: Princeton University Press.

Hirschman, Albert O. 1986 *a*. Against Parsimony: Three Easy Ways of Complicating some Categories of Economic Discourse. Pp. 142–160 in A. O. Hirschman, *Rival Views of Market Society and Other Recent Essays*. New York: Viking.

Hirschman, Albert O. 1986 *b*. The Concept of Interest: From Euphemism to Tautology. Pp. 35–55 in A. O. Hirschman, *Rival Views of Market Society and Other Recent Essays*. New York: Viking.

Hodgson, Geoffrey 1988. *Economics and Institutions: A Manifesto for a Modern Institutional Economics*. Cambridge: Polity Press.

Hollis, Martin and Edward J. Nell 1975. *Rational Economic Man: A Philosophical Critique of Neo-Classical Economics*. London: Cambridge University Press.

Humphrey, Caroline 1995. Creating a Culture of Disillusionment: Consumption in Moscow, a Chronicle of Changing Times. Pp. 43–68 in Daniel Miller (ed.), *Worlds Apart: Modernity through the Prism of the Local*. London: Routledge.

Humphrey, Caroline, and Stephen Hugh-Jones (eds) 1992. *Barter, Exchange and Value: An Anthropological Approach*. Cambridge: Cambridge University Press.

Jameson, Fredric 1991. *Postmodernism, or, The Cultural Logic of Late Capitalism*. Durham, NC: Duke University Press.

Jamieson, Ian 1980. Capitalism and Culture: A Comparative Analysis of British and American Manufacturing Organizations. *Sociology* 14: 217–245.

Kanter, Rosabeth Moss 1977. *Men and Women of the Corporation*. New York: Basic Books.

Keynes, John Maynard 1964. *The General Theory of Employment, Interest, and Money*. New York: Harcourt Brace Jovanovich.

Kirby, Maurice W., and Mary B. Rose (eds) 1994. *Business Enterprise in Modern Britain*. London: Routledge.

Kollock, Peter 1994. The Emergence of Exchange Structures: An Experimental Study of Uncertainty, Commitment, and Trust. *American Journal of Sociology* 100: 313–345.

Kuhn, Thomas 1970. *The Structure of Scientific Revolutions*. Chicago: University of Chicago Press.

Leibenstein, Harvey 1980. *Beyond Economic Man: A New Foundation for Microeconomics*. Cambridge, Mass.: Harvard University Press.

Lindblom, Charles Edward 1977. *Politics and Markets: The World's Political Economic Systems*. New York: Basic Books.

Lindstrom, Lamont 1993. *Cargo Cult! Strange Stories of Desire from New Guinea and Beyond*. Honolulu: University of Hawaii Press.

Lubasz, Heinz 1992. Adam Smith and the Invisible Hand – of the Market? Pp. 37–56 in Roy Dilley (ed.), *Contesting Markets: Analyses of Ideology, Discourse and Practice*. Edinburgh: Edinburgh University Press.

Lukes, Steven 1974. *Power: A Radical View*. London: Macmillan.

Macaulay, Stewart 1963. Non-Contractual Relations in Business: A Preliminary Study. *American Sociological Review* 28: 55–67.

McCloskey, Donald N. 1986. *The Rhetoric of Economics*. Brighton:

Wheatsheaf.

McCloskey, Donald N. 1990. *If You're so Smart: The Narrative of Economic Expertise*. Chicago: University of Chicago Press.

Macfarlane, Alan 1978. *The Origins of English Individualism*. Oxford: Basil Blackwell.

Macfarlane, Alan 1992/93. Louis Dumont and the Origins of Individualism. *Cambridge Anthropology* 16 (1): 1–28.

McNally, David 1993. *Against the Market: Political Economy, Market Socialism and the Marxist Critique*. London: Verso.

Marriott, McKim, and Ronald Inden 1977. Toward an Ethnosociology of South Asian Caste Systems. Pp. 227–238 in Kenneth David (ed.), *The New Wind: Changing Identities in South Asia*. The Hague: Mouton.

Marsden, David 1986. *The End of Economic Man? Custom and Competition in Labour Markets*. Brighton: Wheatsheaf.

Miller, Daniel 1995 *a*. Consumption as the Vanguard of History. Pp. 1–57 in D. Miller (ed.), *Acknowledging Consumption: A Review of New Studies*. London: Routledge.

Miller, Daniel 1995 *b*. Introduction: Anthropology, Modernity and Consumption. Pp. 1–22 in D. Miller (ed.), *Worlds Apart: Modernity through the Prism of the Local*. London: Routledge.

von Mises, Ludwig 1944. *Omnipotent Government*. New Haven: Yale University Press.

Morgan, David, and Mary Evans 1993. *The Battle for Britain: Citizenship and Ideology in the Second World War*. London: Routledge.

Mort, Frank 1986. The Texas Chain Store Massacre. *New Socialist* 35: 15–19.

Nadel-Klein, Jane 1991. Reweaving the Fringe: Localism, Tradition and Representation in British Ethnography. *American Ethnologist* 18: 500–17.

Nadel-Klein, Jane 1995. Occidentalism as a Cottage Industry: Representing the Autochthonous 'Other' in British and Irish Rural Studies. Pp. 109–134 in James G. Carrier (ed.), *Occidentalism: Images of the West*. Oxford: Clarendon Press.

Nash, George H. 1979. *The Conservative Intellectual Movement in America since 1945*. New York: Basic Books.

Nelson, Richard R., and Sidney G. Winter 1982. *An Evolutionary Theory of Economic Change*. Cambridge, Mass.: Belknap Press.

O'Barr, William M., and John M. Conley 1992. *Fortune and Folly: The Wealth and Power of Institutional Investing*. Homewood, Ill.:

Business One Irwin.

Ormerod, Paul 1994. *The Death of Economics*. London: Faber and Faber.

Ouroussoff, Alexandra 1993. Illusions of Rationality: False Premisses of the Liberal Tradition. *Man* 28: 281–298.

Ouroussoff, Alexandra 1995. The Problem of Consciousness in Corporate Rhetoric. Presented at the American Anthropological Association annual meeting, November, Washington, DC.

Pálsson, Gísli 1995. The Virtual Aquarium: Commodity Fiction and Cod Fishing. MS.

Pálsson, Gísli, and Agnar Helgason 1995. Figuring Fish and Measuring Men: The Individual Transferable Quota System in the Icelandic Cod Fishery. *Ocean and Coastal Management* 28: 117–146.

Parry, Jonathan 1986. *The Gift*, the Indian Gift and the 'Indian Gift'. *Man* 21: 453–473.

Pearce, Roy Harvey 1965. *Savagism and Civilization: A Study of the Indian and the American Mind*. Baltimore: Johns Hopkins Press.

Perry, Michael 1994. The Brand Vehicle for Value in a Changing Marketplace. Advertising Association, President's Lecture, 7 July, London.

Polanyi, Karl 1957 *a*. Aristotle Discovers the Economy. Pp. 64–94 in K. Polanyi, Conrad M. Arensberg and Harry W. Pearson (eds), *Trade and Market in the Early Empires: Economies in History and Theory*. Glencoe, Ill.: The Free Press.

Polanyi, Karl 1957 *b*. The Economy as Instituted Process. Pp. 243–270 in K. Polanyi, Conrad M. Arensberg and Harry W. Pearson (eds), *Trade and Market in the Early Empires: Economies in History and Theory*. Glencoe, Ill.: The Free Press.

Polanyi, Karl 1957 *c*. *The Great Transformation: The Political and Economic Origins of Our Time*. Boston: Beacon Press.

Pospisil, Leopold 1963. *Kapauku Papuan Economy*. New Haven: Yale University Press.

Robbins, Joel 1994. Equality as Value: Ideology in Dumont, Melanesia and the West. *Social Analysis* 36: 21–70.

Sahlins, Marshall 1976. *Culture and Practical Reason*. Chicago: University of Chicago Press.

Said, Edward 1978. *Orientalism*. Harmondsworth: Penguin.

Salaman, Graeme 1986. *Working*. London: Tavistock.

Sassen, Saskia 1990. *The Global City*. Princeton: Princeton University Press.

Schneider, David 1980. *American Kinship: A Cultural Account.* Second edition. Chicago: University of Chicago Press.

Schor, Juliet B. 1991. *The Overworked American.* New York: Basic Books.

Seguino, Stephanie, Thomas Stevens and Mark A. Lutz 1996. Gender and Cooperative Behavior: Economic *Man* Rides Alone. *Feminist Economics* 2: 1–21.

Smith, Adam 1976 (1776). *An Inquiry into the Nature and Causes of the Wealth of Nations.* Ed. Edwin Cannan. Chicago: University of Chicago Press.

Smith, Bernard 1985. *European Vision and the South Pacific.* Second edition. New Haven: Yale University Press.

Smollett, Eleanor 1993. America the Beautiful: Made in Bulgaria. *Anthropology Today* 9 (2): 9–13.

Soiffer, Stephen M., and Gretchen M. Herrmann 1987. Visions of Power: Ideology and Practice in the American Garage Sale. *Sociological Review* 35: 48–83.

Spencer, Jonathan 1995. Occidentalism in the East: The Uses of the West in the Politics and Anthropology of South Asia. Pp. 234–257 in James G. Carrier (ed.), *Occidentalism: Images of the West.* Oxford: Clarendon Press.

Strathern, Marilyn 1988. *The Gender of the Gift: Problems with Women and Problems with Society in Melanesia.* Berkeley: University of California Press.

Swedberg, Richard 1987. Economic Sociology: Past and Present. *Current Sociology* 35 (1, Spring): 1–221.

Taussig, Michael 1977. The Genesis of Capitalism Amongst a South American Peasantry: Devil's Labor and the Baptism of Money. *Comparative Studies in Society and History* 19: 130–155.

Taussig, Michael 1980. *The Devil and Commodity Fetishism in South America.* Chapel Hill: University of North Carolina Press.

Tax, Sol 1953. *Penny Capitalism: A Guatemalan Indian Economy.* Washington, DC: Smithsonian Institution.

Thompson, E. P. 1971. The Moral Economy of the English Crowd in the Eighteenth Century. *Past and Present* 50: 76–136.

Tomlinson, Jim 1990. *Hayek and the Market.* London: Pluto Press.

Touraine, Alain 1971. *The Post-Industrial Society; Tomorrow's Social History: Classes, Conflicts and Culture in the Programmed Society.* Translated by Leonard F. X. Mayhew. New York: Random House.

Tucker, Robert C. (ed.) 1978. *The Marx–Engels Reader.* Second edition. New York: W. W. Norton.

Turner, Ralph 1976. The Real Self: From Institution to Impulse. *American Journal of Sociology* 81: 989–1016.

Wade, Robert 1996. Japan, the World Bank, and the Art of Paradigm Maintenance: *The East Asian Miracle* in Political Perspective. *New Left Review* 217: 3–36.

Weber, Max 1958. *The Protestant Ethic and the Spirit of Capitalism.* New York: Charles Scribner's Sons.

Wiley, Norbert F. 1983. The Congruence of Weber and Keynes. *Sociological Theory* 1: 30–57.

Wilk, Richard 1995. Learning to be Local in Belize: Global Systems of Common Difference. Pp. 110–133 in Daniel Miller (ed.), *Worlds Apart: Modernity through the Prism of the Local.* London: Routledge.

Williamson, Oliver 1975. *Markets and Hierarchies.* New York: The Free Press.

World Bank 1993. *The East Asian Miracle.* Oxford: Oxford University Press.

Chapter 1

Demons, Commodities and the History of Anthropology

Joel S. Kahn

In 1980 the American-based Australian anthropologist Michael Taussig published *The Devil and Commodity Fetishism in South America*. Rarely for an anthropological monograph these days, it captured the imagination not just of anthropologists, but of a wider public. Taussig's discussion of the significance of the devil in the myths and rituals of miners and plantation workers, based partly on his own experiences as an ethnographer and partly on the findings of others in the region, most notably June Nash, seemed to strike a chord among many Western intellectuals. The question with which I wish to begin is: what was it about this account of the demonisation of the commodity form in apparently remote regions of South America that so appealed to a reading public that has become decreasingly susceptible to the seductions of a discipline devoted to the exoticisation of the world?[1]

The question is, of course, more difficult than might at first appear to be the case, raising issues to do both with internal developments within the discipline and the external economic, political and cultural environment within which Taussig's work, anthropology more generally and intellectual work as a whole are embedded. But equally intriguing is a paradox to do with what is probably the dominant theme of Taussig's text: why should the particular critical approach to commodities, markets and utilitarianism that Taussig attributes to South American peasants resonate, at least in certain periods, so strongly throughout the community of Western intellectuals?

Why should this resonance seem paradoxical? As the many people who have read the book know, it discusses the ways in

which Afro-American workers on Colombian sugar-cane plant-
ations are believed to enter into Faustian agreements to increase
their output and wages – the fruits of which, precisely because
they are achieved with the help of the devil, are assumed ultimately to be barren. Similarly, formerly-Indian peasants in the
Bolivian highlands are reputed to make ritual offerings to the devil,
regarded as the ultimate owner of the mines in which they work –
offerings which are designed to secure knowledge about the
location of the ore-bearing veins of tin upon which their livelihood
also depends.

What, asks Taussig, are we to make of these beliefs? His answer
is that they must be seen 'as the response of people to what they
see as an evil and destructive way of ordering economic life', or
as the

> collective representations of a way of life losing its life . . . intricate
> manifestations that are permeated with historical meaning and that
> register in the symbols of that history, what it means to lose control
> over the means of production and to be controlled by them. ... [T]he
> devil represents not merely the deep-seated changes in the material
> conditions of life but also the changing criteria in all their dialectical
> turmoil of truth and being with which those changes are associated –
> most especially the radically different concepts of creation, life, and
> growth through which the new material conditions and social
> relations are defined (Taussig 1980: 17).

What then are these new conditions? While for Taussig they
are most often characterised by the term 'capitalism', it is equally
clear that their essence lies in the processes not so much of
appropriation of surplus value, but of 'commodity formation'. The
main opposition between the social lives of traditional South
American peasants and that of those who have been caught up in
the plantation and mining complexes is between two 'radically
distinct ways of apprehending or evaluating the world of persons
and things' which, 'following Marx', Taussig terms *use-value* and
exchange value (Taussig 1980: 18). And these devil beliefs mediate
the oppositions between the two, perhaps even stimulating the
'political action necessary to thwart or transcend' the passage from
the former to the latter. 'The mystical interpretations and rhetorical
figures associated with these two modes [of apprehending or
evaluating] become enormously intensified when they are set into

opposition by the spread of the cash economy and capitalism' (1980: 21).

Moreover, what makes the demonised response particularly apt for Taussig is the fact that it appears better able than ours to recognise the artificiality and even moral bankruptcy of a world structured by exchange value. We in the industrialised West, according to Taussig, apprehend a world in which distinctive objects and particular human beings are evaluated not for the practical uses to which we may put them or the individual ways in which we may relate to them, but also for a value which differs only quantitatively from the value of quite different objects and human beings. All particularity is reduced to mere quantitative difference. Moreover, we take this world of exchange value to be in some sense natural instead of what it 'really' is, an artificial way of arranging our social lives based on the dominance of the commodity form, which is to say the object and the labour-power produced specifically for exchange, and exchange for money itself.

But because we have learned to take such an arrangement as natural we fail to see, in ways so clearly seen by South American peasants, that such an arrangement is distinctly unnatural – more than this, demonic. Thus, while some might suggest that such exotic devil-beliefs and rituals are 'a response to anxiety and thwarted desire' or that they are 'part of an egalitarian social ethic that delegitimizes those persons who gain more money and success than the rest of the social group', Taussig prefers to see them 'in their own right with all their vividness and detail', as 'poetic cadences that guide the innermost course of the world' (Taussig 1980: 15–17 *passim*).

What is distinctive, then, about Taussig's text is the way it apparently speaks the voice of the other. But why should that voice speak so persuasively to us? A clue is provided by an earlier case of the Western consumption of a Spanish-American discourse of demon commodity, provided this time not by an anthropologist but by the novelist B. Traven.

In *The Treasure of the Sierra Madre*, originally published in 1926, the mysterious B. Traven articulated a powerful critique of Western civilisation by means of a narrative device familiar to students of anthropology, by arranging for that critique to be spoken by someone from another culture. This critique is perhaps most clearly present in the words of the 'Indian chief' Aguila Bravo, when he contrasts indigenous and Spanish attitudes towards gold and money:

> I want no gold and I want no silver. I have enough to eat and I have a good and beautiful wife and a son whom I love and who is strong and well formed. What is gold to me? The earth brings a blessing; the fruits of it and my herds of cattle bring blessings. Gold brings no blessing and silver brings no blessing. Does it bring the blessing to you white Spaniards? You murder each other for gold. You hate each other for gold. You spoil the beauty of your lives for gold. We have never made gold our master, we were never its slaves. We said: Gold is beautiful. And so we made rings of it and other adornments, and we adorned ourselves and our wives and our gods with it, because it has beauty. But we did not make it into money. We could look at it and rejoice in it, but we could not eat it. Our people and also the peoples of the valleys have never fought or made wars for gold. But we have fought much for land and fields and rivers and lakes and towns and salt and herds. But for gold? Or silver? They are only good to look at. I can't put them into my belly when I am hungry, and so they have no value. They are only beautiful like a flower that blooms or a bird that sings. But if you put the flower in your belly, it is no longer beautiful, and if you cook the bird it sings no longer (Traven 1980: 115–116).

Traven, by our best account a *nom de plume* adopted by the Austrian anarchist Ret Marut (see Wyatt 1980), chased from first continental Europe and then Britain by the police, apparently spent the rest of his life in Mexico, from where he is thought to have written a large number of popular novels about the travails of Mexican peasants and the destructive effects of North American imperialism. Like Michael Taussig a half a century later, Traven found in the attitudes of indigenous Mexicans a powerful critique of a North American civilisation itself based on greed and the worship of gold and money for their own sake rather than for any inherent use value they might have.

But *The Treasure of the Sierra Madre* is probably better known, at least among members of my own generation, as an Oscar-winning film directed by John Huston and starring Walter Huston, the director's father, and Humphrey Bogart. Also a denunciation of a culture of greed, Huston's screenplay took significant liberties with the novel on which it was based, perhaps inadvertently telling us something about the trope of demon commodity that is concealed by the anthropological device of a Traven or a Taussig. As a disciple of the anarchist theorist Landauer, himself an interpreter of the philosophy of Max Stirner (a 'Young Hegelian' and hence contemporary of Marx), Marut would have been loathe to accept the possibility of an earthly paradise within the United States, where, in his view, society was thoroughly corroded and corrupted by capitalism, commodities and the dominance of instrumental rationality. Instead, he saw in Mexico a terrain that, while certainly under the influence of North America, still had roots in a radical cultural alterity that permitted Mexicans, or at least certain Mexicans, still to see through the sham that is commodity fetishism.

John Huston, while he claims to have met Traven (who was then using the name Hal Coves) in Mexico, and while he claims that Coves approved his screenplay, was nonetheless vehemently opposed to what he took to be Traven's 'bolshevism', and was thus more inclined to see North American society as reformable. The film-maker was therefore more inclined to relocate the terrain of use value in the heartlands of North America. As a consequence, in the Huston screenplay it is among a mythical community of fruit-pickers of the San Joaquin valley, rather than indigenous Mexicans, that true community has been rescued from the depravations of the market, as the following extract shows.

Asked by Howard, played in the film by Walter Huston, what he will do with his share of the fortune in gold that the three prospectors discover (and subsequently lose to bandits) in Mexico, Curtin, the good guy, responds:

Curtin: I figure on buying some land and growing fruit – peaches maybe.
Howard: How'd you happen to settle on peaches?
Curtin: One summer when I was a kid I worked as a picker in a peach harvest in the San Joaquin Valley. It sure was something. Hundreds of people – old and young – whole families working together. After the day's work we used to build big bonfires and sit around 'em and sing to guitar music, till morning sometimes. You'd go to sleep, wake up and sing, and go to sleep again. Everybody had a wonderful time . . ..

That the life of California fruit-pickers represents, for John Huston at any rate, a rejection of the instrumentalism that characterises the life of the market is clearer when Curtin's response is contrasted with that of Dobbs (the Humphrey Bogart

character), a true slave of instrumental calculation. Asked the same
question by Howard, Dobbs responds as follows:

Dobbs:	First off I'm going to the Turkish bath and sweat and soak til I get all the grime out of my pores. Then I'm going to a barber shop and after I've had my hair cut and 've been shaved and so on, I'm going to have 'em douse every bottle on the shelf. Then I'm going to a haberdasher's and buy brand new duds ... a dozen of everything. And then I'm going to a swell cafe – and if everything ain't just right, and maybe if it is, I'm going to raise hell, bawl the waiter out, and have him take it back ... (He smiles, thoroughly enjoying this imaginary scene at the table.)
Curtin:	What's next on the programme.
Dobbs:	What would be ... a dame!
Curtin:	Only one?
Dobbs:	That'll depend on how good she is. Maybe one – maybe half a dozen.
Curtin:	Dark or light?
Dobbs: (the liberal)	I don't care what her nationality is just so long as she's kind of small and plump ... you know ... (his hands describe an hourglass) ... with plenty of wiggle in 'er.

(From John Huston's screenplay 'Treasure of the Sierra Madre',
Scene 47 in Nevemore 1979.)

There are striking parallels between Traven's ideas about the
ability of those still 'outside' modernity to see more clearly through
the smokescreen of market instrumentalism than we moderns born
to it, and the assumptions of anthropologists about their capacity
also to escape into the mindset of cultural otherness and from there
to look back critically on modern society. Taussig's *The Devil and
Commodity Fetishism in South America* is a very apt successor to
Traven's Mexican novels for the ways it places a Young Hegelian
critique of commodities and markets into the mouths of Latin
American peasants. And yet the geographical slippage that occurs
between Traven's text and Huston's film suggests that we do not
need to place that critique in the mouths of others. In attempting
to evaluate the anti-Market discourse of Taussig's peasants or
Traven's indigenous Mexicans, we should instead begin with the
demonisation of the commodity within modern thought itself, and
from there proceed to the terrain of the cultural other. This is

because the debate over the morality of money, exchange, the market and economic rationality has long been a theme *within* Western modernism. Before returning again to the non-West, therefore, I want first to look at the origins of anti-Market discourse in Western thought.

From Expressivism to Demon Commodity

In his Introduction to this volume, James Carrier has suggested that the Market is as much a cultural construction as it is a description of a particular set of economic institutions. As discourse, the 'Market model' represents not just a defence of 'markets', but an elaborated 'theory' about human nature and the best means of promoting human emancipation. Within that model, those who populate this cultural world of the Market are taken as free individuals with their eyes securely on material reward. Whatever sorts of people they may be in their private lives, once they enter the economic realm their manner is one of self-regard and material calculation. In the Smithian version, public life is – or, perhaps better, should be – characterised by impersonal interactions: neither who one is nor considerations of morality should be allowed to influence public behaviour. Indeed, precisely this liberation from social and ethical norms is what constitutes human emancipation in the discourse of the Market.

However, because Market is discourse, perhaps unsurprisingly it can be and has been understood and evaluated very differently, as the other contributions to this volume demonstrate. Carrier's own account of a very different view of the relationship between Market and human sociality and ethics, a view articulated by Mr Hawken, is an important case in point. While, for Mr Smith, market values can and should prevail over all others, for Mr Hawken market orientation must be subsumed to life, understood in Hawken's terms as 'an uncluttered expression of' oneself. And, as the chapter by Alan Smart demonstrates, the direct link posited by Smithian discourse between market economy and a civil society of self-interested individuals has also been challenged outside the West, in Smart's example by certain Chinese representations of the market. Here Smith's arguments for the effectiveness of market mechanisms are not questioned, and yet the assumption that market calculus must prevail in non-market spheres is.

My concern here is also with Market as discourse and, like both Carrier and Smart, I wish to explore alternatives to the Smithian vision. In so doing I want to suggest that contemporary under-standings of the market are informed as much by critical anti-Market strands in modern thought as by the Market triumphalism of Adam Smith and his successors or, perhaps better, that Market and anti-Market polemics stand in an interior rather than exterior relationship one to another. Modern Western understandings of the Market have, as a consequence, been informed as much by modern critiques of the Market as they have by the arguments of its defenders. I shall begin with that version of anti-Market discourse that has its origins in what some have termed an expressivist critique of modernism. This critique, clearly arti-culated in both Traven's 'anthropological' texts and Huston's ethical one, has its origins in probably the first major intellectual challenge to 'modernism', what is often called 'romanticism'. In the final part of this chapter I shall return once again to non-Western critiques of the Market. But having linked the discourse of anti-Market firmly within, rather than outside, modernity, I shall place a very different interpretation on the new waves of anti-Market discourse in, in this case, the Islamic world, by linking them to the phenomenon of cultural globalisation rather than to the 'persistence of tradition'.[2]

That Taussig, and Traven before him, should find in the philosophy of the Young Hegelians inspiration for their critiques of the commodity form is, of course, hardly surprising. For Karl Marx, Moses Hess, Max Stirner and the rest can be said to represent an earlier tradition, particularly among German writers of the first half of the nineteenth century, which saw commodity exchange as something innately immoral in itself. This stance in Marx is most clearly expressed in his earlier work, in which, *contra* Taussig, alienation rather than commodity fetishism is the key concept.

The notion of alienation represented Marx's own ambivalence towards the freedom and emancipation promised by the French Revolution and articulated by the philosophers of the French Enlightenment. Like many German intellectuals of the early nineteenth century, Marx embraced the ideal of human emancipation but wondered whether the French 'freedom of the individual' was really any kind of freedom at all. For, to maintain that freedom of the individual was equivalent to human emancipation was to assume that 'the individual' as known to

Enlightenment philosophy was really the autonomous, pre-social being posited by French and British philosophical constructions of humans in a state of nature. Or rather, was this autonomous self itself something artificial, a socially constructed being whose character derived from the society and culture from which he or she (but mostly he) emanated? In fact, argued Marx very early on, freeing the individual is not to give free expression to basic human needs at all, but merely to give full flight to an individual *alienated* from his or her true 'species being' or nature, free to compete, to do down his neighbour. Human species being, for Marx, was not defined by a Hobbesian or Smithian state of nature. On the contrary, what such philosophers took for humans in a state of nature was really humans in a social state, alienated from each other by the imperative to compete with each other. Marx, following Hegel, termed that social arena modern 'civil society' (the label 'capitalism' was to come later). And reading through the early manuscripts one is constantly struck by the extent to which for Marx, as for Hegel, civil society is defined as the sphere of economic exchange.

Hegel, as we know, saw the path to emancipation through an institution that stood outside civil society, for only in this way could the selfishness imposed on man by the norms of civil society be curbed and true reason (as opposed to understanding) find its fullest expression. That institution for Hegel was, of course, the State. Marx and his fellow left Hegelians, having observed the development of the Prussian state,[3] rejected this solution. They argued that the State, far from being altruistic and standing outside civil society, in fact had its own particular agendas and in any case was the captive of powerful forces emanating from civil society.

We know how Marx later was to discover an alternative vehicle of emancipation in the class of proletarians, that one group within civil society for whom the universal interests of human emancipation corresponded with self-interest. However, this mode of casting civil society as class society characterised Marx's later career. His earlier critique of modern notions of freedom rested instead almost entirely on the notion that money, markets, exchange, commodities and, hence, individualism as competition for individual advantage, represent the main alienating forces in modern society. 'Practical need or egoism', he wrote 'is the principle of civil society and appears as such in all its purity as soon as civil society has completely given birth to the political state. The god of practical need and selfishness is money' (Marx 1971: 112). And this influence is corrosive and corrupting of all forms of human social arrangement. Referring to religion, for example, Marx writes:

> Man emancipates himself politically from religion by banishing it from the field of public law and making it a private right. Religion is no longer the spirit of the state where man behaves, as a species-being in community with other men albeit in a limited manner and in a particular form and a particular sphere: religion has become the spirit of civil society, the sphere of egoism, the *bellum omnium contra omnes* ['the war of everyone against everyone']. Its essence is no longer in community but in difference. It has become the expression of separation of man from his common essence, from himself and from other men, as it was originally (Marx 1971: 95).

That in some of his earliest writings Marx subscribed wholeheartedly to the narrative of demon commodity, a narrative that derives in part from his own attachment to a version of expressivism, is clear. And in this, it must be added, Marx did not depart very far from either his teacher, Hegel, or his contemporaries, the Young Hegelians.

Hegel himself was less critical of civil society than was Marx, for, true to his dialectical understanding of history, he saw individualisation and freedom as necessary to the emergence of a synthetic *Sittlichkeit* that would surpass that of the Greek polis that he admired so much. But precisely because civil society is driven by selfish calculation

> it also leads to the intensification of the division of labour, the increasing subdivision of jobs, and the growth of a proletariat. ... . This proletariat is both materially impoverished, and spiritually as well by the narrowness and monotony of its work. But once men are reduced in this way materially and spiritually they loose their sense of self-respect and their identification with the whole community, they cease to be integrated into it and they become a 'rabble' (Taylor 1975: 436).

As a result, for Hegel as for Marx, it is less a question of turning back than of transcendence, and for Hegel civil society will 'be kept in balance by being incorporated in a deeper community. It cannot govern itself. Its members need allegiance to a higher community to turn them away from infinite self-enrichment as a goal and hence the self-destruction of civil society' (Taylor 1975: 438).

However, the critical attitudes towards civil society, Adam Smith's public sphere of the Market, adopted to some extent by Hegel and to a far greater extent by the Young Hegelians, were not distinctive to Hegelian philosophy. On the contrary, as the work of the philosopher Charles Taylor demonstrates most clearly, these attitudes were absorbed from a movement that was otherwise seen by Hegel and Marx as anathema, namely the romantic movement. In this sense the roots of the important anti-Market strand in modern thought can be traced to what is probably the first major intellectual and cultural challenge to modern culture. I have used the term 'romanticism', although it is debatable whether it is precise enough to have any particular meaning, and its use is likely to be misleading since it is often employed as a term of abuse: to refer to a discourse as 'merely romantic' is to rob it of its critical cutting edge. I will, therefore, use Taylor's notion of the 'expressivist' conception of human life, a conception that develops in explicit opposition to the 'associationist psychology, utilitarian ethics, atomistic politics of social engineering and ultimately a mechanistic science of man' that is commonly traced to the European Enlightenment (Taylor 1975: 539).

There are two aspects of expressivism that are of central relevance here. First, the expressivist critique of what we might call techno-rationalism or instrumental modernism should not be seen as a pre-modern discourse resurrected in the aftermath of modernity. This is because in its developed form it does not merely advocate a return to a pre-modern age, and because it shares a number of often unstated assumptions with the discourse that it seeks to criticise. Second, because the triumphalist Market discourse of Adam Smith and others associated with the English and Scottish Enlightenments shares many of the basic assumptions about human nature and human subjectivity with enlightenment philosophy in general, we would expect to find an expressivist critique of political economy as part of the romantic movement.

Taylor argues that the instrumental mode of evaluation inherited from the Enlightenment, and against which expressivism develops, has become endemic to modern society. In it,

[t]he major common institutions reflect . . . the Enlightenment conception in their defining ideas. This is obviously true of the economic institutions. But it is as true of the growing, rationalized bureaucracies, and it is not much less so of the political structures, which are organized largely to produce collective decision out of the concatenation of individual decisions (through voting) and/or negotiation between groups (Taylor 1975: 541).

At the same time the Enlightenment vision has also informed 'many . . . conceptions of society which have been invoked to mitigate the harsher consequences of the capitalist economy . . . [such as] notions of equality, of redistribution among individuals, of humanitarian defence of the weak' (Taylor 1975: 541).

Taylor wants to argue that, as a consequence, expressivism has been more or less banned from public life, confined to the sphere of the private, where 'Romantic views of private life and fulfilment' proliferate. I, on the other hand, am particularly interested in those periods when the expressivist critique of instrumentalism resonates more strongly beyond the discourse of personal fulfilment; that is to say, those periods when tropes such as 'cultural difference' are marshalled against the very structures of the modern state and modern economy. For we are going through just such a period now, and this explains the seductiveness of invitations to 'listen to the voices' of the cultural other.

The expressivism that a B. Traven speaks through his Mexican peasants and John Huston through the fictionalised fruit-pickers of California, therefore, appears first to have been clearly and publicly articulated by those unhappy either with what they took to be the Enlightenment attitudes towards Man, or with the perceived threat of the emancipatory rhetoric of the French Revolution, particularly in its Jacobin phase. This ground has been covered so many times in recent attempts to specify the nature of modernity in general and of modern conceptions of the self, that it is not necessary to retrace the various strands of the argument here. Suffice it to say that what I, with Taylor, am calling 'expressivism' developed against the perception that an increasingly larger number of humans in the grip of modern ideologies (philosophical or, more important for the masses, theological) were beginning to think of themselves as self-defining rather than being defined from a cosmic order outside themselves.

If human subjectivity comes to be seen as self-definition, the

relationship between humans and the world is radically transformed. Rather than humanity and nature together representing
a deeper meaning whose source is the same, individuals are seen
as autonomous subjects who stand apart from the natural (and
social) world, which now becomes just so many facts that can be
known only by the sensations we as autonomous subjects have of
them. Taylor calls this view of the world of nature 'objectified', by
which he means a vision of nature as lacking in any inherent
meaning and purpose, as characterised merely by contingent
relations or patterns that we can uncover through the processes
of observation. With Newton, Man now gives up the search for
final causes in nature and looks instead merely for efficient causes
among separately observable 'facts'.

However, in this view humans do not merely stand outside
nature, for since the observable world is now totally naturalised,
then Man must also be part of nature, and therefore understandable in the same way that we understand the movements of
the planets. Discovering the nature of humans was conceived by
Enlightenment scholars to be a process like all other forms of
scientific inquiry, since it was assumed that humans were part of
that rational and understandable natural order that it was the task
of philosophers to study.

There were, argues R. G. Weyant (1973), three kinds of approach
to the investigation of human nature during the eighteenth century,
which he terms 'biological', 'psychological' and 'anthropological'.
The first was concerned with the properties that set the human
creature apart from other creatures. Inheritors of the Christian
category of Man as a separate creation of God, these scientists were,
not surprisingly, concerned with biology, not theology. Secondly,
there were attempts to analyse human nature into a small number
of basic abilities, processes or faculties that combined in lawful
ways to produce the complex observable phenomenon of human
behaviour. These Weyant describes as psychological theories.
Finally there were those who focused on the question of what Man
would be, or had been, in a state of nature, without the complications of social contracts or customs. These anthropological (in
the philosophical sense) studies aimed at the determination of
Man's original nature, as a prelude to criticising social institutions
that did not enhance or further that nature.

What were the results of these studies? First, although largely
unified in their approaches to the study of human nature, it can

not be said that Enlightenment philosophers came to any very sophisticated, or even agreed upon, understanding of the 'nature of human nature'. Second, with the benefit of hindsight we can see that this is a consequence of the naive way in which they set about studying it. What is perhaps more important to a character-isation of the age is that there were some widely shared views, namely that:

1. there *is* a fundamental human nature;
2. it is shared by *all of humanity*; and
3. it is the proper task of science to investigate it, just like any other aspect of the natural world.

To this it is important to add two more points of summary. Firstly, and somewhat paradoxically, it can be argued that Enlightenment philosophers believed that 'it is the nature of Man to have no nature'. While not strictly speaking accurate (cf. Weyant 1973), this belief does follow on logically from an extreme version of Lockian sensationalism, a view that Man has no innate ideas. This view holds, in other words, that everything about humans derives from their sensed experience; hence human character, social behaviour and the like are totally *environmentally* determined. Such a view is, for example, implied by the remark of Helvetius, who wrote: 'Born without ideas, without vice, and without virtue, everything in man, even his humanity, is an acquisition' (quoted in Weyant 1973: 32).

But, secondly, if Lockian sensationalism tended to lead Enlight-enment philosophers to the notion of 'natureless humans', most of them also did share a minimalist view of humans, like Huston's Dobbs, as seekers of pleasure and avoiders of pain. Even Locke and Helvetius accepted the universality of pleasure and pain in human nature. Beyond this minimum there were two main tendencies in Enlightenment anthropology, described by Weyant as *egocentric* and *sociocentric*. According to the first, human behaviour stems entirely from personal needs and desires; for the latter, while some human behaviour stems from personal needs and desires, there is also a natural affection for others, a 'social love'. An example here is the Earl of Shaftesbury's distinction between the mutual affections that lead to the good of the public, and the self affections that lead to the good of the private. This sociocentric view of an innate human morality is also found in the writers of the Scottish Enlightenment, including Adam Smith in his *Theory of Moral Sentiments* (a view which he changed later in his better-known work on human economic egoism) and in the thought of Thomas Jefferson.

It is important to see the connection between this Enlightenment anthropology and the new understanding of human freedom that arose in the period. Freedom now becomes the freedom of the individual subject to express his or her human nature most fully; that is, for the minimalist to be free to maximise pleasure and minimise pain. This means that all social, political and religious institutions need to be judged according to whether they do or do not hinder the autonomy of the individual subject. It does not, of course, follow that all such institutions must be destroyed. Instead they must be evaluated according to the principles of reason as to their effects on human individuality. Naturally, those who see human nature as largely egocentric, such as Jeremy Bentham, will find the need for political institutions, even highly repressive ones, in order to maximise the sum total of human happiness rather than allowing the happiness of particular individuals to decrease the happiness of the whole. Indeed this combination of naturalism and atomism brings a new way of making moral judgements, based not now on religion, but on scientific reason itself.

Rather than simply rejecting this Enlightenment formulation of modern subjectivity and advocating a return to the vision of human subjectivity as a mere expression of a cosmic order that is also expressed in nature and in human social arrangements, expressivists in general retained, even if unconsciously, the notion of a self-defining subjectivity. What they appeared to object to most was the separation between subjectivity and the world, between meaning and being, and hence between mind and body posited by Enlightenment anthropology. This is, of course, most radically posited by Kant in his argument that there can be no internal connection between the thing in itself and the knowledge we have of it. But it is generally present in most eighteenth-century philosophy, which, as I have noted, abandoned final for efficient cause and hence saw meaning as a property not of the world itself but only of our propositions about it.

Expressivism takes a view of human life quite different from that implied by Enlightenment anthropology. Rather than seeing human life and activity as essentially without any meaning, expressivism sees them as 'expressions', as realisations of a

purpose or an idea. This notion was unlike pre-modern notions of
expression, in two main ways. First, for the pre-moderns the
meaning or purpose of human life is pre-given; that is, it is already
established outside human subjectivity. For modern expressivism,
on the other hand, the meaning unfolds within human subjectivity,
so that the notion of the self-defining subject is retained. Second,
that meaning is not necessarily known in advance: humans may
grasp it or recognise it as their own only once it has been realised.
It could not have been known in advance. To quote Taylor,

> the notion of human life as expression sees this not only as the
> realization of purposes but also as the clarification of these purposes.
> It is not only the fulfilment of life but also the clarification of meaning.
> In the course of living adequately I not only fulfil my humanity but
> clarify what my humanity is about. As such, a clarification of my life-
> form is not just the fulfilment of purpose but the embodiment of
> meaning, the expression of an idea. The expression theory breaks with
> the Enlightenment dichotomy between meaning and being, *at least as
> far as human life is concerned*. Human life is both fact and meaningful
> expression; and its being expression does not reside in a subjective
> relation of reference to something else, it expresses the idea which it
> realizes (Taylor 1975: 17, emphasis added).

This expressivist critique of Enlightenment anthropology can
lead, as it has led, to a number of somewhat diverse projects: an
intuitionist critique of reason, an extreme romantic individualism,
a particular romantic aesthetics (perhaps the central project of
romanticism), a pantheistic nature-worship and so on. To bring
this back to the particular critique of instrumental reason with
which I am concerned here, it is important to see how expressivism
lay at the foundation of two ideas – first, what we might call the
meaning of human cultural life and, second, the diversity of human
groups – which in turn provide the basis for the kind of anthropological (now using the term in our twentieth-century sense)
critique of the commodity with which I began.

As Taylor demonstrates, these ideas are first clearly articulated
by Herder, and it is therefore worth looking briefly at his discussion
of them.[4] In Enlightenment philosophy language is seen simply
as a set of arbitrary signifiers whose meaning is those objects and
ideas to which it refers. The idea that language could itself have a
meaning or purpose would have been nonsensical within this view.
It is this instrumental understanding of language as 'referential

sign', as a mere tool kit, with which Herder took issue. For him language is not just a way of operating in an objectified world; it is itself an expression of human capacity or potential; more than that, it is its embodiment. Language does not merely represent thought; in some sense it actually is human thought. As part of the world, it is outside us, but it is also our expression, and so can not be reduced to its instrumental function. It has purpose in the pre-modern sense, but that purpose is not divinely pre-given, being rather created by human subjectivity.

It is significant that Herder used language as his main example of human expression for a number of reasons. First, because language is necessarily created by humans in social groups, it, more clearly than art, can be seen to be not just the expression of a highly individualised romantic subjectivity. Second, the recognition of the interior relationship between language and human thought leads one to reach conclusions about other spheres of shared meaning similar to those reached about language; in other words, recognition of the non-instrumental, expressive dimensions of language leads almost inexorably to a view of human culture as a whole as expression in the romantic sense (a conclusion drawn by successive generations of linguists and anthropologists). Third, the fact that there are many languages in the world leads the expressivist, unlike the instrumentalist, to the view that humanity (or, better, modes of thought and systems of meaning) can be differentiated. Combined with our first point, this leads less to a private or highly individualised expressionism and more to a public one, a division of the public into different linguistic and, hence, cultural groups. This in turn marks the beginning of a second, if related, critique of Enlightenment anthropology, that is of its universalistic presuppositions. That the English, French and Germans have different languages is no longer just an accident, an arbitrary or contingent point of difference among them: it is a fundamental difference, since, in Herder's system, linguistic differences speak of differences in the modes of thought or *volksgeist* of different peoples.

As I have suggested, expressivism represents a critique of an Enlightenment anthropology in which the world is objectified and subjected to human reasoning and manipulation. But it is more than epistemological critique. Expressivism is also a heartfelt despair at the world-view propounded by eighteenth-century philosophy. To quote Taylor once again:

The Enlightenment developed a conception of nature, including human nature, as a set of objectified facts with which the subject had to deal in acquiring knowledge and acting. [It created a] rift . . . between nature, whether as plan or instrument, and the will which acted on this plan.

It was this rift which the originators of expressivist theory . . . could not tolerate. They experienced this vision of things as a tearing apart of the unity of life in which nature should be at once the inspiration and motive force of thought and will. It was not enough that nature provide the blueprint for the will, the voice of nature must speak through the will (Taylor 1975: 22–23).

But this rift between humans and nature was not the only rift decried by expressivism. As the discussion of Herder shows, expressivism also decried the rift among humans themselves created by the Enlightenment vision of human nature. As Taylor points out,

what has been said of communion with nature applies with the same force to communion with other men. Here too, the expressivist view responds with dismay and horror to the Enlightenment vision of society made up of atomistic, morally self-sufficient subjects who enter into external relations with each other, seeking either advantage or the defence of individual rights. They seek for a deeper bond of felt unity which will unite sympathy between men with their highest self-feeling, in which men's highest concerns are shared and woven into community life rather than remaining the preserve of individuals (Taylor 1975: 27–28).

The very notion of freedom espoused by the Enlightenment and the French Revolutionaries was, according to expressivism, only negative, and hence meaningless. That freedom meant only the unshackling of the individual free to pursue his or her own private ends. But where did these ends come from if not from the communities and languages in which they were embedded? And if so, then unshackling all human bonds in the name of freedom is to create a new kind of slavery in which humans are now left only with their natural desires and inclinations, pursuing these goals and these goals alone in purely instrumental fashion. This is what is left by Enlightenment reason and the emancipation promised by the French revolution.

It can now, I think, be seen fairly clearly that the trope of demon commodity represents a direct development out of an emerging expressivist critique of instrumental rationality of the late eighteenth century. This anti-instrumentalism found its way into the explicitly anti-romantic philosophy of Hegel and the more radical Young Hegelians. From there it found its way into anarchist thought, itself carried from its European origins to Mexico by B. Traven, and again through Marx's writings on alienation by Taussig to South America. Dobb's pursuit of base self-interest embodies all that the expressivists were reacting against – a crude materialism, a desire to satisfy the baser wants against the higher potential of human subjectivity, competitive and atomistic individualism, conflict and competition. John Huston's more conservative version of the critique was transported to the mythical communities of fruit-pickers in California's San Joaquin valley.

The expressivist critique of modernity that arose first in late eighteenth-century romanticism has been more or less contained by the increasing dominance of techno-rationalism in the public sphere on the one hand and, on the other, by the pre-eminence of the Enlightenment project of emancipation in the aims of the most significant opposition movements, including Marxism. However, it must not be assumed that the critique has disappeared. On the contrary, it is my contention that expressivism remains a con-stitutive element in the formation of a modern (and post-modern?) culture, not confined solely to private life as Taylor suggests. Instead, expressivism, particularly in the form of the critique of commodification and instrumental reason, has been a more or less constant presence in the history of modern culture, never resolved, taking different forms and being articulated by radically different political forces, but always an undercurrent that resonates particularly in times of perceived crises of modernity. That expressivism continues to resonate in modern culture (at least among intellectuals) is evident, as I have suggested, in the reception accorded the works of 'anthropologists' like B. Traven and, more recently, the writings of post-colonial and multicultural theorists. Marx's account of the alienating qualities of modern civil society was not the end but only the beginning of this expressivist current in modern thought.

While the Hegelian version of expressivism may not have survived the disasters of 1848, the negative vision of commod-ification and instrumental reason did not disappear, even in nineteenth-century Germany. It was manifest, for example, in the development of a renewed critique of the discipline of economics by the so-called younger generation of 'historical economists' in Germany, a group that included Karl Bücher and Gustav Schmoller. These and other members of the school directed their critiques not at classical political economy, but at the Austrian marginalists, arguing once again against the false universalisation of a basic human propensity to truck and barter created by the assumption of a *homo oeconomicus*. Implied in the writings of this school was also a critique of the effects of the spread of market rationalism for its corrosive effects on German 'community' (see Kahn 1990).

The concerns of this group of historical economists appear in a somewhat different form in the critiques of instrumental reason found in the writings of both Werner Sombart and Max Weber. Both were direct intellectual descendants of the earlier historical economists; indeed, Weber's earlier writings fell squarely within the tradition established both by earlier writers like Roscher and Knies, and by later theorists such as Schmoller (see Oakes 1975). And the expressivist critique of the commodity has re-emerged in this century in different forms and in different places. Combining the concerns of the Young Hegelians and of Weber characteristic of all Frankfurt School exponents, we have Adorno's critique of mass culture and Habermas's critique of instrumental rationality. For Adorno protection against infection by instrumental reason is to be found in high art, for Habermas in the sphere of communicative action.

More direct twentieth-century heirs of the German economists include: the Russian 'neo-populist' A. V. Chayanov, arguing for the unique features of the peasantry, which can not be subsumed in a general economic theory that presupposes a universal *homo oeconomicus* (either liberal *or* Marxian); Karl Polanyi, who brought many of the ideas of historical economics into American anthropology, instigating the so-called substantivist critique of formalism (once again a critique of instrumental rationality, and especially of attributing it to non-Western peoples), leading in turn to Marshall Sahlins's critique of 'practical reason' and Clifford Geertz's attack on economism.

Parallels are evident in the critiques of the consumerism of Western, particularly American, society, from Thorstein Veblen to the so-called 'institutionalists' and also to the *Monthly Review* economists, particularly Paul Baran and Paul Sweezy, and among the anthropological heirs of Durkheim in France, especially Marcel Mauss, whose analysis of the gift was formulated in direct opposition to the instrumental mode of commodity exchange.

Finally, reference should be made to more recent developments in post-modern and post-colonial critiques of modernity and the 'West'. As I have suggested elsewhere (Kahn 1995), both have tended too quickly to equate modernity or the West with Enlightenment philosophy, which in turn is associated with an instrumentalist techno-rationalism. In this way the significant expressivist strands in modern thought, within which at least certain versions of post-modernism and post-colonialism might be fruitfully located, are all too frequently ignored, thus, among other things, concealing the Western or modern roots of their own critiques.

However, rather than pursuing the expressivist critique of markets and commodities through the history of Euro-American thought, I want to return to the terrain of the non-West. However, by refocusing on places outside the traditional heartlands of modernism I am not advocating a return to the classical anthropological project of a Traven or a Taussig, if only because I think that the problematic nature of any project that seeks to subsume genuine cultural alterity to the concerns of modern cultural critique makes such a project both ethically and epistemologically unacceptable. Instead, by offering some observations on recent Asian critiques of instrumental reason I wish to draw attention to the genuine globalisation[5] of the critique, a critique that we can now see emanates from inside rather than outside modernity. In this way the reasons for the parallels between 'Western' and 'non-Western' points of view become explicitly historical, and we do not need to rely on those sorts of problematic assumptions about human 'species being' that undermine the expressivism of the traditional anthropological project of cultural critique.

The Globalisation of Anti-market Discourse: Islam and the Market

As the work of anthropologists such as Taussig shows, there are significant parallels, as well as differences, between Western and non-Western representations of the Market. South American peasants use a metaphor of the devil to express their experience of the alienation brought by processes of commodification, a metaphor which for them captures the artificiality of a cultural system that reduces everything to quantified exchange value. What allows South American peasants to see so clearly what most Westerners can not, according to Taussig, is that they remain entwined in pre-modern communities, while Westerners occupy social spaces where Market calculus has been so thoroughly routinised that they take it as part of their natural environment.

And yet this notion that there are non-modern terrains in the remoter regions of South America, and that their occupants have an external perspective on modernity, is highly problematic. Such occupants prove remarkably difficult to locate in a region of the world that has been effectively re-made by European conquest, the forced movement of peoples, the extraction of wealth, the rise of 'modern' nation-states, the activities of multinational corporations over a period of almost 500 years, to say nothing of processes of cultural imperialism and cultural globalisation that began with the Iberian missionaries.

It is, however, only within the anthropological frame adopted by Taussig that the apparent coincidence between a non-modern and a distinctly modern (Young Hegelian) critique of the Market appears to be so paradoxical. Indeed, to the extent that we work within a frame in which the fact of the globalisation of modernity is explicitly recognised, the parallels and divergences between 'Western' and 'non-Western' discourses of the Market become not only unsurprising, but thoroughly understandable.

A central issue here, as Smart argues in his chapter on Chinese representations of the market, is what James Carrier has elsewhere described as 'occidentalism' (see Carrier 1992). In an important sense the contemporary Asian and Islamic constructions of 'the West' play much the same role in current expressivist discourse as the (negative) constructions of Market instrumentalism did for early European critics of the Enlightenment.

A case in point is the emergence of a discourse of an Islamic economics where greed is replaced by moral relations within the Islamic *ummat*. The plea for a distinctively Islamic economics has been part of the global Islamic revival, itself associated with political developments in the aftermath of the Arab–Israeli war, the oil price shocks and the Islamic revolution in Iran. Perhaps not surprisingly, the rediscovery of an Islamic economics first took place in the Middle East and Pakistan, beginning in the 1970s. But what is particularly interesting about these developments is the extent to which they take place in conscious opposition to materialism, instrumentalism and the Market, this time conceived of as distinctively Western artefacts (although having also penetrated into the Islamic world). The parallels with the earlier internal critique of the Market in Europe are, however, evident. The label 'fundamentalism', often applied particularly to current Islamic attempts at the 're-enchantment of the world' (see Tibbi 1995), suggests that we have here to do with a simple return to the classical age of Islam. However, as the following quotes extracted from recent textbooks on 'Islamic economics' make clear, the emerging Islamic critique of the West must be considered in its contemporary context, and hence as part of a process of cultural globalisation (a process that must of necessity encompass cultural movements that derive their impetuses precisely from a rejection of globalisation):[6]

> Conventional economics ignores ethical values and assumes all economic agents to be pursuing self-interest while seeking to maximise private gain. Islamic economics takes a moral view of man and studies the behaviour of the money-holder, consumers, producers, labourers etc. as influenced by Islamic moral teachings (Justaneiah 1988: 3).

> The Holy Qur'an takes cognizance of the fact the man is greedy, impatient, and violent in his love of wealth. Islam has endeavoured to subject this instinct to a moral purpose in order to restrain greed (Nazar 1981: 6).

> In an Islamic economy, the complete spirit will be accompanied by an overriding sense of co-operation, which is more than just an act. It is at once a mood and a motive, a principle and a psychology (Nazar 1981: 14).

> The dichotomy of Ethics and Economics in the western mode of thought which underlies the evolution of the capitalistic economic thinking has done incalculable harm to the evolution of an appropriate human environment. It has practically amounted to a defence of exploitation, rapacity and extreme materialism of the capitalist economic system . . ... Devoid of any ethical validity, the 'economic' becomes synonymous with the selfish, the material and the monetary (Nazar 1981: 15).

> Western economists since time immemorial have concerned them-
> selves only with the view of man as *homo economicus*. This was
> sufficient for erecting their structure of market mechanism. Everything
> else that was beyond empirical analysis was excluded. Schumpeter's
> well-known work ... discerned a complete removal of matters of
> ethics and values in the economic system on grounds that were
> empirical (Choudhury 1986: 8).

The discourse of an Islamic economics is occidentalist in the
way it constructs Western and Islamic worlds as inversions one of
the other. In the former, individuals when entering the market must
leave all that is not 'rational' behind – in Carrier's terms, whatever
they are in private life, in the public sphere of market exchange
they are reduced to self-interested economic maximisers. In the
Islamic world of the 'Islamic economists', on the other hand,
Market actors are expected to re-infuse the Market sphere with
values deriving from outside it, especially religious values. In the
world of Islamic economics, then, believers are invited to imagine
a re-enchanted civil society, and hence an end to the Smithian
privileging of the economy; indeed, a complete dissolution of the
public–private divide.

This, however, is not the only possibility. As Smart demonstrates, more recent Chinese representations of the Market (as
opposed to Maoism, in which something surprisingly close to the
Islamic project of re-enchantment of the public sphere was
envisaged) the distinction between the Market and the non-Market
is preserved, only now normative valuation is reversed. Like some
European romantics, representatives of the Communist state in
China see the Market as dangerous for its potential to dissolve
Chinese culture and society, yet they are also keen to promote the
Market model, since they share with the Smithian paradigm a
highly optimistic view about its developmental potential. China's
rulers, then, become twentieth-century Hegelians, looking not to
ethicise the realm of Market transaction but to contain its influences
in society as a whole. And like Hegel, they see the State as the
force that, because it alone stands outside civil society, can
effectively perform that containing function. For China's rulers,
then, something like the public–private distinction must remain;
indeed, the boundaries between the two must be policed.

It is almost precisely in this paradigm of the Market that current
neo-modernist discourses in the industrialising nations of South-

east Asia are also apparently cast. In modern Malaysia, for example, we have witnessed the development of a notion of a particularly Malaysian, or Asian, path to modernity, which at the same time avoids the materialism and instrumentalism of the West.

The call for a uniquely Malay, Malaysian, Islamic trajectory of modernisation inevitably implies an expressivist rejection of what is perceived to be the meaninglessness of development 'Western-style'. At least in most official pronouncements, however, this does not mean a rejection or even re-enchantment of the Market, but rather its containment. Certainly in Malaysia there have for some time now been moves to promote economic institutions that operate according to the principles of Islam. But the promotion of Islamic values in business dealings does not seem to be a major priority. Indeed, the Prime Minister, Dr Mahathir Mohamad, has on numerous occasions castigated the Islamic world for its continuous critiques of the Western world, arguing that only economic development will make Islamic countries important players on the world stage.[7]

In the working paper that formed the basis for his now well-known Vision 2020 speech, in which he put forward the view that Malaysia should strive to become a fully developed, industrialised country by the year 2020, Dr Mahathir urges the establishment of a fully competitive economy, one which is diversified and balanced, quick on its feet, technologically proficient, characterised by escalating productivity and low inflation. In particular, Malaysia should strive for 'an entrepreneurial economy that is self-reliant, outward-looking and enterprising ... *subjected to the full discipline and rigour of market forces*' (Mahathir 1991: 5, emphasis added). Nowhere in this extremely significant and widely-cited document is there any question of modifying or inflecting what are assumed to the laws of operation of a Market economy in any significant way – this from a leader who is increasingly willing to invoke Islam politically, whose actions are seen by some astute observers to be leading towards the imposition of an 'Islamic State' (see Hussin 1993).[8]

And yet, official Malaysian advocacy of 'the full discipline and rigour of market forces' does not imply a whole-hearted acceptance of the Smithian model of the Market as unencumbered public space. On the contrary, Mahathir's admiration for the economic and developmental potential of Market forces coexists with a demonisation of instrumentalism and materialism in a vision of the West as 'transcendental evil' (see Yao 1994). Mahathir's occidentalism is of a particular kind, one that we might call 'cultural', in the sense that he separates out the Market, as universal and culturally-neutral, from a culture that is individualistic, competitive, amoral. His admiration and demonisation are not contradictory, but are simply different aspects of a view of the proper place of economic and Market forces within a social and cultural whole. Like the ideologues of the Chinese Communist Party, Mahathirism parts company with Smithianism on the normative evaluation of the Market actor and, like the Chinese leadership, Mahathir wants to privilege Malaysian, Islamic culture over the culture of the Market.

This 'civilisational' dimension of Mahathirism was neatly encapsulated by the term 'Melayu Baru' (New Malay), coined several years ago by the prominent Malay sociologist and influential adviser to Mahathir, Rustam Sani. In a book published in 1993, and in numerous speeches, seminars and workshops, Rustam has argued that development can not and must not be pursued as a purely economic goal. On the contrary, the goal of becoming a fully industrialised country must be also a political, religious, spiritual and cultural one (Rustam 1993: 3). The politically-dominant but, at least previously, economically-weak Malays must not allow the economic success brought by twenty years of pro-Malay policies to destroy Malay culture. In other words, economic success must not led to individualism and competitiveness in the non-economic spheres. The 'New Malay', therefore, will be a Malay who can compete in the market with the best of them; but Market culture will not come to define who a Malay really is. The dividing line between public and private must be maintained, even policed (by the State and, increasingly, by State-sponsored religious officials), and the former must not be allowed to determine the contours of the latter.

These assumptions equally characterise Mahathir's own vision. The document on which the Vision 2020 speech was based does not even discuss economic development until a whole series of 'non-economic' goals have already been set, among them 'the challenge of establishing a fully moral and ethical society, whose citizens are strong in religious and spiritual values and imbued with the highest ethical standards' (Mahathir 1991: 2). He goes on to say:

Since much of what I say this morning will concentrate on economic development, let me stress yet again that the comprehensive development towards the developed society that we want – however each of us may want to define it – cannot mean material and economic advancement only. Far from it. Economic development must not become the be-all and end-all of our national endeavours (1991: 3).

There is no space here to develop the analysis of these features of contemporary Malaysian representations of the Market and of the relationships between a Market-determined civil society and the other spheres of social existence. I have, for example, not examined the variety of such representations, having chosen instead only to focus on what now appear to be the hegemonic ideas of Mahathir and the current ruling faction. Nor have I looked at the reception accorded Mahathir's own ideas outside élite circles. I hope, however, to have demonstrated that a particular version of Market and anti-Market discourse has emerged in Malaysia over the last decade or so not because Malaysia constitutes some non-modern terrain outside the reach of global modernism, but precisely as a consequence of the globalisation of both economic institutions and representational practices.

This chapter began with a particular representation of the Market, one that has emerged to challenge 'Western thought' from within, and one that demonises the Market for its tendency to privilege techno-rationalism, instrumentalism and the atomised economic actor unencumbered by bonds of community, ethics and morality. I have suggested that our modern understandings of the Market have been informed at least as much by this anti-Market discourse as they have been by the Market triumphalism of classical political economists.

I have also suggested that viewing the expressivist critique of Market ideology in these terms leaves us in a better position to evaluate non-Western representations of the Market than does the traditional anthropological approach, one that conceives of itself as studying cultures and societies located outside modernity. The case of a neo-modernist discourse in contemporary Malaysia, combining an advocacy of the Market as an engine of economic development with an expressivist *angst* about the potentially damaging effects of a Market culture if it is not confined within the Market sphere, can not be understood on its own, as though

Malaysia were a site of radical alterity in the modern world. Rather, it can be understood only in the context of the globalisation of both Market relations and modern Market and anti-Market discourses that all have their origins in Europe, but are no longer exclusively, or even mainly, Western.

Notes

1. See for example Marcus and Fischer (1986).
2. The case for such a 'non-anthropological' approach to the non-West is a complex one, and can not be fully argued here (cf. Kahn 1993, 1995).
3. Taylor gives the lie to the simplistic assumption that Hegel's philosophy represented merely a defence of the Prussian state (Taylor 1975: Chap. 16).
4. Others have seen in Herder an antecedent of contemporary notions of cultural and linguistic relativism. Anthony Darcy (1987), for example, notes the similarities between Boasian notions of culture and Herder's ideas about *Volksgeist*, while Brian Whitton (1988) has seen Herder's early work on language as anticipating in significant ways the ideas of Lyotard (and, one might add, the earlier ideas of Wittgenstein, Sapir and Whorf).
5. I do not want to suggest that non-Western expressions are necessarily always a result of the direct diffusion of Western ideas. More significantly, it seems that the social conditions of (late) modernisation frequently give rise to indigenous forms of expressive critique (for a fuller discussion, see Kahn 1995).
6. This distinction between pre- and anti-global is nicely made by Robertson (1992).
7. See reports of Mahathir speeches in *The New Straits Times*, 9 March and 13 April 1991.
8. This attempt to hive off the Market from a more general process of modernisation is analogous to the general views of science and industrialisation held by Mahathir and his ruling faction, namely that they are global phenomena, not just part of Western modernity, and that therefore science, economic development,

the Market, industry can all be brought into Malaysian development without at the same time importing Western cultural values and social forms (see for example, various contributions in IKIM 1993; International Institute of Islamic Thought 1994).

References

Carrier, James G. 1992. Occidentalism: The World Turned Upside-Down. *American Ethnologist* 19: 195–212.

Choudhury, Masudul Alam 1986. *Contribution to Islamic Economic Theory: A Study in Social Economics*. Houndmills, Hants: Macmillan.

Darcy, Anthony 1987. Franz Boas and the Concept of Culture: A Genealogy. Pp. 3–17 in Diane J. Austin-Broos (ed.), *Creating Culture: Profiles in the Study of Culture*. Sydney: Allen & Unwin.

Hussin Mutalib 1993. *Islam in Malaysia: From Revivalism to Islamic State?* Singapore: Singapore University Press.

IKIM (Institute of Islamic Understanding) and Economic Planning Unit of the Prime Minister's Department 1993. *Industrialisation from an Islamic Perspective*. Conference Proceedings. Kuala Lumpur.

International Institute of Islamic Thought and Civilization 1994. *Symposium on Islam and the Challenge of Modernity: Historical and Contemporary Contexts*. Kuala Lumpur.

Justaneiah, Darwish S. 1988. *Islamic Economics: Important Issues Facing Islamic Societies*. Working Paper No. 11. Christchurch: Australasian Middle East Studies Association.

Kahn, Joel S. 1990. Towards a History of the Critique of Economism: The Nineteenth Century German Origins of the Ethnographer's Dilemma. *Man* 25: 230–249.

Kahn, Joel S. 1993. *Constituting the Minangkabau: Peasants, Culture and Modernity in Colonial Indonesia*. Oxford: Berg.

Kahn, Joel S. 1995. *Culture, Multiculture, Postculture*. London: Sage Publications.

Mahathir Mohamad 1991. Malaysia: The Way Forward. Presented at the inaugural meeting of the Malaysian Business Council, 28 February, Kuala Lumpur.

Marcus, George, and Michael J. Fischer 1986. *Anthropology as Cultural Critique: An Experimental Moment in the Human Sciences*. Chicago: University of Chicago Press.

Marx, Karl 1971. *Early Texts*. Edited and translated by David McLellan. Oxford: Basil Blackwell.

Nazar, Mian M. 1981. *The Islamic Economic System: A Few Highlights*. Islamabad: Pakistan Institute of Development Economics.

Nevemore, J. (ed.) 1979. *The Treasure of the Sierra Madre*. Wisconsin/Warner Brothers Screenplay Services. Madison: University of Wisconsin Press.

Oakes, Guy (ed.) 1975. *Max Weber, Roscher and Knies: The Logical Problems of Historical Economics*. New York: The Free Press.

Robertson, Roland 1992. *Globalization: Social Theory and Global Culture*. London: Sage Publications.

Rustam A. Sani 1993. *Melayu Baru dan Bangsa Malaysia: Tradisi Cendekia dan Krisis Budaya*. Kuala Lumpur: Utusan Publications & Distributors.

Taussig, Michael 1980. *The Devil and Commodity Fetishism in South America*. Chapel Hill: University of North Carolina Press.

Taylor, Charles 1975. *Hegel*. Cambridge: Cambridge University Press.

Tibbi, Bassam 1995. Culture and Knowledge: The Politics of Knowledge as a Postmodern Project? The Fundamentalist Claim to De-Westernization. *Theory, Culture and Society* 12 (1): 1–24.

Traven, B. 1980. *The Treasures of B. Traven*. London: Jonathan Cape. (Contains English versions of *The Treasure of the Sierra Madre* [1934]; *The Death Ship* [1940] and *The Bridge in the Jungle* [1940].)

Weyant, R. G. 1973. Helvetius and Jefferson. Studies on Human Nature and Government in the 18th Century. *Journal of the History of Behavioral Sciences* 9: 29–41.

Whitton, Brian 1988. Herder's Critique of the Enlightenment: Cultural Community versus Cosmopolitan Rationalism. *History and Theory* 27 (2): 146–168.

Wyatt, Will 1980. *The Man Who Was B. Traven*. London: Jonathan Cape. (Published in the United States as *The Secret of the Sierra Madre*. New York: Doubleday.)

Yao, Souchou 1994. *Mahathir's Rage: Mass Media and the West as Transcendental Evil*. Working Paper No. 45. Murdoch, WA: Murdoch University Asian Research Centre.

Chapter 2

The Free Market as Salvation from Government: The Anarcho-Capitalist View

Susan Love Brown

The Free Market is a powerful icon in Western civilisation, especially for Americans, because it incorporates and integrates the three important core principles of American culture: self-reliance (individualism), equality and resistance to authority (Hsu 1969). In the United States these core principles have always accommodated the idea of a duly constituted government designed to allow these principles to balance one another within the cultural mosaic. However, anarcho-capitalism throws these three principles out of balance with one another, privileging individualism and ultimately sacrificing equality in an effort to eschew all authority. The view taken of the Free Market by anarcho-capitalists, therefore, makes more striking the strengths of other versions of the Free Market model, especially that of limited government libertarianism.[1]

Anarcho-capitalism is a form of anarchism whose prime tenet is that the free market, unhampered by government intervention, can coordinate all the functions of society currently being carried out by the state, including systems of justice and national defence.[2] Anarcho-capitalists believe that a system of private property based on individual rights is the only moral system – a system that implies a free market, or total voluntarism, in all transactions. Such a system, according to anarcho-capitalists, minimises coercion and maximises individual liberty, while government intervention disrupts the natural and benevolent process of voluntary human exchange and creates new problems that then have to be corrected by further interventions, leading to the growth of government power and the ultimate eclipse of human freedom. For anarcho-capitalists the Free Market is defined not only by its economic attributes but by its polar opposition to government. It is through this good vs. evil opposition that anarcho-capitalism establishes itself and the Free Market as morally superior to all other human arrangements.

This chapter explores how the dichotomy between market and state reveals the tensions and the contradictions within this approach that ultimately lead to problems: (1) the lack of acknowledgement of collective action as a legitimate way of establishing and enforcing individual rights; (2) the failure to recognise rights and law as a pre-condition of the market; and (3) the dichotomising of human nature in such a way that only very good people can operate in a market environment. But at the root of this dichotomy is the principle of anti-authoritarianism.

Anti-Authoritarianism[3]

Anarcho-capitalism emerged and gained force in the 1970s in the United States with the appearance of key books elaborating it from three viewpoints: *The Market for Liberty* (1970) by Morris and Linda Tannehill, which had an Objectivist viewpoint; *Power and Market* (1970) and *For A New Liberty* (1973) by Murray N. Rothbard, which had a natural rights viewpoint; and *The Machinery of Freedom* (1973; second edition 1989) by David Friedman, which had a utilitarian viewpoint.[4] The rise of anarcho-capitalism was a response to conditions following the cultural and political turmoil of the 1960s. The events of that decade pulled apart many assumptions about society and its institutions. Young people unleashed a current of anti-authoritarianism that was deep and followed many paths.

Anarcho-capitalism grew from the soil of that anti-authoritarian garden, but the spores of its existence had been a part of American soil for a very long time. Escape from unjust authority is an old and enduring theme in the United States, one that springs from the enduring Western debate about the individual in society and the extent to which one or the other should prevail.

Anarcho-capitalism has cultural roots in the formation of the nation itself and its origins in the prevailing philosophies and experiences of the centuries that pre-date nationhood, going back as far as the dissenting religious tradition in England, which was an important reason for emigration to the New World (Bailyn 1967: 53–54). An enduring American myth concerns Pilgrims coming to America to escape from religious persecution.

Bernard Bailyn devotes an entire chapter of *The Ideological Origins of the American Revolution* to the concern that American colonists had about power, which they defined as 'the dominion of some men over others, and the human control of human life: ultimately force, compulsion' (1967: 56). They saw power as inherently aggressive, creating 'its endlessly propulsive tendency to expand itself beyond legitimate boundaries' (1967: 56). Power was legitimate only when exercised by 'mutual consent'. The learned citizens of the American colonies were personally aware of the consequences of the illegitimate use of state power, and they were wary of its dangers. Thus, their quest for justice in their dealings with England was framed within the context of this understanding. The Declaration of Independence was a direct result of perceived acts of despotism on the part of England.

So the problem of the individual and society emerged early in American history, with individuals through their mutual consent becoming a collectivity to constrain the abuses of power among themselves and to establish the extent of its legitimacy. The protection of the individual can occur, in this standard American view, only through people's own collective action. This irony or paradox is acknowledged from the beginning of the union, but becomes muddled with the growth and change of cultural symbolism.

Geoffrey Gorer, in his national character study, *The Americans*, likens the birth of the United States to the Oedipal struggle so central to psychoanalytic interpretations of human development:

> England, the England of George the Third and Lord North, takes the place of the despotic and tyrannical father, the American colonists that of the conspiring sons, and the Declaration of Independence and the American Constitution that of the compact by which all Americans are guaranteed freedom and equality on the basis of the common renunciation of all authority over people, which had been the father's most hated and most envied privilege (Gorer 1948: 18).

The cost of freedom and equality is the renunciation of authority. But this origin story is even more psychologically resonant because of its wider symbolism – a symbolism invoked again and again in the development of the individual, in the breaking away of immigrant sons from their non-English-speaking fathers and in the escape of slaves from their masters. Gorer observed that among Americans one of the 'major psychological truths' that prevailed was 'the belief that authority over people is morally detestable and should be resisted' and 'that those who occupy the necessary positions of authority within the state should be considered as potential enemies and usurpers' (1948: 18–19).

As the United States took form, the degree to which its citizens expressed their feelings of anti-authoritarianism ebbed and flowed with historical events. As the new republic consolidated its own legitimacy, resistance to authority also broadened to become an incipient resistance to any rules or regulations that hampered individual freedom or expression, whether these came from government officials or titans of industry. Speaking of Americans in the nineteenth century, Henry Steele Commager says: 'The American's attitude toward authority, rules, and regulations was the despair of bureaucrats and disciplinarians... . His disrespectful attitude toward authority and his complacent confidence in the superiority of his institutions combined with prosperity and well-being to make the American lenient toward dissent and non-conformity' (Commager 1950: 19–20).

The great epics of the American nation emanate in part from the resistance to authority implicit in the stories of the Underground Railroad by which slaves escaped from the South in defiance of federal law, the formation of outlaws and their gangs in reaction to the coming of the railroads, cowboys who defied the closing of the open range, union members who defied the power of industry and draft protesters who sprang up with almost every war.

Americans in the mid-twentieth century still believed that 'authority is inherently bad and dangerous', according to Gorer (1948: 20). This attitude on the part of Americans, Gorer claimed, was not a matter of 'abstract idealism' but a profoundly moral belief: '[P]eople, or institutions, who "push other people around" are bad, repugnant to decent feelings, thoroughly reprehensible. Authority over people is looked on as a sin, and those who seek authority as sinners' (1948: 21).

This moral fervour against authority is bound up with Puritan foundations and a Protestant work ethic (Weber 1958) conflated with the ideology of individualism. Gorer argues that the American desire for private enterprise 'is no reasoned belief in the superiority of one method of production or distribution over another; it is not necessarily a screen behind which personal interests and hopes for profits are defended; it is a deeply sincere, quasi-religious moral attitude, as little susceptible to rational argument as the Hindus' aversion to killing cows' (Gorer 1948: 24).

Ironically, this anti-authoritarianism came to serve as the basis for *two* views of the market. A negative view emerged as a critique of the power of business over the individual, captured in such works of literature as *The Octopus* (1901) by Frank Norris, which portrayed the story of California wheat farmers pitted against powerful railroad companies with the power to block the farmers' access to their markets, and *The Jungle* (1906) by Upton Sinclair, which exposed the wretchedness of the Chicago meat-packing industry, and the myth of the Robber Barons, powerful men of industry who built their wealth at the expense of others. In this negative view, the Market, in the guise of business, is the usurper of rights and the practitioner of excessive power, and the state, through reform legislation, is the saviour. The idea that government can remedy the problems caused by the growth of big business became a powerful model in the minds of some Americans, one that co-exists with and stands in direct opposition to the Free Market model, allowing Americans to manoeuvre culturally between either extreme as necessary.

Free Market supporters (both the limited governmentalists and anarchists) had an uphill battle fending off the effects of this negative view generated by the urbanisation and industrialisation of the United States. They attempted to replace it with a view in which the Free Market was the solution to excesses made possible by the collusion of business and government (essentially Adam Smith's argument). But anarcho-capitalists are the descendants of earlier individualist anarchists who related to Smith's work in quite a different way. When anarchism first appeared in the United States in the nineteenth century, it did not focus on the Market at all, but on the rights of individuals to their labours and the property it produced.

Antecedents

Although part of the classical liberal tradition, contemporary anarcho-capitalists are descendants of nineteenth-century individualist anarchists such as Josiah Warren, Lysander Spooner and

Benjamin Tucker.[5] Individualist anarchism was, in itself, an entrepreneurial act within a system that encouraged experiments in economics, religion and even politics, as long as they were contained within a range of acceptable options.

These early anarchists, though staunchly individualistic, did not entertain a penchant for the Market or capitalism. Rather, they saw themselves as socialists opposed to the state socialism of Karl Marx. The individualist anarchists saw no contradiction between their individualist stance and their rejection of capitalism. Though the ideal image of the Free Market derives to a great extent from Adam Smith's *Wealth of Nations*, this work represented something different to the individualist anarchists: it was a scathing indictment of the dangers of government power, particularly the power to set up and maintain monopolies, preventing private individuals from competing and labourers from realising the fruits of their labours.

These early anarchists took from Adam Smith the labour theory of value, which to them meant that workers created value through their labour, a value appropriated by owners of businesses, who paid their wages.[6] The individualist anarchists blamed capitalism for creating inhumane working conditions and for increasing inequalities of wealth. Their self-avowed 'socialism' was rooted in their firm belief in equality, material as well as legal. But the concept that identified them as a group was an absolute commitment to the sovereignty of the individual and to voluntary behaviour as a moral good.

The earliest anarchism in the United States was experimental. Less attuned to political doctrine and theorising and more attuned to actual ways of living, this kind of anarchism is typified in the work of Josiah Warren, who is often cited as the first American anarchist. Warren was an inventor and founder of three intentional communities: Equity, Utopia, and Modern Times. In Warren we have the beginning of an anarchist tradition that tried to demonstrate that alternatives to government were possible.

Warren, a businessman, joined Robert Owen in the formation of the New Harmony community, Warren's first experience with communal living (Bailie 1972 [1906]: 1–8). But New Harmony failed, and Warren concluded that a major cause of this failure was 'the suppression of individuality, the lack of initiative and responsibility. What was every one's interest was nobody's business' (Bailie 1972 [1906]: 6).

In 1827 Warren experimented with his Equity store, which became known as the 'time store' because of his use of clocks to measure the amount of labour to be exchanged. People purchased products in exchange for grants of their own labour in an amount equal to the time required to produce the product they were purchasing. Labour notes were issued on this basis. People were also allowed to advertise in the store for certain labour or products that were needed, and the store became a locus of labour exchange. Thus, Warren implemented a method of exchange based not only on the labour theory of value but on the concept of individual contractual relationships. Warren also established trade schools so that young men could learn trades without going through what anarchists of the day considered long and exploitative apprentice-ship programmes, which Warren believed were means of obtaining cheap labour from children and women.

Believing in the 'decentralization of manufactures', he was opposed to monopolies established by patents on machinery, ownership of land by those who were not actually working it and craft monopolies (Martin 1970: 53–54). He was clearly motivated by his concern for equality and equity, as well as anti-authoritarianism. He made efforts to reduce the inequality attributed to capitalism and the power of business over labour.[7]

Warren envisioned the 'ultimate reorganisation of society on the basis of decentralised local communities in which the needs and capabilities of all might be readily learned' (Martin 1970: 52–53). Whereas anarcho-capitalists assume the implementation of their principles within a complex society much like the one we live in, individualist anarchists seemed to recognise that their ideas were more appropriate in small-scale communities. This was in part nostalgic desire to maintain the intimacy of the agrarian life against the encroachments of the impersonal urban life; but there was also a basic recognition that anarchism was more appropriate on this scale (see Brown 1989).

Warren's model of the market, in spite of its anarchistic orientation, was closer to the mainstream view of the Free Market than to the anarcho-capitalist one. However, some of Warren's community failures point to weaknesses in his model that presage those of anarcho-capitalists: namely, his failure to see that communities failed because they were not perceived as part of a larger collectivity – that individuals, even in communities, are part of a society with which they must become reconciled. Warren believed that peace required liberty, but that 'it can never be realized under any organization of society known to us' (Warren from *True Civilization* cited in Schuster 1970: 82). Spooner, another individualist anarchist, was to reach a similar conclusion.

Lysander Spooner was a prolific contributor to the theory of individualist anarchism in his day. In 1844 he started a private mail service, American Letter Mail Company, only to lose his money fighting a congressional act of 1845 that prohibited competition with the government postal service. From this personal experience Spooner became keenly aware of the nature of monopolies, poverty and injustice, and came to see the government as the creator of these major obstacles to human liberty (Shively 1971: 15–62). He saw banks as state monopolies granted to the rich to allow them to control money. He saw slavery as unconstitutional, and declared that the Supreme Court had the power to end it at any time. It was in Spooner that a strong, clear anti-authoritarianism emerges with government as its target.

Spooner eventually stopped supporting the idea of a constitution and all legislation, because he considered them

> the assumption by one man, or body of men, of a right to abolish outright all the natural rights, all the natural liberty of all other men; to make all other men their slaves; to arbitrarily dictate to all other men what they may, and may not, do; what they may, and may not, have; what they may, and may not, be (Spooner 1882: 20).

This passage illustrates an extreme, the declaration that natural rights can not be protected through mutual consent if that consent is in the form of a constitution or laws. Like today's anarcho-capitalists, Spooner did not provide a credible answer to the dilemma of who will enforce the contracts, freedoms, and property rights that he sees as natural. Indeed, by asserting the natural rights position, Spooner sidesteps the issue of why such rights are not forthcoming, but are circumvented by the actions of the very people in whom they should be manifest. Buried within Spooner's viewpoint, then, is an assumption about human nature that is contradictory. The last major individualist anarchist, Tucker, would, like Spooner, have to come to terms with such thinking.

Benjamin Tucker, the best-known of the early individualist anarchists, was the founder, publisher and editor of *Liberty*, the most successful anarchist publication of its day. In the pages of

Liberty anarchist ideas were presented and debated from 1881 to 1908 (McElroy 1981: 7–39). Tucker was initially attracted to anarchism through contacts with Josiah Warren, William B. Greene and Ezra Heywood (Martin 1970: 203). In 1874 he went to Europe, where he studied the work of Pierre-Joseph Proudhon. When he returned to the United States, he published a translation of Proudhon's *What Is Property?* in 1876, whereupon he achieved immediate attention from the anarchist community (McElroy 1981: 11).

Tucker also became involved in issues of free speech of his day.[8] But as an individualist anarchist, Tucker disagreed with the anarcho-communists, who had been mostly foreign-born. According to William Kline, 'the groups could not reconcile their differences, the Communist Anarchists dedicated to a community of property and the Individualist Anarchists deeply committed to private property and individual effort. They never again found any basis for an attempt at rapprochement' (Kline 1987: 58–59).[9]

In his 'State Socialism and Anarchism' (1972 [1893]: 3–18) Tucker made the distinction between the two forms of socialism on the grounds that state socialism was based on the principle of authority, while anarchism was based on the principle of liberty. The common basis for the two, said Tucker, was the labour theory of value. Tucker thought that Marx had followed the path of authority in which 'the remedy for *monopolies* is Monopoly' (Tucker 1972 [1893]: 7). By this he meant government, the greatest monopoly of all. On the other hand, for individualist anarchists the remedy for monopoly was individual liberty and private ownership established through labour.

Once again, the priority given to anti-authoritarianism becomes clear. Tucker's arguments with the Single Taxers and labour unions involved the willingness of both of these groups to use the coercive powers of the state (through taxation and legislation) to achieve their ends. But Tucker also took issue with the great individualist thinker Herbert Spencer for dismissing socialism without making the distinction between state socialism and the 'higher' order of socialism, which was anarchism. As can be seen with Tucker, the individualist anarchists, even relatively late in the day, were still fervent anti-capitalists. According to Tucker, Spencer failed adequately to indict the 'capitalistic class'.

Finally, in 1886 Benjamin Tucker adopted Max Stirner's egoism, and 'this rejection galvanized the movement into fierce debates,

with the natural rights proponents accusing the egoists of destroying libertarianism itself' (McElroy 1981: 11).[10] They made this
claim because, without natural rights, the danger of the use of
force as the only other alternative seemed imminent. However,
Tucker fell back on the idea of contract as a solution to the problem,
and with it faced the same problems as Spooner, how to enforce
such contracts and how to distinguish them from other forms of
mutual consent, such as constitutions or compacts. But toward
the end of his life, Tucker declared, 'Capitalism is at least tolerable,
which cannot be said of Socialism or Communism' (cited in Martin
1970: 275), providing the shift further illuminated in the 1970s by
anarcho-capitalists.

As McElroy notes: 'In many ways, Tucker exemplified the
golden age of libertarianism which faltered in the face of growing
statism and militarism... . His death, like that of Herbert Spencer,
marked the end of an era. Libertarianism as an organized movement would not appear again for many years' (McElroy 1981:
33–34). Individualist anarchism spanned an era marked by
oppositions – pro-slavers against abolitionists; Union against
Confederacy; farmers against railroads, labour against business;
rural against urban; rich against poor; agrarian against industrial
– an era finally eclipsed by the First World War, the firm establishment of capitalism and the rise of the Free Market as a mythic
American institution.

When libertarianism arose again, one of its threads was
anarchistic. But this time, the anarchists defined themselves almost
totally by reference to the Free Market. These anarchists derived
their evidence for the Free Market from two powerful schools of
economics, the Chicago school and the Austrian school.

Part of what made the ascendancy of the Free Market model
possible was the rise of a prestigious science of economics, the
shift into an era of prosperity following the Second World War
and the coming-of-age of the baby-boom generation that took such
prosperity for granted and clearly saw government and its role in
racial segregation and the Vietnam war as oppressive. As anti-
authoritarianism grew more extreme during and after the 1960s,
the character of the Free Market model did as well, until it came
to epitomise the total freedom from restraint that characterised
the ethos of the boomer revolt in the United States (Brown 1992).

In the presence of a more sophisticated science of economics,
anarcho-capitalists took every advantage to prove their case that

the Free Market is the only moral basis for a free society. But they did so by contrasting it with the state and by creating a dichotomy that can only be sustained by internal contradictions that undo the Free Market model itself.

Context and Contradiction

Failure to recognise the context in which the Market must exist leads anarcho-capitalists into contradictions from which they can not extract themselves. The Free Market model of the anarcho-capitalists arises from the logical connection between the positive right to acquire property and the negative sanction against the initiation of force, or violation of the rights of others. The right to own property is the right on which the right to life and liberty depend, even though it derives from these rights; therefore, anarcho-capitalists take great pains to explain that there are no distinctions between so-called *human* rights and *property* rights. In regard to individual rights and the importance of property rights, anarcho-capitalists do not differ from libertarians in general. In order to exercise one's rights to life and liberty, one must do so through material means; therefore, one must have the right to own property.

> Material goods are necessary to sustain life, and so are the ideas which a man generates. So, man invests his time in generating ideas and in producing and maintaining material goods. A man's life is made up of time, so when he invests his time in material or intellectual property (ideas) he is investing parts of his life, thereby making that property an extension of his life. The right to property is part of the right to life. There is no conflict between property rights and human rights – property rights *are* human rights (Tannehill and Tannehill 1970: 11).

This quotation is straightforward: property is necessary to sustain life and assure rights. But from the careful delineation of individual rights comes the prohibition on the initiation of force. It follows that the only system possible in a free society is one that also recognises the freedom to dispose of one's property as one wishes and to acquire property through non-coercive exchange with others. This is a free market, the natural expression of voluntary exchange within a free society.

If one is not free from the incursions of others, one can not implement one's freedoms. Behind the assertion that the market is the natural outgrowth of the recognition of rights is an equally powerful proposition: the necessity of establishing or defining rights as the common basis of behaviour and pre-condition for the market. The Free Market symbolises the very freedom that comes with the recognition of rights that is a pre-condition of its own existence. In conceiving of the Market as a symbol of freedom, a certain conflation occurs in anarcho-capitalist thinking between the freedom necessary to sustain the Market and the Market itself. Thus, at least in this one sense, the establishment and protection of individual rights, a pre-condition for the Market, depends on collective action.

However, anarcho-capitalists often equate collective action with the social, and they often deny that the social exists. Anarcho-capitalists believe that reality is vested only in individuals and that society is an abstraction, a collection of individuals who simply interact. They do not consider society to have any characteristics or operating principles distinct from those of individuals; and since it is individuals who act within the market, all human activity becomes market activity.[11] For example, Rothbard explains that society 'denotes a pattern of interpersonal exchanges among human beings. It is obviously absurd to treat "society" as "real", with some independent force of its own. There is no reality to society apart from individuals who compose it and whose actions determine the type of social pattern that will be established' (1962: 71).

But to define society solely as 'interpersonal exchanges' is to define it in terms of the market and the principle of exchange, and to confuse the market with all social activity, rather than seeing the market as one kind of social activity. According to Rothbard, a 'network of voluntary interpersonal exchanges forms a society; it also forms a pattern of interrelations known as *the market*' (1962: 77). There is already a one-to-one correspondence between the free society and the free market, and it is in this closeness of definition surrounding 'exchange' that we find the slippage in which one is confounded with the other.

If society is simply an aggregation of individuals who live in proximity to one another and who participate in exchanges with one another, then we lose sight of the fact that these associations create a relational entity that emerges when people have set relationships with one another. For example, market principles can be delineated without any reference to specific individuals, because they constitute a level of operation beyond the level of individual action, though constituted by it. An example would be the way in which the market determines price through supply and demand. These relationships and related actions constitute a structure, a system or an organisation that can be studied in and of itself and from which principles of operation can be derived.

Indeed, this is what Rothbard does in his magnum opus, *Man, Economy, and State* (1962). 'Society' or 'the market' might be just an abbreviated way of referring to any group of individuals who interact, but both of these concepts seem to entail a specific group relationship that is synergistic in a way that a mere aggregation of individuals is not. While societies do not exist without individuals (nor individuals without society for that matter), societies do seem to constitute a level of organisation above the individual level, a level that can be fruitfully studied. To invoke an analogy made famous by Herbert Spencer (1886: 437–450), that of society to an organism, the existence of cells does not revoke the existence of the organism that comprises them.

Society, market and state may all be seen as objectively real entities by virtue of their relational, structural and systemic natures. Even if they are not materially real, they denote different kinds of relationships, all of which involve the same groups of individuals and rely upon some form of solidarity for their maintenance. That is, people are bound by more than just exchange; they are bound by common understandings and expectations; in a word, culture.

It is commonplace within anthropology to define a society as an organised group of people sharing a common culture and a common language and occupying a specific territory, evoking an understanding that these people in some way rely upon one another. The things that people have in common tie them together psychologically.[12] It is attachment and affiliation, not just exchange, that characterises the social.

Likewise, culture prevents people from being only unrelated individuals and ties them together with common understandings. Only by ignoring culture can anarcho-capitalists see the world so atomistically and, therefore, reduce it to interacting automata. This pushes individualism so far that they can not find a way in which individuals can come together to implement the protection of rights without which freedom and the Market can not exist.

The Obliteration of Mutual Consent

The social relationship among individuals implies a common interest that is manifested in the social controls that societies develop in order to maintain themselves even before states arise (see Hoebel 1964). Whether they are informal or formal, these controls or rules (norms) can be referred to as law. But law poses a problem for anarcho-capitalists, since all law implies the use of force, 'the legitimate use of physical coercion by a socially authorized agent' (Hoebel 1964: 26).

For anarcho-capitalists, this legitimate force must be retaliatory only. But there is a further problem for anarcho-capitalists in deciding where such law must come from, for in acknowledging the need for law they enter the murky waters of mutual consent and enforcement, which automatically imply constraints. Since in an anarchistic society no governmental body (a legislature, for example) will exist to enact laws, anarcho-capitalists must solve the problem of how to establish law without initiatory force.

The Tannehills see the only legitimate law as 'natural law', which is derived from the discovery of principles in nature. Having told us that human beings require freedom and property rights to live and that initiatory force must be proscribed, they have said everything they think is necessary to establish what constitutes law. They object to any statutory law whatsoever (1970: 116). They assert that all one has to do is ask if one is aggressing against another in order to decide if an act is right or wrong. They see the market as evidence of the existence of natural law, as well as a model of how people should act in other domains of their lives (1970: 124–125).

This approach is tantamount to no approach at all, because it evades the real problem of how people are going to know a natural law when they see it, how they are going to be sure that others agree with them, and how they are going to settle disputes when the parties do not agree on whether an act of aggression has been committed.

Rothbard at least addresses this issue. He proposes a system in which a commonly agreed-upon legal code is available before-hand, but enforcement is private. 'Within the framework of such a code, the particular courts would compete on the most efficient procedures, and the market would then decide whether judges, juries, etc., are the most efficient methods of providing judicial services' (1973: 235). In proposing a universally accepted legal code, Rothbard avoids the lack of answers provided by the Tannehills. Therefore, his case for private police and courts that abide by the common laws of society is much more reasonable and, therefore, stronger than theirs. But he still faces the problem of how such a code would be developed.

An obvious solution to Rothbard's problem would be for a group of wise people to sit down to draft a common agreement to which other members of society would then subscribe. However, he can not get around the facts that such law must be arrived at through some collective practice, or that adherence to it must be enforced. He is noncommittal in revealing the exact process through which this would happen.

On the other hand, Friedman proposes that law should be generated in the Free Market itself. 'The answer is that systems of law would be produced for profit on the open market, just as books and bras are produced today. There could be competition among different brands of law, just as there is competition among different brands of cars' (1989: 116–117). Different systems of laws would be represented by different courts. Individuals would subscribe to defence agencies according to the type of law they offered and the courts with which they were associated.

The problem with this approach is that it assumes that the Market itself exists somewhere outside a legal system. If it is to be the generator of laws, then presumably it does not require a legal context in which to flourish. This approach also does not deal adequately with the necessity of mutual consent or equality before the law, which are two requirements for the establishment of individual rights and a pre-condition for the market.

This vision of the creation of laws on the market itself is the most extreme of all the anarcho-capitalist views, because, unlike the Tannehills and Rothbard, Friedman does not assume a common code in a given society. Rather, in such a system people who are part of the same society will have competing legal codes available to them, provided by private defence agencies and courts. Indeed, Friedman's approach brings about the very conditions that anarcho-capitalists are attempting to avoid, the necessity of individuals answering to a law to which they have not agreed (see Beaird 1975; Machan 1975, 1989).

With Friedman's solution, it becomes conceivable that rich people could buy their way out of crimes in the market, which constitutes a contradiction to the principle of equal justice that necessarily follows from the argument for individual rights. Thus, this approach commodifies the law and transforms it from a form of social control, providing norms to regulate behaviour so that rights can be assured, into a market good available only to those who can afford it.

Both Rothbard and Friedman find it necessary to buttress their cases for law with historical examples. To address the problem of how a common legal code would arise, Rothbard tells us that it will arise in the way that other law has, for instance, Anglo-Saxon common law (1973: 236). However, Rothbard notes, 'the basic legal code would not rely on blind custom, much of which could well be antilibertarian' (1973: 239). Rather, this code would have to be based on 'reason'. Rothbard cites ancient Celtic Ireland as an example of a *'state-less* and libertarian society – in short, a society of virtual "free-market anarchism" '. Rothbard bases his argument on a paper by Joseph Peden entitled 'Stateless Societies: Ancient Ireland' (1971).

In an earlier work I responded to this claim by noting that Rothbard and Peden had misunderstood the nature of ancient Ireland. There I noted that 'not only did ancient Ireland have all of the characteristics of a chiefdom or primitive state, but seems to have had a structure like that of a feudal state' (Brown 1989: 65–66). In fact, I pointed out that D. A. Binchy (1970: 90) preferred not to call the *tuath* a state, because of its lack of administrative apparatus. But rather than the defence agencies that Rothbard envisions, private enforcement of claims in ancient Ireland often amounted to blood feud, a common approach in non-state societies around the world (for example, see Hasluck 1967; Karsten 1967).

Beyond this, Rothbard fails to note (as do all the anarcho-capitalists) that truly acephalous societies (bands and tribes) all exist at levels of less structural complexity than the market systems he is familiar with (Barclay 1990; Brown 1989). Furthermore, customary law exists at all levels of social organisation, and so operates with or without state administration (see Bohannan 1967; Hoebel 1964; Nader 1969). But the fact that law exists and operates without the state should not be construed as a function of the Market, but rather of the very custom that Rothbard said he wanted to avoid.

Like Celtic Ireland, ancient Iceland, Friedman's example, was a chiefdom, a stratified society without a state. The legal system that Friedman so much admires was a system of codified custom-ary law that was orally spoken in total each year by law-speakers and eventually put into writing. But it was nevertheless a common code, even though enforcement of it was private. Ancient Iceland had a general assembly of thirty-six chieftains, who nominated judges for the courts. However, enforcement of decisions was strictly private (Durrenberger 1988: 246–247). The Icelandic commonwealth also had a tithing system that constituted a form of taxation to take care of impoverished members of the population. While Iceland existed in this situation for 300 years, it did so at a much lower level of complexity than states of today. Iceland was primarily an agricultural society, in which both blood feud and sorcery were options for settling differences (Barclay 1990: 95–96).

Although the people of both ancient Ireland and ancient Iceland manifested a good deal of autonomy within their societies, they were not essentially different from societies in other parts of the world at similar levels of complexity. Seeing them as examples of either anarchy or free markets is possible only if other societal features are ignored.

The Free Market model of the anarcho-capitalists does not acknowledge that law arises in a social context. Law, which is the way societies maintain social control over their members, appears to be a necessary condition for the successful operation of societies *and* markets. Without social controls, whether formal or informal, people fall into constant conflict. One of the things that society requires is the mitigation of interpersonal conflicts and the encouragement of cooperation, although these two goals are achieved in varying degrees by different societies at different times.

Anarcho-capitalists would have us believe that the Free Market is the source of cooperation rather than the beneficiary of it. But whenever sustained conflict becomes truly great within a society – let us say, for example, with the outbreak of continuous war – the market is adversely affected, and often disrupted altogether. When crime becomes so great that property rights can no longer be protected, then markets as peaceful systems of exchange cease to exist. Therefore the means of mitigating conflict, a crucial part of social existence, is a necessary pre-condition for the market.

Creating law through problem-solving and private approaches such as mediation and arbitration or by custom is not the same as *producing* law on the open market for profit. The difference lies in mutual consent and common agreement, two characteristics that anarcho-capitalists undermine in their efforts to avoid anything that looks governmental. In so doing, they highlight the reasonableness of libertarians who acknowledge that mutual consent is the basis for maximum individual liberty and even for limited governments. Without mutual consent, not even anarchy is possible.

Anarcho-capitalists and the State

The anarcho-capitalist Free Market model reveals a great deal about the way in which extreme anti-authoritarianism results in a hyper-individualism that undermines even the anarcho-capitalists' own professed view of human nature. Both Rothbard and Friedman make a point of saying that the Free Market does not require especially good people, yet the dichotomisation of market and state belies this claim. Anarcho-capitalists can not explain the existence of the state, but nevertheless demonise it, even as they sanctify the market:

> [T]he free market is a society in which all exchange voluntarily. It may most easily be conceived as a situation in which no one aggresses against person or property. In that case, it is obvious that the utility of all is maximized on the free market (Rothbard 1970: 14).

> [A] truly free market is totally incompatible with the existence of a State, an institution which presumes to 'defend' person and property by itself subsisting on the unilateral coercion against private property known as taxation (Rothbard 1970: 6).

Because of its nature as a producer of wealth, the Market tends to create only extremely beneficial situations for everyone:

> [A] free market tends to lead to abundance for all of its participants, and . . . violent intervention in the market and a hegemonic society tend to lead to general poverty (Rothbard 1962: 70).

> On the market all is harmony. But as soon as intervention appears and is established, conflict is created, for each may participate in a scramble to be a net gainer rather than a net loser – to be part of the invading team, instead of one of the victims (Rothbard 1970: 12).

The Tannehills define the Free Market in a similar way, as 'a network of voluntary exchanges; it includes all willing exchanges which do not involve the use of coercion against anyone' (1970: 16). If, as anarcho-capitalists claim, both markets and states are made up only of individuals acting, then it must follow that such actors are capable of committing offences in either realm of action, that criminal activity can invade both the market and the state. But for anarcho-capitalists criminal activity can never be conceived of as arising *in* the market.

This view further promotes the contradiction arising from confusing the market with the conditions under which it might exist. It leads anarcho-capitalists into the very thing they were trying to avoid, namely, the hypostatising of the market.

In opposition to the market, there is an institution that is characterised solely by its violation of property rights and the initiation of force. For anarcho-capitalists the insidious nature of the state is made worse by the fact that it is considered legitimate. Anarcho-capitalists do not define the state or government differently from others, but they often equate it with criminal activity:

> *Government is a coercive monopoly which has assumed power over and certain responsibilities for every human being within the geographical area which it claims as its own* (Tannehill and Tannehill 1970: 32).

> *Government is an agency of legitimized coercion.* I define 'coercion', for the purposes of this definition, as the violation of what people in a particular society believe to be the rights of individuals with respect to other individuals (Friedman 1989: 112).

> Government consists largely of various forms of legalized theft (Friedman 1989: 153).

Anarcho-capitalists do not conceive, as do other Free Market supporters, of the possibility of a limited government. Government, as we have seen, is by definition coercive. But there is a problem here in the use of the word 'coercive'. A monopoly on the use of force is coercive in an unacceptable way *only* if its coercion is not defensive. Governments use force both defensively (to defend the rights of their citizens) and offensively (aggressing against rights of their own citizens and others). Therefore, it seems reasonable to conclude that coercion limited to legitimate defence would be acceptable.

By defining the government or the state as capable only of offensive coercion, anarcho-capitalists effectively erase part of the justification for believing governments to be legitimate. Without making this distinction, anarcho-capitalists can not account for the legitimacy of the state in the eyes of most people. Indeed, Friedman admits that 'the special characteristic that distinguishes governments from other agencies of coercion (such as ordinary criminal gangs) is that most people accept government coercion as normal and proper. The same act that is regarded as coercive when done by a private individual seems legitimate if done by an agent of the government' (Friedman 1989: 112). But, in fact, not all government actions are offensive: some are defensive. In failing to distinguish between offensive and defensive coercion in their model of government, the anarcho-capitalists preclude the legitimacy of any organised group designed by mutual consent for the purpose of defence.

Rothbard, in his essay, 'The Anatomy of the State' (in Rothbard 1974), puts forth Franz Oppenheimer's (1975 [1942]) distinction between the economic means and political means for acquiring wealth. The economic means is through production and exchange, the equivalent of what Rothbard refers to as 'power over nature' (1970: 171). But the political means 'does not require productivity; it is the way of seizure of another's goods or services by the use of force and violence. This is the one-sided confiscation, or theft of the property of others' (Rothbard 1974: 36). The political means is what Rothbard refers to elsewhere as 'power over men' (1970: 171). The political means is a device of the state. But, Rothbard tells us, 'It should be equally clear that the coercive, exploitative means is contrary to natural law; it is parasitic, for instead of adding to production, it subtracts from it' (1974: 36).

Oppenheimer's distinction between the economic and political means is the introduction to his theory of the origin of the state, a theory that clearly identifies the state as coming into existence through coercive means. Although Oppenheimer's theory has been refuted, the theory of circumscription advanced by Robert Carneiro (1970) also supports the coercive origins of the state. Moreover, Carneiro's theory presents the origin of the state as an unintended consequence of human action. If Carneiro is correct, the rise of the pristine state is a 'natural' occurrence, generating not only stratification but a more specialised division of labour, which eventually includes the complex economic phenomenon known as the market. Thus, the market arises within the context of the state. The market is a function of the complexity of the society in which it arises – a complexity based on an elaborate division of labour whose original impetus may have been the warfare that resulted in the state itself.

If this is the case, then the dichotomy between market and state fostered by the anarcho-capitalist view (summarised in Table 2.1) is an arbitrary one. Ironically, Oppenheimer took the position that although the state had arisen by coercive means, it ultimately gives way to democratic institutions, because of the eventual identification of the dominant party with those it dominated. Oppenheimer further suggested that, following this trend, the state might eventually be reduced to almost nothing. Thus, Oppenheimer saw some relationship between the state and society that led him to postulate that the political means would eventually be replaced or minimised by the economic means.

In spite of the fact that he quotes Oppenheimer at length, Rothbard does not address the aspects of Oppenheimer's argument that I have described. Anarcho-capitalists almost never explain the ubiquitous presence of the state or address it as a possible 'natural' phenomenon like the market. Although the mere presence of the state does not necessarily prove that the state *must* exist, its presence does require an explanation. By failing to provide

Table 2.1. The Characteristics of the Market and the State from the Writings of Anarcho-Capitalists

The Market	*The State*
Economic means	Political means
Voluntarism	Coercion
Harmony	Discord
Produces wealth	Plunders wealth
Operates by competition	Operates by monopoly
Beneficial	Exploitative
Power over nature ('creative')	Power over people ('parasitic')
Individual gains social utility	Individual loses social utility
Social power	Political power
Peaceful	Warlike
Advance in living standards	Regression of living standards
Freedom	Slavery
Natural	Unnatural

one, anarcho-capitalists increase their own lack of credibility and that of their Free Market model.

> The logic of governments is to grow. There are obvious reasons for that in the nature of government, and plenty of evidence. Constitutions provide, at the most, a modest and temporary restraint . . .. Anarchy at least might work; limited government has been tried (Friedman 1989: 147).

> Any attempt to devise a government which did not initiate force is an exercise in futility, because it is an attempt to make a contradiction work. Government is, by its very nature, an agency of initiated force (Tannehill and Tannehill 1970: 33).

> Government isn't a necessary evil – it's an unnecessary one (Tannehill and Tannehill 1970: 42).

American Culture and the Free Market[13]

The internal contradictions of the anarcho-capitalist view of the Free Market, with its radical dichotomy of economy and state, are only part of the problem anarcho-capitalists face within American culture. The Free Market as cultural artefact informs a number of different cultural perspectives and integrates itself into a number of different national myths. The anarcho-capitalist construction of the Free Market has never been fully acceptable, because (1) it appears to vest too much power in business, (2) it appears to lead to disintegration of community, and (3) it contradicts other American myths, and must become reconciled with them in a fashion acceptable to the general public before such a pure version of the market can be culturally embraced. I want to discuss a range of views that integrate the Free Market in both positive and negative ways with other American cultural elements.

A particularly negative view of the Free Market is held by those who see power and authority as concentrated in the market, allowing business to ride roughshod over innocent individuals – a juggernaut that threatens to run away with society, crushing the masses beneath its weight. They often advocate eliminating the Free Market altogether and replacing it with government-controlled enterprises. This is a minority position, because it represents the kind of totalitarianism that Americans abhor and that interferes with the core principle of individualism and substitutes one unacceptable authority for another. It is generally held by socialists, communists and others who promote an uncompromising version of those philosophies with government control at the centre.

More moderate proponents of the Free Market seek to harness its power and efficiency while keeping it from going too far, and they use government regulation as the means of controlling the 'excesses' of the market. They tend to be biased in favour of workers (labour) rather than corporations and tend to invoke anti-trust legislation to keep too much economic power from being concentrated in too few hands. While generally wanting government to uphold civil liberties and stay out of people's personal lives, they support minimum wage laws, child labour laws, redistributive taxation and other policies that reflect the core principle of equality and Christian charity and concern for the weak that is at the root of American culture. This view tends to be associated with those who call themselves welfare statists, social democrats, or liberals (in the American sense).

Other proponents of the Free Market see it as a positive vehicle for the growth of national prosperity, but feel it is necessary to protect the market from foreign incursions through the use of protective legislation such as tariffs and import restrictions, limitations on immigration, and the military protection of overseas American businesses. Supporters of this view tend to be biased in favour of corporations over labour. They support bail-outs for corporations in financial trouble and subsidies to key industries, but otherwise want to minimise government participation in the market, the educational system and social welfare programmes, believing in personal responsibility in these areas. This view tends to be associated with conservative politics, and it honours the core principle of individualism and the idea of Americans banding together to defeat outside interests.

Of the three models sketched above, Americans tend to fluctuate between the so-called liberal and conservative views of the Free Market, although there are many variations within these models. In *Tales of a New America*, Robert B. Reich (1987) states that four national myths (he calls them 'morality tales') inform the American view and are used to interpret the world around them. These are (1) 'the mob at the gates', the idea that the United States is a 'beacon light of virtue in a world of darkness, a small island of freedom and democracy in a perilous sea' that must stave off those on the outside who threaten it; (2) 'the triumphant individual', the idea that an individual is self-made and can become successful through hard work and risk-taking, triumphing over nay-sayers, associated with the American core principle of self-reliance and the Protestant work ethic; (3) 'the benevolent community', the idea that Americans cooperate as 'neighbors and friends rolling up their sleeves and pitching in to help one another' and show 'essential generosity and compassion toward those in need', associated with Christian charity and the core principle of equality; and (4) 'the rot at the top', the idea associated with the core principles of anti-authoritarianism and equality that holds as suspect 'the malevolence of powerful elites, be they wealthy aristocrats, rapacious business leaders, or imperious government officials' (Reich 1987: 8–13).

Both liberals and conservatives have successfully interpreted these myths in their turn. Reich makes the case that the shift from liberalism to conservatism since the Second World War constitutes a reinterpretation of these four myths from the liberal perspective to the conservative perspective, reflecting changes in the world and America's place within it. The shift from the affluence of the post-war years to the recessions of the 1970s, the rise of Japan as an economic competitor and the shift in the perception of the effectiveness of social welfare programmes all led to a massive reinterpretation that made more sense to Americans in view of their experiences.

In terms of the Free Market model, Reich states that the tendency to have to choose between a totally free market and a government-controlled market 'infuses issue after issue with mythic overtones, and excites debates over where we dare and where we must abandon other social concerns in favor of the vigor of the market, or abandon free enterprise to pursue a higher public good' (1987: 222). The anarcho-capitalists, by defining the market as pure and outside society (or co-terminous with society), are unable to integrate it with non-economic concerns that are nevertheless influenced by economics and of deep concern to most Americans. They are capable of imagining an ideal world in which a Free Market has been achieved, but they are not very good at defining the Free Market within a moral community and suggesting how to achieve it without sacrificing deeply held cultural beliefs.

All three of these models of the market would be considered impure and erroneous approaches by those who call themselves classical liberals, who would argue that attempts to control the market, whether to stem its power or to protect its operation, will result in the expansion of government power and the corruption of the Free Market, as well as interference with the civil liberties of individuals. Within the classical liberal camp, with its libertarian outlook, government always constitutes the greater power and, thus, the greater threat to individual liberty, because of its inherently coercive nature.

Yet, whatever their empirical case may be, anarcho-capitalists have no morality tales sufficiently engaging to sway the majority of Americans into their camp. They have failed to provide an explanation of the world in terms that people can relate to culturally. Thus their model of the Free Market exists within a cultural void.

Conclusion

The growth of civilisation and the concomitant growth of emphasis on the individual in contradistinction to society constitutes one of the thorniest problems in Western thought. No one has yet suggested a solution we can all agree on, and in fact this may never happen. Still, the anarcho-capitalist view of the Free Market and its internal contradictions makes clear the contingent nature of the market with regard to the state, to individual rights and to the core principles of American culture.

In the end, anarcho-capitalism fails to resolve the great problem of the individual and society, because it can not accept the social and cultural aspects of the very human nature that it purports to take for granted. Anarcho-capitalists can not accept that human beings both generate market phenomena and disrupt them, design governments as a solution and use the solution to worsen the problem. Instead, they invest all that they admire, their cultural ideals, into the Free Market model, and slough off all that they disdain on to the weary bones of the state.

By dichotomising human activity in such a way as to create binary opposites out of the market and the state, anarcho-capitalists commit an act comparable to severing the two sides of the brain. Both sides continue to function in theory, but the functions are incomplete and do not really permit the mutual benefits of understanding that existed when they were related.

Notes

1. F. A. Hayek, a Nobel-prize winning economist, and Tibor Machan, a philosopher, would be representatives of this point of view. See Hayek's three-volume *Law, Legislation, and Liberty* (1973–1979) or Machan's *Human Rights and Human Liberties* (1975) and *Individuals and Their Rights* (1989).
2. I do not distinguish 'state' and 'government' here.
3. Anarcho-capitalism should not be confused with the anti-government militias that have formed in the United States. These militias are one variant of the anti-authoritarian principle that underlies much of American thinking. Generally, anarcho-capitalism is a theoretical position without implications for specific action.
4. Objectivism is the philosophy of Ayn Rand, who believed in limited government and regarded anarchists of any stripe as irrational. The natural rights position of Rothbard follows from his grounding in classical economic theory and classical liberal political theory. Rothbard, who died in 1995, is a scion of Austrian economics. Friedman's utilitarianism is of a practical nature. He rejects utilitarianism as a moral principle but believes that utilitarian arguments are the best way to defend his views (Friedman 1989: 181). Friedman is a scion of the Chicago school of economics.
5. Although I have chosen to focus on these three individuals, there were many more individualist anarchists whose ideas are worth exploring. For example, Stephen Pearl Andrews and Ezra Heywood were disciples of Josiah Warren but also presented provocative ideas of their own. Also, J. K. Ingalls and William B. Greene made substantial contributions (Martin 1970: 103–167). One also can not overlook Voltairine De Cleyre (Avrich 1978).
6. Adam Smith wrote, 'The value of any commodity, therefore, to the person who possesses it, and who means not to use or consume it himself, but to exchange it for other commodities, is equal to the quantity of labour which it enables him to purchase or command. Labour, therefore, is the real measure of the exchangeable value of all commodities' (Smith 1981 [1776]: 47). This view of value was later corrected by Carl Menger's theory of subjective value. Menger wrote, 'The measure of value is entirely subjective in nature, and for this

reason a good can have great value to one economizing individual, little value to another, and no value at all to a third, depending upon the differences in their requirements and available amounts' (Menger 1950: 146). People often attribute the labour theory of value to Karl Marx, who, in fact, came up with the theory of surplus value built upon the labour theory of value. His explanation can be found in *Capital* (Marx 1932: 39), which is available in many editions. Marx's economics is an offshoot of classical economics.

7. It is interesting to note that the Free Market model put forth by the anarcho-capitalists does not seem to take the viewpoint of the worker explicitly, in spite of its emphasis on individualism.

8. In 1882, when Walt Whitman's *Leaves of Grass* was censored under the Comstock law, Tucker openly criticised the act in *Liberty* and then published the work himself, in violation of the law. 'Thus Tucker earned Whitman's life-long esteem' (Kline 1987: 58).

9. Indeed, by the heyday of early twentieth-century anarchism, the individualist anarchists had been totally eclipsed by anarcho-communists such as Emma Goldman and Alexander Berkman.

10. Max Stirner (1806–1856) was a German philosopher whose doctrine that individuals constituted the only social reality was called egoism and was presented in *The Ego and His Own* (1963 [1845]). Karl Marx took exception to much of what Stirner had to say in *The German Ideology* (Marx and Engels 1947).

11. This view of individuals accounts for the lack of interest among anarcho-capitalists in the work of sociologists and anthropologists. While they rarely think of the work of anthropologists at all, they have occasionally made negative statements about the discipline of sociology, primarily because they associate it with a tradition of socialism and hostility to individualism.

12. F. G. Bailey has noted how relationships that start off as transactional often become moral over time (1969). See also Dore (1983) and Granovetter (1985).

13. A key problem that seems to go unremarked is the equation of the free market with capitalism. This is a probably precisely because most capitalistic countries do not have free markets in the libertarian sense. Capitalism then comes to stand for

those systems with industrialised economies, even when
markets are relatively unfree. Consequently, negative economic results that can be specifically attributed to government
controls are usually attributed to the free market.

References

Avrich, Paul 1978. *An American Anarchist: The Life of Voltairine de
Cleyre*. Princeton: Princeton University Press.

Bailey, F. G. 1969. *Stratagems and Spoils*. Oxford: Basil Blackwell.

Bailie, William 1972 (1906). *Josiah Warren: The First American
Anarchist*. Boston: Small, Maynard, and Company. (Reprinted
by Arno Press and The New York Times.)

Bailyn, Bernard 1967. *The Ideological Origins of the American
Revolution*. Cambridge, Mass.: Harvard University Press.

Barclay, Harold 1990. *People Without Government: An Anthropology
of Anarchy*. London: Kahn & Averill.

Beaird, Paul 1975. On Proper Government. MS.

Binchy, Daniel A. 1970. *Celtic and Anglo-Saxon Kingship*. Oxford:
Oxford University Press.

Bohannan, Paul (ed.) 1967. *Law and Warfare: Studies in the Anthropology of Conflict*. Garden City, NY: Natural History Press.

Brown, Susan Love 1989. The Impossibility of Anarchy In Complex
Society: An Anthropological Critique of Political Philosophy.
Unpublished master's thesis, Department of Anthropology,
University of California, San Diego.

Brown, Susan Love 1992. Babyboomers, American Character, and
the New Age: A Synthesis. Pp. 87–96 in Gordon Melton and
James R. Lewis (eds), *Perspectives on the New Age*. Albany: SUNY
Press.

Carneiro, Robert 1970. A Theory of the Origin of the State. *Science*
169: 733–738.

Commager, Henry Steele 1950. *The American Mind*. New Haven:
Yale University Press.

Dore, Ronald 1983. Goodwill and the Spirit of Capitalism. *British
Journal of Sociology* 34: 459–482.

Durrenberger, E. Paul 1988. Stratification Without a State: The
Collapse of the Icelandic Commonwealth. *Ethnos* 53: 239–265.

Friedman, David 1989. *The Machinery of Freedom: Guide to a Radical
Capitalism*. Second edition. La Salle, Ill.: Open Court.

Gorer, Geoffrey 1948. *The Americans: A Study in National Character.* London: Cresset.

Granovetter, Mark 1985. Economic Action and Social Structure: The Problem of Embeddedness. *American Journal of Sociology* 91: 481–510.

Hasluck, Margaret 1967. The Albanian Blood Feud. Pp. 381–408 in Paul Bohannan (ed.), *Law and Warfare: Studies in the Anthropology of Conflict.* Garden City, NY: Natural History Press.

Hayek, F. A. 1973–1979. *Law, Legislation and Liberty.* Three volumes. Chicago: The University of Chicago Press.

Hoebel, E. Adamson 1964. *The Law of Primitive Man: A Study in Comparative Legal Dynamics.* Cambridge: Harvard University Press.

Hsu, Francis L. K. 1969. *The Study of Literate Civilizations.* New York: Holt, Rinehart, and Winston.

Karsten, Rafael 1967. Blood Revenge and War among the Jibaro Indians of Eastern Ecuador. Pp. 305–325 in Paul Bohannan (ed.), *Law and Warfare: Studies in the Anthropology of Conflict.* Garden City, NY: Natural History Press.

Kline, William Gary 1987. *The Individualist Anarchists: A Critique of Liberalism.* Lanham, Md: University Press of America.

McElroy, Wendy 1981. Benjamin Tucker's Individualism and *Liberty: Not the Daughter but the Mother of Invention. Literature of Liberty* IV (3): 7–39.

Machan, Tibor 1975. *Human Rights and Human Liberties: A Radical Reconsideration of the American Political Tradition.* Chicago: Nelson-Hall.

Machan, Tibor 1989. *Individuals and their Rights.* LaSalle, Ill.: Open Court.

Martin, James J. 1970. *Men against the State.* Colorado Springs, Col.: Ralph Myles.

Marx, Karl 1932. *Capital and Other Writings of Karl Marx.* New York: Carlton House.

Marx, Karl, and Frederick Engels 1947. *The German Ideology.* New York: International Publishers.

Menger, Carl 1950. *Principles of Economics.* Glencoe, Ill.: The Free Press.

Nader, Laura (ed.) 1969. *Law in Culture and Society.* Chicago: Aldine.

Norris, Frank 1901. *The Octopus.* Garden City, NY: Doubleday.

Oppenheimer, Franz 1975 (1942). *The State.* New York: Free Life Editions.

Peden, Joseph 1971. Stateless Societies: Ancient Ireland. *The Libertarian Forum* 3 (4): 3–4, 8.

Reich, Robert B. 1987. *Tales of a New America*. New York: Times Books.

Rothbard, Murray N. 1962. *Man, Economy, and State*. Los Angeles: Nash Publishing Company.

Rothbard, Murray N. 1970. *Power and Market: Government and the Economy*. Menlo Park, NJ: Institute for Humane Studies.

Rothbard, Murray N. 1973. *For a New Liberty*. New York: Macmillan.

Rothbard, Murray N. 1974. *Egalitarianism as a Revolt against Nature*. Washington, DC: Libertarian Review Press.

Schuster, Eunice Minette 1970. *Native American Anarchism: A Study of Left-Wing American Individualism*. New York: Da Capo Press/ Plenum.

Shively, Charles 1971. Biography. Pp. 15–62 in *The Collected Works of Lysander Spooner*. Weston, Mass.: M & S Press.

Sinclair, Upton 1906. *The Jungle*. New York: Doubleday, Page, and Company.

Smith, Adam 1981 (1776). *An Inquiry into the Nature and Causes of the Wealth of Nations*. Vol. I. Indianapolis: Liberty Classics.

Spencer, Herbert 1886. *The Principles of Sociology, Volume I*. Third edition. New York: D. Appleton.

Spooner, Lysander 1882. Natural Law: or the Science of Justice. In *The Collected Works of Lysander Spooner*. Volume 1. Weston, Mass.: M & S Press.

Stirner, Max 1963 (1845). *The Ego and His Own*. Translated by Steven T. Byington. New York: New Edition.

Tannehill, Morris, and Linda Tannehill 1970. *The Market for Liberty*. Lansing, Michigan: no publisher listed.

Tucker, Benjamin 1972 (1893). *Instead of a Book by a Man too Busy to Write One: A Fragmentary Exposition of Philosophical Anarchism*. New York: Arno Press and The New York Times.

Weber, Max 1958. *The Protestant Ethic and the Spirit of Capitalism*. New York: Charles Scribner's Sons.

Chapter 3

Mr Smith, Meet Mr Hawken

James G. Carrier

As noted in the Introduction to this collection, the model of the Free Market is a powerful element of Western culture, and one that has deep roots. However, the fact that it is powerful and long-lived does not mean that everyone believes in, espouses and adheres to it all the time. Rather, there are alternative understandings of what economic life is and ought to be like, understandings that range from the mildly revisionist to the wholly condemning. In this chapter I investigate one particular American alternative, which is more revisionist than otherwise. This is the alternative associated with an image of the petty entrepreneur that is romantic, concerned with sentiment rather than reason (see Campbell 1987; Kahn, this volume, Chap. 1).

Petty entrepreneurship, starting your own business, was especially visible and popular in the United States in the 1980s. Part of the reason for this doubtless was the fit between being a petty entrepreneur and important American values like self-reliance (see Berthoff 1980). However, part of the reason also was the fact that American managers were being fired as large corporations sought to maintain their profits by cutting labour costs (Fefer 1994). According to one report, corporations in the United States eliminated about two million positions in the middle levels of management from 1985 to 1991. Further, while those who were fired in the early stages of this process generally were able to find comparable jobs with comparable pay, as the 1980s progressed those who were fired increasingly had to take substantial cuts in pay and prestige, if they found work at all (*Business Week* 1992). Even those who did not lose their jobs in these rounds of firing saw that their positions were insecure and their prospects were uncertain (*Economist* 1993; Lublin 1993). Starting your own business was an attractive option for many of these people, and they were receptive to flattering portrayals of petty entrepreneurs.

Popular publications for and about petty entrepreneurs range from the technical to the hortatory. Implicitly or explicitly, however, they all contain an image of what petty entrepreneurship is, an image of how petty entrepreneurs do or ought to conduct their business. Consequently, they contain models of economic actors, models that can depart from the assertions and assumptions of the model of the Free Market. In presenting one description of petty entrepreneurs in this chapter, I seek to show the existence of alternatives to the notion of the impersonal, calculating actor that is a feature of the Market model. Even though it is worthwhile showing that there is a romantic alternative to the Market model, that is not my sole purpose here. In addition, I seek to show the lineage of that alternative. Although petty entrepreneurship may have flourished as an idea in the United States late in the 1980s, some of the literature that deals with it reflects cultural understandings that have been important for almost 300 years. Moreover, describing this lineage helps reveal the ways that the romantic image of the petty entrepreneur fits with and draws on established cultural conceptions of what people are like – conceptions of the self that lie within Market actors, the understanding of their nature, mentality and sources of motive.

Mr Smith

The 'Smith' of my title is Adam Smith. He is the founder and pre-eminent luminary of Market thought, and I use him to stand for the conventional Market model. Famous in the lore of that model is Smith's assertion: 'It is not from the benevolence of the butcher, the brewer, or the baker, that we expect our dinner, but from their regard to their own interest' (Smith 1976: 18). Here, Smith describes a world in which people are free from the claims of friendly and social obligation. The Smithian Market actor is an autonomous being not bound to others in any significant way. Our relations with them, as economic actors, are impersonal, for we can induce them to act only by way of the trade of equivalents. We can get our meat, our beer and our bread only by giving what they want to those who possess them. 'Whoever offers to another a bargain of any kind, proposes to do this. Give me that which I want, and you shall have this which you want, is the meaning of every such offer' (Smith 1976: 18). As Jonathan Parry (1986: 454) notes, relationships among such people are construed as 'essentially *dyadic* transactions between *self-interested individuals*, . . . premissed on some kind of *balance*'. To recall a point from the Introduction to this collection, this is a world of Benthamites who bestir themselves to carry out their trade only when lured with the offer of a reward. They personify the calculus of gain and loss, pleasure and pain.

Those who populate this cultural world of the Market are taken as free individuals with their eyes securely on material reward, interested in what will 'empty [or] fill the pocket' (Adam Ferguson, quoted in Silver 1990: 1484). Whatever sorts of people they may be in their private lives, once they enter the economic realm their manner is one of self-regard and material calculation. This rendering of Market actors and the public, commercial world in which they operate does not exist by itself. Rather, it co-exists with common understandings of a non-economic, social realm, exemplified by private, domestic life, ultimately life within the family. These understandings of the economic and the social realms are not neutral reflections of people's existence in different areas of their lives. Rather, as was noted in the Introduction to this collection, they define each other in a dialectical process that exaggerates and stylises the difference between the two (Carrier 1995). But even though the opposition may be artificial in many ways, it remains pervasive in Western thought.

This stylised rendering of the public, economic sphere is pronounced in high academic thought. For example, Max Weber argued that a key aspect of the genius of the modern West lay in the tendency of its public institutions to be characterised by instrumental rationality and the bureaucratic ethos (Weber 1978: Chap. 11). These are distinguished by thoroughgoing impersonality and the adherence to formal rules and regulations, for it is only this disregard for persons as individuals that allows the organisation to pursue the goals set for it, free of the vagaries of personal circumstance and allegiance. Similarly, and perhaps more familiarly, he argued in *The Protestant Ethic* (1958) that the feature that distinguished modern capitalism is the rational, ascetic and single-minded pursuit of material gain for its own sake. Karl Marx made analogous points repeatedly. Thus, in a famous passage in the *Manifesto*, he observed that the rising bourgeoisie 'has drowned the most heavenly ecstasies of religious fervor, of chivalrous enthusiasm, of philistine sentimentalism, in the icy waters of egotistical calculation. It has resolved personal worth into exchange value' (Marx and Engels 1948: 11). Even Emile Durkheim, not renown for his criticism of modern economic life, argued in *The Division of Labour* (1984) that commercial, industrial society is characterised by the decay of common moral sentiment and the growing importance of sectional self-interest.

In this world, people are evaluated not in terms of what Marx called their 'personal worth', but in terms of 'exchange value' – that is, their ability to conform to the impersonal rules and regulations of Weber's bureaucratic organisation, their competence at the task assigned to them, the task for which they receive their pay. Talcott Parsons (1959: 261) echoed this point when he said that, in such organisations, 'roles are organized about standards of competence or effectiveness in performing a definite function. That means that criteria of effective performance . . . must be predominantly universalistic and must be attached to impersonally and objectively defined abilities and competence through training.'

This notion that the public realm is one of impersonal rationality is not restricted to academic thought. David Schneider (1980: 47) says that it exists among ordinary Americans as well. As he summarises one of the results of this research, the people he studied believed that 'at work, it is what one does and how he does it that counts. Who he is is not supposed to really matter.' Steve Barnett and Martin Silverman (1979: esp. 51) reflected on this distinction between who one is and what one does, and concluded that it is associated with a particular, bifurcated view of human beings, a particular construction of the self that contains two distinct parts. They argue that in the public world of economic activity people engage what they take to be only one particular aspect of the self, its superficial aspect. This is a collection of personal attributes and activities that are conceived as being distinct and separable from the real self.

The real self, on the other hand, is the self that is constituted 'of things which people believe to be real things, which are in an important sense thought to be internal to the individual or continuous with the individual as a concrete being' (Barnett and Silverman 1979: 51). This is the self of Marx's 'personal worth'. The 'real self' that Barnett and Silverman describe is not just different from the superficial aspects that are at issue in the economic realm. In addition, this self is associated with the social world, the realm of social relations that is distinct from the realm of economic actions and transactions. In Schneider's study of American kinship, respondents saw this real self as associated with the home and family, the quintessence of the social world. Parsons (1959: 262) put it thus:

> Broadly speaking, there is no sector of our society where the dominant patterns stand in sharper contrast to those of the occupational world than in the family. The family is a solidary group within which status, rights, and obligations are defined primarily by membership as such and by the ascribed differentiations of age, sex, and biological relatedness. This basis of relationship and status in the group precludes more than a minor emphasis on universalistic standards of functional performance.

In the family, then, and in the social world more generally, it is not what you do that is important, but who you are and how you are related to those around you.

I have taken Adam Smith to stand for a particular aspect of common Western understandings of the Market. That is, the notion that Market actors are dispassionate, autonomous and unconstrained beings who evaluate each other impersonally and instrumentally, only in terms of the task at hand. Moreover, this Smithian rendering of the self that the self-regarding Market actor regards is part of a distinction between economic and social aspects of life. Self-regard, rationality and the methodical, impersonal pursuit of material reward are features of the Market self, which is opposed to the affective, personal expression that is a feature of social life. Schneider (1980: 46) summarises the distinction thus: 'Home is not kept for money and, of those things related to home and family, it is said that there are some things that money can't buy! The formula in regard to work is exactly reversed at home: What is done is done for love, not for money! And it is love, of course, that money can't buy.'

Mr Hawken

As I have taken Mr Smith to stand for important features of the Market model, so I take Mr Hawken to represent a more romantic view of Market actors. Mr Hawken is Paul Hawken, who presents himself as an American entrepreneur, and it is what he has to say about himself and his world that is at issue here, not the facts of his personal and commercial history. Americans who know of Hawken are most likely to do so because of his mail-order company, called 'Smith & Hawken', which is based in California. This was founded late in the 1970s to sell gardening tools, but has since expanded to sell a range of garden-related accessories and implements, from clothing to lawn furniture.

Paul Hawken, however, is not only an entrepreneur. In addition, he makes a living as a commentator on and adviser of American business. As a part of these activities, he was involved in the 1980s in a television series on the Public Broadcasting Service in the United States. Associated with the series, he wrote a book, *Growing a Business* (Hawken 1987). Like the television series, the book deals with how to start and run a small business, and it is in this book that Mr Hawken lays out his vision of petty entrepreneurs and the commercial world that they inhabit – a vision very different from that associated with Mr Smith.

Growing a Business is no ready manual of ways to negotiate with banks and landlords or how to advertise and distribute a product; it is not impersonal and utilitarian, it is not concerned with what you do and how you do it. Rather, and like the catalogue of the Smith & Hawken company (see Carrier 1994: 131–134), it is social and personal, and it is about sociability and personality. It is a story of Paul Hawken's personal and business life, and it is his personal reflections on business and the ways to make a business a success. It is this personality that makes Hawken's book an intriguing statement of a particular view of Market actors. Throughout *Growing a Business*, Hawken denies the image of impersonal calculation and pursuit of profit that characterises the more conventional view of Market actors. Profit is there, as it must be in a book about being a petty entrepreneur. However, for Hawken profit is a not a self-evident goal that the good entrepreneur struggles to achieve in the manner of Weber's ascetic Protestant capitalist. Rather, it is almost an afterthought, the consequence of being a good entrepreneur, and a good human being. 'Being in business is not about making money. It is a way to become who you are' (Hawken 1987: 19). Indeed, 'profit' never appears in the book's index.

There is much in *Growing a Business* that emphasises personality in business, that emphasises the 'who you are' rather than 'what you do'. Perhaps the most striking, at least from the perspective of this chapter, is what Hawken has to say about the identification of the firm with the entrepreneur. Such identification could take many forms. For instance, the identification might emerge in the minds of the public who associate the firm with its owner, the sort of identification that goes with companies with names like 'Smith & Hawken' rather than with names like 'General Electric'. Equally, it might emerge as the owner shapes the firm over the course of time, marking it with his or her identity. Unlike these sorts of identification, which are built gradually through a shared history, the identification that Hawken describes is personal and immediate. This is because the firm embodies the owner, 'an uncluttered expression of yourself' (Hawken 1987: 61). The 'best idea for a business will be something that is deep within you... . The idea itself is just the tip of the iceberg. The iceberg is your life' (Hawken 1987: 61, 62).

In other words, this book contradicts the cultural assumption that Schneider describes and that is part of the Smithian understanding of the Market actor. This is because, for Hawken, what is noteworthy in the economic realm is who you are, the self of which the firm is an uncluttered expression. However, to say that a firm is an expression of the owner does not exclude the possibility that it reflects careful, dispassionate and impersonal calculation. It does not tell us what kind of self these Market actors have. Logically speaking, after all, the would-be entrepreneur who carefully calculates the way to achieve the greatest possible return on investment, and lays out a business plan accordingly, is engaged in self-expression. The business that results expresses the orientation and calculation of the entrepreneur as surely as a portfolio of stocks expresses the orientation and calculation of the market speculator. The distinctiveness of what Hawken describes, then, is not just the fact that the firm expresses the owner. Rather, it is the kind of owner that it expresses.

A story that Hawken tells about himself will illustrate what kind of owner. The story concerns the founding of the Smith & Hawken company. Hawken was associated with a non-profit California organisation that, as a source of income, set up a store selling gardening equipment, including Bulldog garden tools, manufactured in England and purchased from an American distributor. However, the distributor went out of business, and Hawken wrote to Bulldog Tools saying he wanted to place an order.

Bulldog eventually replied and the order was placed. By this time Hawken had taken on as a partner Dave Smith, the man who became the 'Smith' in 'Smith & Hawken'. Also, he learned that he would have to establish a commercial firm to import the tools, in order to protect the non-profit status of the California organisation. As a result, 'it looked as if we'd have to go into regular business, complete with shareholders, capital and an official plan. That was not at all what we had had in mind' (Hawken 1987: 60). Hawken had a problem:

> Nobody wanted to own the company . . .. That night I took a five-hour bath as my wife Anna brought in steaming tea kettles after the hot water heater had run out. I tried to soak myself out of this dilemma. In the end the conclusion was simple. Dave Smith and I had given our word to the English suppliers, so we would form a company (1987: 60).

Here is a self that does not impersonally calculate profits and losses. Indeed, here is a self for whom the very apparatus of profit and loss is distasteful. Hawken did not decide on his course of action because it was good business sense, did not decide for reasons that were economically rational, but because his course of action was moral. He as a person had given his word, and he would keep it.

It should not be thought that Hawken's concern with the expressive self is restricted to entrepreneurs, who, as bosses, are in a position to make their own decisions and to make decisions for their subordinates as well. Rather, Hawken is thorough in his vision of Market actors, for employees need to express their selves as well. Here too, who you are is more important that what you do and how you do it. Writing of employment policy at Smith & Hawken, he says: 'We're more interested in what kind of person a potential employee is than in where the person worked before or what he or she has or hasn't accomplished' (Hawken 1987: 214). Reliance on credentials and specific skills, a core of bureaucratic practice, is displaced by a concern for Barnett and Silverman's 'real self'. The result, Hawken says, is that the firm often employs people who have done poorly in their previous work, people who positively depart from rational bureaucratic criteria. His explanation of the firm's policy revolves around the need that employees share with entrepreneurs: to express themselves.

When hiring at Smith & Hawken, we will often look for people who have not thrived in the conventional business world. ... Not being able to adjust to a hierarchical organization means that a person didn't get into the habit of self-denial for the sake of employment. They are the changelings of the world of commerce, people who couldn't find a job or a company that allowed them to be as expressive of their humanity and their selves as they needed to be (Hawken 1987: 215).

Likewise, customers, the other party to the business, have selves that are important. The firm's relationship with them should not just entail the transaction of money for object, it should not be what Hawken (1987: 200) sees as 'a world of commerce between machines. The customer might as well be a machine.' Rather, the firm should allow them to express themselves, even if they do so with the aid of the entrepreneur:

> [N]eeds are *drawn out* of the customer and *into* the business, and then fulfilled. This does not call for reading the customer's mind or doing surveys. More important is to watch the customer's hands, eyes, feet, and body. See what people do and don't do, the attractions and repulsions, and observe the minutiae of daily life so that you can say before the buyer even knows it, 'This is what you want' (Hawken 1987: 177).

The Soul of the Entrepreneur

Hawken presents an image of the entrepreneur that he sees as new, as a rejection of the conventional ways that people act in and think about their Market selves. He expresses this novelty in various ways. For instance, he says that, in contrast to the 1950s and 1960s, 'the ability to strike out on one's own will be the most dynamic means of developing a "career" in the late 1980s and 1990s'. This dynamism is not just attractive, it is also necessary, for those who do not adopt it 'may be left behind' (Hawken 1987: 13). It is not just individuals who need this novel approach; firms do too, for those who lack it 'are dinosaurs' (1987: 199). But even though he treats his entrepreneur as a novel form, what Hawken says is novel only in part. In an important way it is a re-affirmation of the Market-model belief that the entrepreneur, like all Market actors, is autonomous, acting on the basis of internal motives and desires rather than external ties and obligations. Here is a sense of self that resonates not only with Market thought, but with Western individualism more generally. It is worth tracing some of the history of this sense of self.

Marcel Mauss (1985) has charted the nature and emergence of that sort of individualism in Western Europe in the seventeenth and eighteenth centuries, appropriately enough a period that saw a rapid spread of capitalism. It was during this period that some people began to hold that the self springs from individual consciousness as an irreducible being. Consequently, the only valid source of motivation was the individual. People began to identify themselves and others in terms of their personal wills, and were concerned to be what Lionel Trilling (1972) calls 'authentic', were concerned not to hide that will or mislead others about it. Prior to this change it appears to have been common to see the self not as autochthonous, but as springing from and defined by the webs of social relationships in and through which people lived their lives, most notably the webs of family, kinship and patronage. Under this older view, people's social locations were their only valid source of motivation. Consequently, people tended to identify each other in terms of their locations in an encompassing social frame, and they were concerned to be, again in Trilling's terms, 'sincere', concerned not to hide that location or mislead others about it.

Colin Campbell's study of English thought in the eighteenth century traces aspects of the emergence of the idea that the individual will is the legitimate source of motive. In particular, early in the 1700s people began to believe that humans have an innate moral sense, and an innate drive to do what is good and avoid what is bad. Campbell presents Lord Shaftesbury as an exemplar of this attitude, most notably in his *Characteristics of Man, Manners, Opinions, Times*, published in 1711. Shaftesbury, says Campbell, asserted that the operation of this inherent moral sense meant that 'virtuous behaviour can only be conduct which is freely chosen, arising directly out of one's very being' (Campbell 1987: 150). Or, as Shaftesbury said of the good man: 'He never deliberates . . . or considers the matter by prudential rules of self-interest and advantage. He acts from his nature, in a manner necessarily, and without reflection; and if he did not, it were impossible for him to answer his character, or be found that truly well-bred man of every occasion' (quoted in Campbell 1987: 150).

This philosophy is a charter of autonomous individualism. Because moral behaviour springs from individual will and its innate moral sense, it is freedom that best allows right thought and action.[1] Constraint and external obligation are bad. This elevated the social and moral virtue of the landed patriots, secure in the economic independence guaranteed by their estates (Pocock 1975: Chap. 13, 1979), just as it tends to elevate, more recently, the virtue of those who are secure in the economic independence generated by their capital (Hirschman 1977: 127–128). In the New World, this philosophy was best exemplified, perhaps, by Thomas Jefferson, who was influenced by it and who was instrumental in incorporating it into the Declaration of Independence and American thought more generally (Wills 1978: Chaps 13, 16, 21).

This belief in the morality of the autonomous individual attracted the thinkers of the Scottish Enlightenment, including Adam Smith through the influence of his teacher Francis Hutchison (Myers 1983: 68). According to Allan Silver (1990), these thinkers also saw an older sort of self being displaced by a newer. In the older, people were defined by their positions in a structure of faction or patronage. These positions were the source of people's motive, for they not only defined people as social beings, but also shaped expectations of their behaviour. Moreover, under such a system people's relationships with each other, as ally or enemy, were defined in advance by their faction membership. For the members of the Scottish Enlightenment, and especially Ferguson, Hume and Smith, a new form of identity and sociality was emerging. People were no longer members of factions or bound to patrons, but were independent individuals. The stranger, then, was no longer necessarily friend or enemy in advance. Instead, social relations of amity and enmity emerged through 'natural sympathy', the sentiment that emerges unbidden as we deal with each other. Adam Smith (quoted in Silver 1990: 1481) describes this as 'an involuntary feeling that the persons to whom we attach ourselves are the natural and proper objects of esteem and approbation'.

For these thinkers, a important factor that allowed for the play of natural sympathy was the growing separation of economic from social areas of life. Thus, for example, Adam Ferguson said that, under the decaying order, people's relationships with each other were shaped by economic necessity and the desire for gain. Consequently, 'one has no choice but to be, in Ferguson's disapproving phrase, "interested and sordid" in all interactions' (Silver 1990: 1484). However, as 'the economy becomes progressively disembedded from society, . . . economic relationships become increasingly differentiated from other types of social relationships' (Parry 1986: 446). With the emergence of the impersonal Market, people had a distinct sphere in which to secure their livelihood, leaving the social sphere to be ruled by the heart.

Thus far I have argued that Hawken's image of the autonomous entrepreneur, though presented as a novel vision springing from the fact that 'the world of commerce is changing radically' (Hawken 1987: 113), echoes a view of the self that emerged at about the same time as capitalism was undergoing an important period of growth in the West, and especially in Britain. Under this view, people are autonomous beings whose identities and motives spring from within themselves, rather than from the web of relationships in which they live their lives.

The webs of relationships that concerned people like Lord Shaftesbury, Adam Ferguson, Adam Smith and the rest were the webs of kinship, faction and patronage, not the sort of webs that might constrain Hawken's entrepreneur. However, Hawken is concerned with constraining webs even so. These are the webs that constrain individuals within firms, which can be glossed generally as bureaucracy. Ralph Turner has described some American conceptions of the self. One such conception reflects the self that exists within organisations, which he calls the 'institutional self'. He says that this is the self that is recognised and realised 'in the pursuit of institutional goals and not in the satisfaction of impulses outside institutional frameworks' (Turner 1976: 991). Such a self was caricatured in William Whyte's *The Organization Man* (1956), but it can be characterised more positively as a self that realises itself in the seeming contradiction of self-abnegation in the fulfilment of duty and responsibility to something larger than itself.

Hawken will not have it. 'We were not created in order to spend half or more of our working lives in such constricting circumstances, and we know it' (Hawken 1987: 13). (Paul Hawken is hardly the first to comment on the contrast between the freedom of the entrepreneur and the subordination of the worker. See Marx, *Capital*, Vol. I, Chap. 6, in Tucker 1978: 336–343.) Those who may think that they take pride and pleasure in such self-denying work are fooling themselves, are, in Trilling's terms, inauthentic, and Hawken reduces them to the sort of 'person who chooses to hide within some bureaucracy' (1987: 13). The constraints that people face are not just those emanating from the formal rules of bureaucratic organisation such as Weber described. For Hawken, they are more pervasive, and their result is a lack of self-fulfilment, a denial of the expression of the self.

> Ask someone who works for a company if 100 percent of his or her intelligence, creativity, energy, and abilities is being utilized and nurtured. Most people, most of the time hold something back or even a lot back from their employers. This doesn't mean they are not bone-weary at night; they are, and part of the reason they are is because of this restraint. It's tiring not to put your heart and soul into your work. It's enervating to play office politics, to have to create power bases for yourself, to compete with others for position and salary, to worry about your backside when you are trying to get a job done (Hawken 1987: 113–114).

Smith vs. Hawken

I have pointed out the way that Hawken's image of the entrepreneur echoes a central feature of the Market model that is in turn a durable Western notion, that of the autonomous individual who is free from constraints imposed by relationships with others. Equally, however, Hawken's image departs from some of the features of the Market model in some important ways.

One of these features is the belief that Market actors are Benthamite rational calculators who seek to gain as much utility for as little cost as possible, a calculating rationality that becomes possible because of the cultural splitting of social and economic areas of life in the West. People are supposed to be free to follow their sentiments in social life because the rise of commercial, capitalist society meant that there was a distinct, economic sphere in which they could pursue their material interests in an impersonal and calculating way. However, the image that Hawken presents is somewhat different. Certainly Hawken's entrepreneur seeks to secure wealth, even if only as an afterthought, and certainly Hawken asserts that those who follow his advice will be more likely to succeed in business. Equally, however, Hawken's presentation is notable for the way that it slights rationality and calculation.

Instead, Hawken's entrepreneur seems to live in a world in which the social and the economic, so carefully separated by people like Smith and Ferguson, are rejoined. Entrepreneurs, for Hawken, thrive precisely because they do not act in accord with their better judgement and the careful plan. It is rather as if they had taken to heart Shaftesbury's injunction that the good man 'never deliberates . . . or considers the matter by prudential rules of self-interest and advantage', but instead 'acts from his nature, in a manner necessarily, and without reflection'. Hawken's entrepreneur is a creature of the social, not the economic world, embodying Adam Smith's 'natural sentiment'. Thus, for instance, Hawken (1987: 18) says: 'I believe that most, if not all, of the successful new businesses are operating with values that go beyond opportunism. In fact, I believe they are successful *because*' they do so. His view of the bureaucratic side of business illustrates the same orientation. 'All businesses involve such factors as cash flow, accounting, and marketing . . ... But these things no more describe your business than household shopping lists and errands describe your family' (1987: 14). And just as freedom from constraint is a moral good because it allows the play of innate moral sense, so the business world is morally good because it is free. A 'business is the most unencumbered institution in the United States. The self-owned and -operated business is the freest life in the world' (1987: 18). This moralisation of economy is made complete when Hawken says: 'Being a good human being is good business' (1987: 16, emphasis omitted).

This denigration of prudential, impersonal calculation serves in effect to move the entrepreneur out of the economic realm as Schneider and as Barnett and Silverman construe it. And as Hawken speaks of much more than bosses, entrepreneurs, so he moves substantial areas of commerce out of the cultural realm of economic life. Regarding employees, I have already noted his point that they need a job that allows them to express 'their humanity and their selves'. This view that relations between firm and employees ought to be personal rather than bureaucratic, founded on the employees' 'real self' rather than their conformity to the rule book, recurs. Hawken says, for instance, that a good firm shares more than its profits with its employees. It also shares 'responsibility, authority, praise, credit, and a good joke' (Hawken 1987: 115). And again: 'You must give permission to your employees to do what they think is right . . ... No policy book could cover all . . . contingencies. Don't even try to concoct one. Our policy book [at Smith & Hawken] says this: it has to feel right' (1987: 202–203).

Indeed, in a sort of triumph of the fetishism of commodities, Hawken strips away an important part of the economic relationship between entrepreneur and worker: 'You make your profit on your product, not on your people' (1987: 200).

The same applies to the relationship between the firm and its customers. Hawken's world is not one of Smith's butcher, brewer or baker, self-interested and impersonal, confronting equally self-interested and impersonal buyers. Rather, firm and customer should have a durable relationship built over time. Speaking of advertising, but reflecting his more general orientation, he says you should 'proceed as though you are having a dialogue with your customer. Let your ads have the expansiveness of a friendship. Write copy that respects this relationship' (1987: 178). From such a perspective, the impersonality of the mass market is an affront.

> One of the great frustrations in commerce today is that our patronage and loyalty don't add up to anything. No matter how many years you shop at a chain store, nothing will ever change in your relationship with that store or with those people (you will have lasted a lot longer than the employees anyway). The sameness of experience is the whole idea behind the store. McDonald's does not and cannot care how many times you bought a Big Mac. Of course the franchise wants you to return tomorrow for another dose, but if you don't, someone else will. But we as human beings don't feel, act, and comprehend with such uniformity. We would like our activities, even such mundane ones as shopping for food, to add up, to build a relationship, to establish trust (Hawken 1987: 201).

Hawken's moving of the firm out of the economic realm, as culturally construed, is illustrated by something that I mentioned briefly previously, his systematic denigration of profit and the systematic pursuit of money. This denigration is manifest in Hawken's story of his founding of Smith & Hawken. Recall that he established that firm as a business corporation almost in spite of himself. He had, after all, been working with a non-profit organisation, and found the prospect was 'not at all what we had had in mind' (Hawken 1987: 60). This valuation of money echoes what Schneider says of American beliefs about the difference between domestic and economic areas of their lives. As he describes it, home is about the love and affection that binds people, while the economic world is about money, the lure that brings our meal from the butcher, the brewer and the baker. However, the situation 'is exactly reversed at home: What is done is done for love, not for money!' (Schneider 1980: 46). Money thus has a distinct meaning. It 'is material, it is power, it is impersonal and unqualified by considerations of sentiment or morality' (1980: 48). It is, in short, culturally the ideal medium in which to conduct Market transactions. The sentiment that binds people in the social world is very different, for it 'is highly personal and is beset with qualifications and considerations of . . . morality' (1980: 48).

Schneider's invocation of morality indicates that sentiment is not distinct from money simply in a negative sense, is not distinct simply because it is not material. Rather, sentiment differs from money in a positive sense, because it entails a spiritual relationship between people's real selves that is lacking in the world of money. This spiritual, moral element means that relations of sentiment 'transcend small and petty considerations of private gain or advantage or mere gratification' (1980: 49) – precisely the sort of considerations that motivate actors in the Smithian Market model. (For a more extended consideration of the uneasy relationship between money and durable, spiritual relations, see Parry and Bloch 1989.)

Hawken echoes clearly the belief in the moral dangers of money that Schneider describes. He says that it is a polluting substance that weakens the distinctly human side of the organisation, its spirit and imagination, as surely as husbands and wives paying each other for cooking meals, fetching the children from school or taking out the trash would weaken the human side of marriage and the family, would weaken the expression and affection that make it special and that bind its members together.

> It's true: for the small business, too much money is worse than too little. I disagree with the old saw that the major problem afflicting small businesses is lack of capital. The major problem affecting businesses, large or small, is a lack of *imagination*, not capital. A ready supply of too much money in start-ups tends to replace creativity. Companies with money buy solutions by buying consultants, lawyers, clever accountants, publicity agents, marketing studies, and on and on. Companies without money dream and imagine (Hawken 1987: 33).

> [A]fter the business is established you will understand that it wasn't new sources of money that held the key, after all, but the pluck and initiative you had to develop along the way. With low overhead, frugal

means, and fragile budgets, you can't buy your way out of problems. You have to learn your way out. The creativity and tenacity you have to develop will make it hard for you to be put out of business (Hawken 1987: 127).

The Machine in the Ghost

I said that Hawken's sentimentalisation of the entrepreneur is one of the important ways that his image departs from the Market model. Another is that, while Hawken's entrepreneurs are autonomous, they are by no means free of constraint. Thus, when Hawken says that the entrepreneur leads 'the freest life in the world', he is telling only part of the truth. External, legal regulation may be relatively weak, but if constraint means a compulsion to act in some way rather than another, then constraint exists. Such constraint is implicit in the self that is part of the sentimental individualism that Hawken espouses. Shaftesbury's good man, for instance, 'acts from his nature, in a manner necessarily', while for Adam Smith natural sympathy rests on 'involuntary feeling'.

For Hawken, the firm may be 'an uncluttered expression of yourself', for Hawken being an entrepreneur may be 'a way to become who you are' (Hawken 1987: 61, 19). This does not mean, however, that the self is something that one has fashioned consciously or something over which one has any control. Rather, such a person possesses something that Ralph Turner has called an 'impulsive self', which he says is one of the important ways that the Americans he describes construe selves. Under this construction, the self has a distinctly Freudian air, for it is rooted in 'deep, unsocialized, inner impulses' (Turner 1976: 992). Hawken's story of his own first business, a health-food store, shows how these impulses can be wholly beyond conscious control and consideration.

> When I started my first company. . . I was just trying to restore my health. Hindered by asthma since I was six weeks old, I had begun experimenting with my diet and discovered a disquieting correlation. When I stopped eating the normal American diet of sugar, fats, alcohol, chemicals, and additives, I felt better . . .. I was left with a most depressing conclusion: if I wanted to be healthy, I'd have to become a food nut. I bid a fond farewell to my junk foods (Hawken 1987: 9).

These impulses speak of a form of constraint that springs from within the individual entrepreneur's 'real self', made up of 'things which people believe to be real things, which are in an important sense thought to be internal to the individual or continuous with the individual as a concrete being' (Barnett and Silverman 1979: 51).

However, while the real self may spring from within and while it may be an internal source of constraint, part of its constraining force impinges on the entrepreneur from without as well, though this force operates differently from the compulsion of Paul Hawken's asthma. This is because there is a link between these unbidden internal motives and entrepreneurial performance. Acting in terms of them is linked to commercial success. In fact, if there were to be a subtitle to *Growing a Business*, it would be something like 'Trust your Instincts'. Thus, Hawken says: 'A successful business *pulls* you toward it . . .. I am suggesting that your best idea for a business will be something that is deep within you' (Hawken 1987: 61). That is, the 'successful business', the 'best idea', come from the entrepreneur's inner self. And as I noted already, this concern with inner feeling applies not just to the entrepreneur, but to the employee as well, who is encouraged with the rule, 'it has to feel right' (1987: 202).

Just as trusting your instincts, being true to your self and your feelings, is, for Hawken, the route to good business, so the failure to do so is dangerous. Thus, for example, Hawken advocates having employees own shares in the entrepreneur's company, and says that firms with passive stockholders are both old-fashioned and probably doomed to extinction (Hawken 1987: 199). However, he says such a plan will work only if it expresses the entrepreneur's inner orientation, only if the plan is an authentic outward sign of inward sentiment.

> There is no point in sharing equity if it does not stem from your sense of fairness. If you are not a fair person, don't fake it. Employees resent hypocrisy more than greed.
>
> Fairness is something people feel. You cannot fool workers with fancy titles, by calling people 'associates' or holding pep rallies, or by convoluted profit-sharing schemes that vest on the seventieth birthday (Hawken 1987: 114).

And again, at greater length, he links this concern for authenticity with the shortcomings of mere money and the material world that it represents:

No rules, charter, precepts, tenets, or corporate hoohaw will make you or anyone else a better person. Either you are a good company to work for or you are not; you are either good to your employees or you are not; you either share with others or you do not. No amount of puffery can hide the facts. So if you are going to have a profit-sharing program in your company, be sure you want to share . . .. Money is never a substitute for esteem, pride, and dignity, and profit sharing without a sense of sharing is nothing but piecework (Hawken 1987: 115–116).

Hawken's message, that following one's inner sense is linked to business success, has a logical inverse, that failure to trust one's instincts is the path to business failure. Hawken himself does not make this point, but others have made it for him. *Inc.* is a magazine for entrepreneurs. In the July 1994 issue, Gregory Braendel told what happened when he stopped trusting his instincts. In November 1986, Braendel set up a company with borrowed money to sell toilet partitions, and thought he was on the road to success. 'Halfway through our second year, our sales were on track to increase by 300%, and it looked as if we'd continue that pace for several more years' (Braendel 1994: 21). Problems began shortly thereafter, when a prestigious accountancy firm persuaded Braendel to take them on. They came, and brought their consultants with them.

'Since I thought the experts knew more than I did, I listened to what they said, even when it went against my gut feelings' (Braendel 1994: 21). For example, Braendel said that he wanted to resign as president so that he could concentrate on sales and let someone better suited to the task handle the oversight of the company. The consultants said 'No'. He took their advice. 'That was when I first started to relinquish control without understanding, without going with my own feelings. Until then I had disregarded advice that didn't make sense to me' (1994: 22). Things went from bad to worse. Heeding consultants' advice, he hired 'M.B.A.'s, people with big corporate ideas', even though 'I knew whom I wanted to hire', and it was not them (1994: 22). By the middle of 1989 he found his firm short of cash, and ended up selling a 30 per cent share to a large company for $3 million. Not only was the buying company several months late in paying; they did not offer the sort of advice that Braendel anticipated. 'The thing that needed to be done was to go out and get sales. Instead we had to spend money on consultants and come up with answers to [their] questions, because they owned 30% of the company . . . . It was unbelievable. Every board meeting was an attack on me. Worst of all, I was beginning to question myself' (Braendel 1994: 22).

Finally, fed up, he re-established control of the firm, hired the kind of president he wanted, and brought the company back into profit sufficiently that he could sell it to a competitor for enough to pay off his investors. The lesson he draws echoes closely what Hawken says about the relative importance of money and sentiment in business life:

> People say that the worst thing in starting a company is to be undercapitalized. Well, that's not true. The worst thing is listening to the wrong people and not going with your gut feelings when you make your final decisions – and then losing your enthusiasm. That's the worst thing. I am absolutely certain I would still be in business if I had stuck with my own intuition (Braendel 1994: 22).

For Hawken, then, and for those who seem to think like him, entrepreneurs are not Weber's ascetic Protestants, driven by the desire for material gain. Entrepreneurs are driven, like those Protestants. However, they are beings of sentiment, driven by something different, the felicitous combination of their instincts, the success that comes from following those instincts and the failure that comes from ignoring them. One could, if one wished, incorporate the sentimental entrepreneur into Market terms, one could say that such an entrepreneur is best understood as seeking in his or her economic activity the greatest possible reward that is available in the circumstances. Such an incorporation has a logic to it; but it would blur distinctions that appear to be important to many people in Western societies, and that ought to be important to those who want to understand how economic actors think about their actions. Incorporating Hawken's sentimental entrepreneur into the Benthamite calculus would make it difficult to distinguish that entrepreneur from, for instance, someone who speculates in land or shares solely for monetary profit or from the part-time retail clerk who simply can not find a better job. The entrepreneur, the speculator and the clerk do have things in common, including the fact that all have made choices from the options that they see around them. But to reduce them to this similarity makes it too hard to discern the differences between them, which are probably more important for understanding their economic actions.

Mr Hawken, Meet Mr Smith

Paul Hawken sees what he presents in his book as a model that is valid for small business and, arguably, for all businesses. He does so when he puts a general stress on sentiment as a crucial element of commercial success. This sentimentality is individualistic, in the sense that it attends to the importance of individuals rather than collectivities. Indeed, Hawken tells us, 'I wrote a book about the effect that individuals, as opposed to institutions, have on the future' (Hawken 1987: 11). But while this individualism resonates with powerful elements of American culture and Western culture more generally, it remains ideological. It remains a distortion of an economic world in which collective forces have a powerful, even overwhelming impact.

This ideology of individualism helps illuminate the distinction between what Hawken says about commercial activity and the conventional Market model. That model is built upon the actions of autonomous individuals, the butcher, the brewer, the baker on one hand, hungry people with money on the other. However, it moves beyond them when it recognises the ways that individual Market actors are constrained by what are referred to in the Introduction to this collection as structural forces, forces over which they have little control, forces that are alien and even threatening to the world that Hawken constructs.

An illustration of this point comes from a story presented in the same issue of *Inc.* that contains Gregory Braendel's tale of what happened when he stopped trusting his instincts. The story is of another American mail-order firm, Hanna Andersson, which sells costly cotton children's clothes. The founders of the firm, Tom and Gun Denhart, ran it in a way that expressed their sentiments, sentiments of which Paul Hawken would approve. Gun Denhart said this was not a company intended to pursue high profits. 'It's been a way to grow. A way to create opportunities for people to be fulfilled at work and find some deeper meaning in what they do' (quoted in Murphy 1994: 38). Likewise, the Denharts' first employee, Gail Johnson, said of the early years of the company: 'We'd be packing orders and . . . we'd discuss how we would want to be treated and how we would treat employees as we hired more. We would dream of the kind of environment we wanted to work in. We wanted it to be a human place, a place where people felt comfortable being themselves, could grow, have fun' (quoted in Murphy 1994: 38). The assumption made by the founders of the firm echoes Hawken's attitude: 'We always thought the money would come to us if we did the right thing' (Gene Denhart, quoted in Murphy 1994: 38).

While Hanna Andersson was an expensive company to run, the main problems that appear to have led to its economic difficulties sprang from events outside the firm and beyond its control. One problem was the recession of the early 1990s, which reduced demand for the expensive children's clothes Hanna Andersson sells. The other was the growing competition in their part of the market for children's clothes. In 1984, when the company started to trade, they were just about the only firm selling cotton clothes for children. However, by the early 1990s there were a number of powerful firms competing with Hanna Andersson, many of them much bigger, better known and thoroughly established with the social class at which the company was directing its efforts.

The firm learned its lesson. 'By 1992 the Denharts realized that being in business was not purely a matter of satisfying customers and motivating employees. It was also a game of numbers and a never-ending series of compromises . . .. Winning the numbers game required a new discipline' (Murphy 1994: 40). As a result, 'this ideal employer is, indeed, getting real about business' (Murphy 1994: 42). This has meant that the firm has become involved with many of the things that irritate Hawken: planning, including a three-year strategy; contention over the budget; more aggressive marketing; firing many employees and reducing the benefits of the rest. Gun Denhart summarises the new regime of cost-consciousness: 'I want people here to feel the money, you know' (quoted in Murphy 1994: 43). For the people at Hanna Andersson, money has come to mean something very different than it does for Hawken's entrepreneur.

This case of the failure of sentiment and sociability when they are confronted with the *force majeure* of the Market points up a more profound problem, one that Paul Hawken shares with the durable thread of Western individualism that he embodies. That problem is the conflict between sentimental individualism on the one hand, and on the other the fact that people live only by the cooperation of those around them. As I have described, Hawken assumes that acting upon one's sentiments is a key to economic success, to attracting motivated employees and enthusiastic customers. Likewise, Shaftesbury assumes that the good man will find a good life in a community of like-minded fellows, just as Smith assumes that the person with natural sympathies will find a social life of sympathetic friends. Authentic selves will attract. Hawken illustrates this assumption clearly when he says that the clearest way to express 'the key to all business success' is this: 'While you can "approximate" the customer, you can know only yourself. So stay close to the person you understand and market products for yourself' (Hawken 1987: 178). In other words, market products for yourself and you will have customers; be yourself and you will attract others.

But what if you market for yourself and nobody buys? What if you be yourself and nobody comes? The case of Hanna Andersson indicates that the authentic expression of sentiments that are human and held strongly can produce not the success that, for Hawken, they merit, but the indifference of potential customers. For Shaftesbury's good man, for the person endowed with Adam Smith's natural sympathies, the issue is confronted when such a one meets only with rebuff and isolation. How can we assume that acting on one's sentiments will meet with the approbation of those around one? As indicated by the passage from Habakkuk in the Introduction to this collection, the thinkers of the Scottish Enlightenment resolved this question by an act of faith, assuming that the hand of Providence assured that the moral and desirable results ensued. The entrepreneur that Hawken describes would seem to have no such guarantee.

Conclusion

My purpose in this chapter has been to present one popular alternative to the construction of the self contained in the Market model, the alternative contained in Paul Hawken's *Growing a Business*. I do not present this alternative as representative of any mass movement that has been hidden from the academic eye. Rather, I take it only to indicate one sort of message about economic actors that has been sent to the American public, one sort of statement of what economic life is about.

Hawken's statement is not interesting only because it is an alternative to the Market model. It is interesting also because of the way this message about the new way to run a business in new economic circumstances resonates so clearly with an old set of Western cultural conceptions of the nature of the self and of relationships between selves. In a sense, Hawken is re-inventing the wheel, a device built much earlier by Shaftesbury and, curiously enough, by Adam Smith. This is the sentimental self, Shaftesbury's good man who acts not prudentially but in accord with his inner nature, the sort of person who responds to life in terms of Smith's natural sympathy.

In saying that Hawken is re-inventing the wheel, I do not mean that he is doing nothing noteworthy. Although the notion of the self that he propounds has a long history and wide currency in the West, Hawken invokes it in an interesting way. In particular, he applies to the economic realm a notion of the self that generally had been seen as suited only to the social realm. Hawken's sentimental entrepreneur looks especially suited to what Schneider describes as the American conception of sociable, and especially family, relationships. Hawken, then, appears to be transgressing an important cultural boundary, one that was promulgated by Adam Ferguson and Adam Smith and that is accepted and espoused by the Americans that Schneider describes. This is the boundary between social and economic life, a boundary that is a prime element of the Market model. And the lesson of Hanna Andersson is that we transgress that boundary at our peril. At some point, not too far in the future, the impersonal forces of the Market will cause even the 'ideal' employer to stop play-acting and get 'real' about business.

If you will, Hawken is a social imperialist, for he argues that the sorts of selves and relationships characteristic of the social realm, at least as that realm is imagined culturally, are, if the truth were known, the sorts of selves and relationships that are most suited to the economic realm. In his imperialism, he stands diametrically opposed to those who argue that the sorts of selves and relationships characteristic of the economic realm pervade the social realm, or ought to. The most famous of these economic imperialists is probably Gary Becker, the economist who analyses children as durable consumer goods (Becker 1976: 169) and who won a Nobel prize for his economics. A passage by Mark Lutz (1992: 118) explains Becker's economic imperialism nicely. Lutz points to Becker's perception that all human behaviour can be analysed economically, as in the Preface to his *A Treatise on the Family*: 'The economic approach provides a framework applicable to all human behaviour – to all types of decisions and to persons from all walks of life' (Becker 1981: ix). As Schor notes, 'This approach effectively obliterated the idea of "an economy" . . .. [The economy] is everywhere and everything, because it is just a way of behaving' (Schor 1989: 18).

Equally, however, this economic imperialism occurs outside academic economics. A striking example is the sociological literature on social exchange, which says that people in social relations behave very much like Adam Smith's butcher, brewer and baker. Richard Emerson (1976: 337) says that this literature revolves around concepts like 'resource, reward, reinforcement, cost, utility, opportunity, profit, outcome, transaction, payoff, etc.' (see also Davis 1992: 73–74). Thus, for example, George C. Homans (1958: 603) explains social exchange behaviour by invoking the equation 'Profit = Reward - Cost.' Peter Blau (1964: 91) says we must see this behaviour as 'voluntary actions of individuals that are motivated by the returns they are expected to bring and typically do in fact bring from others'. Even Alvin Gouldner (1960: 164) says that understanding such relationships 'requires investigation of the mutually contingent benefits rendered and of the manner in which the mutual contingency is sustained'.

Growing a Business is not interesting only because of the way it leaps the boundary between social and economic lives and selves. It is interesting also because its thoroughgoing sentimentality encourages the reader to consider a notion that is important in the Market model, the notion of freedom. Proponents of the Market tout it as a guarantor of freedom. For extremists like Hayek and the anarcho-capitalists (see Brown, this volume, Chap. 2), but also for liberals of all sorts, the Market protects us from an intrusive state (see also the discussion of tributary systems in Smart, this volume, Chap. 4). We appear to need this protection because the state is a constraint that is beyond individual control and choice. However, *Growing a Business* raises the point that a notion of freedom needs to be complemented by a notion of the person who can be free. Hawken's sentimental entrepreneur is not free in the absence of external constraint, any more than is Shaftesbury's good man or Smith's person endowed with sympathies. All confront a constraint that is beyond their control and choice, just as do

Weber's ascetic Protestants driven by the need to discover their eternal fate through the methodical pursuit of competitive commercial success. Similarly, as I have shown in this chapter and noted in the Introduction to this collection, the Market itself exercises powerful constraints that are also beyond the power of the affected individuals to influence. In presenting so clearly the issue of the self of economic actors, Hawken encourages us to view the stress on freedom among Market advocates sceptically. Their concern with freedom needs to be interrogated rather than assumed – interrogated in terms of the selves who are to be free or constrained.

Growing a Business is no reasoned statement of a philosophical position. Rather, it is ephemeral, a book for a passing moment intended for a popular readership. Even so, it is a book that is worthy of consideration. In the very extremity of its romantic picture of the sentimental entrepreneur, it does not only provide evidence of popular alternatives to the Market model. In addition, it raises issues that allow us to begin to address the nature, underpinning and limitations of that model.

Note

1. It is worth noting that this conception of natural, spontaneous sentiment appears to be subject to the same criticism that Pierre Bourdieu (1984: 68) makes of the notion of the connoisseur and natural taste. He says:

   > The ideology of natural taste owes its plausibility and its efficacy to the fact that . . . it *naturalizes* real differences, converting differences in the mode of acquisition of culture into differences of nature; it only recognizes as legitimate the relation to culture (or language) which least bears the visible marks of its genesis, which has nothing 'academic', 'scholastic', 'bookish', 'affected' or 'studied' about it, but manifests by its ease and naturalness that true culture is nature – a new mystery of immaculate conception.

References

Barnett, Steve, and Martin Silverman 1979. Separations in Capitalist Societies: Persons, Things, Units and Relations. Pp. 39–81 in S. Barnett and M. Silverman, *Ideology and Everyday Life*. Ann Arbor: University of Michigan Press.

Becker, Gary 1976. *The Economic Approach to Human Behavior*. Chicago: University of Chicago Press.

Becker, Gary 1981. *A Treatise on the Family*. Cambridge, Mass.: Harvard University Press.

Berthoff, Rowland 1980. Independence and Enterprise: Small Business in the American Dream. Pp. 28–48 in Stuart W. Bruchey (ed.), *Small Business in American Life*. New York: Columbia University Press.

Blau, Peter 1964. *Exchange and Social Power*. New York: John Wiley and Sons.

Bourdieu, Pierre 1984. *Distinction: A Social Critique of the Judgement of Taste*. London: Routledge & Kegan Paul.

Braendel, Gregory G. 1994. How I Lost It. *Inc: The Magazine for Growing Companies* (July): 21–22.

Business Week 1992. Downward Mobility. *Business Week* (23 March): 56–63.

Campbell, Colin 1987. *The Romantic Ethic and the Spirit of Modern Consumerism*. Oxford: Basil Blackwell.

Carrier, James G. 1994. *Gifts and Commodities: Exchange and Western Capitalism since 1700*. London: Routledge.

Carrier, James G. 1995. Maussian Occidentalism: Gift and Commodity Systems. Pp. 85–108 in J. G. Carrier (ed.), *Occidentalism: Images of the West*. Oxford: Oxford University Press.

Davis, John 1992. *Exchange*. Buckingham: Open University Press.

Durkheim, Emile 1984. *The Division of Labour in Society*. London: Routledge & Kegan Paul.

Economist 1993. The Death of Corporate Loyalty. *The Economist* (3 April): 63–64.

Emerson, Richard M. 1976. Social Exchange Theory. *Annual Review of Sociology* 2: 335–362.

Fefer, Mark D. 1994. Wall Street Loves Layoffs. *Fortune* (24 January): 12.

Gouldner, Alvin 1960. The Norm of Reciprocity: A Preliminary Statement. *American Sociological Review* 25: 161–178.

Hawken, Paul 1987. *Growing a Business*. New York: Simon and Schuster.

Hirschman, Albert 1977. *The Passions and the Interests*. Princeton: Princeton University Press.

Homans, George C. 1958. Social Behavior as Exchange. *American Journal of Sociology* 63: 597–606.

Lublin, Joann S. 1993. Survivors of Layoffs Battle Angst, Anger, Hurting Productivity. *Wall Street Journal* (6 December): A 1, A 16.

Lutz, Mark 1992. Humanistic Economics: History and Basic Principles. Pp. 90–120 in Paul Ekins and Manfred Max-Neef (eds), *Real-Life Economics: Understanding Wealth Creation*. London: Routledge.

Marx, Karl, and Frederick Engels 1948. *Manifesto of the Communist Party*. New York: International Publishers.

Mauss, Marcel 1985 (1938). A Category of the Human Mind: The Notion of Person; the Notion of Self. Pp. 1–25 in Michael Carrithers, Steven Collins and Steven Lukes (eds), *The Category of the Person*. Cambridge: Cambridge University Press.

Murphy, Anne 1994. Too Good to be True? *Inc: The Magazine for Growing Companies* (July): 34–43.

Myers, Milton L. 1983. *The Soul of Modern Economic Man: Ideas of Self-Interest, Thomas Hobbes to Adam Smith*. Chicago: University of Chicago Press.

Parry, Jonathan 1986. *The Gift*, the Indian Gift and the 'Indian Gift'. *Man* 21: 453–473.

Parry, Jonathan, and Maurice Bloch (eds) 1989. *Money and the Morality of Exchange*. Cambridge: Cambridge University Press.

Parsons, Talcott 1959. The Social Structure of the Family. Pp. 241–274 in Ruth Nanda Anshen (ed.), *The Family*. New York: Harper and Row.

Pocock, John G. A. 1975. *The Machiavellian Moment*. Princeton: Princeton University Press.

Pocock, John G. A. 1979. The Mobility of Property and the Rise of Eighteenth Century Sociology. Pp. 141–166 in Anthony Parel and Thomas Flanagan (eds), *Theories of Property: Aristotle to the Present*. Waterloo, Ont.: Wilfred Laurier University Press.

Schneider, David 1980. *American Kinship: A Cultural Account*. Second edition. Chicago: University of Chicago Press.

Schor, J. 1989. On the Definition of the Boundaries of an Economic System. Mimeo, Harvard University.

Silver, Allan 1990. Friendship in Commercial Society: Eighteenth-

Century Social Theory and Modern Sociology. *American Journal of Sociology* 95: 1474–1504.

Smith, Adam 1976 (1776). *An Inquiry into the Nature and Causes of the Wealth of Nations.* Chicago: University of Chicago Press.

Trilling, Lionel 1972. *Sincerity and Authenticity.* Cambridge, Mass.: Harvard University Press.

Tucker, Robert C. (ed.) 1978. *The Marx–Engels Reader.* Second edition. New York: W. W. Norton.

Turner, Ralph 1976. The Real Self: From Institution to Impulse. *American Journal of Sociology* 81: 989–1016.

Weber, Max 1958. *The Protestant Ethic and the Spirit of Capitalism.* New York: Charles Scribner's Sons.

Weber, Max 1978. *Economy and Society.* Berkeley: University of California Press.

Whyte, William H. 1956. *The Organization Man.* New York: Simon and Schuster.

Wills, Garry 1978. *Inventing America: Jefferson's Declaration of Independence.* Garden City, NY: Doubleday.

Chapter 4

Oriental Despotism and Sugar-Coated Bullets: Representations of the Market in China

Alan Smart

The significance of the expansion of markets within the People's Republic of China, the nation with the largest population and the last important Communist-dominated society, is obvious and has received a great deal of attention.[1] The purpose of this chapter is not to reiterate these issues, but rather to explore the meanings that are ascribed to the creation of these markets. There are important representations that lie behind the ways in which the market reforms are lauded or berated, representations that partake of long-standing ideas about Orient and Occident, civil society and despotism, citizens and subjects, commodities and tribute, commerce and power. Increasingly China, as well as the post-socialist republics of Eastern Europe and the former Soviet Union, is seen as representing continuities with the national past as much as or more than revolutionary change: the lack of separation between economics and politics, and the failure to create an autonomous space for civil society, are seen as sharing features of earlier imperial forms.

Together with ideas about the traditional character of socialisms come ideas of the dramatic implications of commodification. Markets, once released from the social, political and cultural constraints of traditionalism, are seen as having remarkable transformative powers to erode social forms and morality, or to produce efficiency and abundance, depending on one's point of view (see Kahn, this volume, Chap. 1). The socialist state acts as a bulwark against the corrosive effects of commodification and markets, and against the imperialism of the developed capitalist nations. China, however, has opted to use market-based reforms to help stimulate its productive forces and 'catch up' with the developed nations. Given the previous deprecation and fear of markets and the 'possessive individualism' and limits on state power that they bring with them, their instrumental use creates ambivalence and contradictions that have unfolded over the last decade and a half.

As Carrier indicates in his Introduction, participants in markets are commonly seen as 'autonomous, rational calculators of their own best material advantage', and as producing relationships that are impersonal and instrumental, the mirror image of the societal solidarity and collective struggle for a common goal that is the vision of socialist movements. More positively, markets are seen by many not just as economic mechanisms that increase efficiency, but as guarantors of individual liberty, as essential protections from the fiat of oppressive governments, as essential to the 'pursuit of happiness'. While decision-makers and commentators in the West have often had such versions of the Market in mind in their celebrations of China's economic reforms, the Chinese Communist Party (CCP) has seen these precisely as dangers accompanying the desired benefits of increased efficiency and 'socialist modernisation'.

A central question, then, is whether the Market can be implemented as only an 'economic mechanism' – a narrow, if powerful, technical institution or set of practices – or if the many social, cultural and political implications often associated with marketisation are inevitably bound up with this technical effectiveness.

The process of constructing markets in China has diverged dramatically from textbook descriptions. This process has involved personal relations, transactions that can be described as corruption,[2] and very little attention to legal formalities. I do not want this account, however, to be interpreted as saying that these divergences are simply a result of China's peculiarities, and thus can be dismissed as inconsequential for assessments of the Market model. Instead, the conditions in China make dramatically apparent processes and circumstances that are much more general, even if less explicit elsewhere.

The social constitution of markets in China does indeed vary from Western textbook descriptions and from the policy recommendations of the International Monetary Fund and the World Bank. But much of this divergence can be seen as congruent with newly emerging Market models, models associated with ideas of 'the Pacific Century' and the 'Asian economic miracles', and more generally with ideas of 'the social economy'. Before examining ideas about how East Asian capitalism operates and the relevance of these ideas for China, it will be necessary to examine, in the next section, ideas about the operation of Asian non-market, non-capitalist economies. I will suggest that ideas of 'Oriental Despotism', the contrast between tribute and commodity, and the liberating potential of markets, pluralism and individualism form a cultural backdrop to certain interpretations of the economic transformation of socialist and post-socialist societies.

In the third section, I turn to ideas about economic development in East Asia and the intersection between state and market that is generating debate about whether East Asia offers new models for the organisation of competitive capitalist economies, before I move to their specific application in the economic transformation occurring in China. Finally, I will examine in more detail the meaning of 'the market' for policy-makers and ordinary people in China.

Oriental Despotism and Market Liberation

James Carrier adds to Edward Said's (1978) idea of 'Orientalism' the need for attention to 'Occidentalism', 'the essentialist rendering of the West by Westerners' (Carrier 1992 *a*: 199). Carrier recognises that there are varieties of Occidentalism, but focuses upon the variety that is most salient in Melanesia: the representation of Western societies as based upon 'independent individuals who transact freely with one another' (1992 *a*: 200), in contrast with gift societies dominated by kinship relations and gift exchanges that obligate and associate giver and receiver.

Although the dichotomy of commodity and gift is important for many of the societies that anthropology conventionally studies, for the non-Western civilisations (and for the pre-modern West) the dichotomy between commodity and tribute is much more important. In the context of analyses of socialist and post-socialist reforms, this dichotomy has maintained its significance, and can help to explain the positive, emancipatory interpretation of the possessive individualism of the Market model in a way that the contrast with gift societies can not.

The distinction between gifts and commodities in anthropology still draws strongly on the work of Marcel Mauss (1990). This distinction contrasts situations where people and things are bound to each other 'by durable links that provide a personal identity towards one another' (Carrier 1992 *b*: 539), and that are created and maintained through the exchange of gifts. Gift exchanges are socially embedded and partake of a sacred nature, in this view, while commodity relations are impersonal, alienated and profane.[3] Social solidarity is contrasted with individualism, social obligations with instrumental goals. Both commodity and gift exchange share, though, the abstraction of power from exchange relations, at least in the Maussian interpretation. One does not receive a gift or a commodity because one is more powerful than the exchange partner, but because the prestation is socially expected (for the gift) or is seen as being adequately compensated by the counter-prestation (for the commodity).

Power is central to the third form of exchange identified by Karl Polanyi (1957), redistribution. While gift exchange and market exchange are both symmetrical and reciprocal, redistribution is characterised by 'centricity', where some individual or institution collects and redistributes the goods and services (1957: 49). In state-level societies, this pattern is obligatory, is supported by coercion and is referred to as the collection of taxes or tribute. While there is commonly a return to those who are not part of the 'centre', in the form of services such as banquets, ceremonies, roads or defence, those at the centre obtain greater power through these exchanges.

In tributary modes of production, the producer 'is allowed access to the means of production, while tribute is exacted from him by political or military means' (Wolf 1982: 80). In such systems the relations of production are based upon the direct use of political authority or force to extract surplus from the producers, with the result that there is no separation of economics and politics as separate spheres of activity: the integration of the economy is accomplished through a direct and visible use of power. The amount of surplus collected by non-producers is not determined by economic processes of generating profits through the employment for wages of free labourers, but by the balance of power within the society. Often, though not inevitably, direct producers are bound to the land and to their lord, and have few alternatives available to them. From this description, it is easy to see how critics can emphasise the common features of communist nations and pre-capitalist tributary system. For example, Ernest Gellner (1994: 145) asserts: 'A command-administrative system is not an invention of Lenin or Stalin; it is simply the normal condition of humanity. . . .. It is the liberation of economic relationships from social and political ones, not their subjugation to them, which is exceptional and requires elucidation.'

Since Machiavelli, there has been an intellectual tradition in Europe that links these evaluations of tributary states with the distinction between East and West. Asian societies have commonly been represented as the Other of the West, and Oriental Despotism is contrasted to Western democracy, private property in land and civil liberties, and to the feudalism from which these emerged.

The focus was first on the Ottoman Empire, and commentators suggested that the basis of tyranny was 'the absence of private property in land' (Anderson 1974: 399). Later this idea was expanded to all the empires of Asia. Montesquieu contrasted Asian despotism with the principles born of European feudalism, suggesting that 'Asia is that region of the world where despotism is so to speak naturally domiciled' (quoted in Anderson 1974: 400). Hegel wrote that in China the state and its laws belonged to the emperor, and these laws 'ruled the subject individuals as if from the outside, and the subject individuals were like children obeying their parents, without will or insight' (Duara 1993: 788). The view was very generally held that Oriental despots were not hampered by civil society, by 'independent intermediaries between themselves and their subjects' as in the feudal West (Abrahamian 1974: 3).

Perry Anderson suggests that 'from Hegel onwards most of the same basic conceptions of Asian society were retained, whose intellectual function was always to draw a radical contrast between European history . . . and the destiny of other continents' (Anderson 1974: 401). Although not all features appeared in the work of all authors, common elements in European accounts of Asian political systems were: state property in land, lack of judicial restraints, the absence of hereditary nobility, public hydraulic works and historical immutability (Anderson 1974: 472). The Orient was seen as being both despotic and stagnant, in contrast with the divided powers leading to democracy and the historical development of the West. Both the stagnation and the despotism were explained by 'a series of missing institutions or beliefs' which 'prevented or misdirected the process of modernisation' (Turner 1981: 264).

In Karl Marx's work, Asiatic society was presented as 'arbitrary, despotic and stagnant', ideas which justified colonisation, since 'external intervention is a necessary, however unfortunate, condition for external change' (Bottomore 1983: 33). The Asiatic mode of production was one in which communities were largely self-sufficient, but their surplus product was appropriated in the form of taxation by the state. Engels wrote that, associated with the Asiatic mode of production, is 'the crudest form of the State, Oriental despotism' (quoted in Antoniadis-Bibicon 1977: 364). In his view, Asiatic societies were 'typified by an overdeveloped state apparatus and an underdeveloped "civil society", whereas in Europe the obverse obtained. In Asiatic society, those social arrangements which were closely associated with the rise of a bourgeois class – free markets, private property, guild structure and bourgeois law – were absent, because the centralized state dominated civil society' (Bottomore 1983: 33–34). Marx concluded that 'there was no potential for autonomous development within societies based on the Asiatic mode of production', and only European colonialism could serve 'to end the age-old stagnation of Asiatic society' (Melotti 1977: 114–115).

In China studies, ideas of the unchanging character of society took the form of 'the dynastic cycle', in which the basic forms of society were reproduced despite invasion, civil war and dynastic succession. Although both feudalism and the Asiatic mode of production can be seen as variants of Wolf's concept of tributary modes of production, they represent two poles of a spectrum defined by the degree of concentration of power (Wolf 1982: 80).[4] In contrast to European feudalism, with its parcellated sovereignty of lords and overlords,

> [t]he Chinese empire was a centralized power unrestricted by privilege, religious power, or rivals of a equal stature, and served by a scholar bureaucracy recruited by merit rather than by birth. The longevity, administrative articulation, and efficiency of the empire were wonders of the premodern world . . . . The state was not externally limited, nor was there an incipient, autonomous civil society (Womack 1991: 57).

While he applied the concept of Oriental Despotism to Chinese history, Karl Wittfogel (1957) also argued for its relevance to an understanding of Stalinist Russia, since 'the idea of a ruling class controlling the means of administration without ownership of private property indicated a continuity of political power from Tsarist to Stalinist Russia' (Bottomore 1983: 35). The persistence of elements of the Asiatic mode of production has also been used to explain why 'real socialism' has not been achieved in Russia or China (Bailey 1981; Melotti 1977).

With the Communist revolutions in Russia and China, the dichotomy of Oriental Despotism and Western liberty was replaced with the contrast between totalitarianism and central planning on the one hand, and on the other democracy and free markets. Both Oriental Despotism and socialism shared the characteristics of arbitrary state power and the absence of private property, especially in land and the other factors of production. The positive evaluation of the individual in the Market model as 'autonomous, rational and self-reliant' can be much more easily understood in the contrast with despotic societies than in comparisons with stateless societies. It is not so much the fact that people are free of social ties and moral obligations that is seen as good; after all 'family values' and 'community' are still important rhetorical concepts in the West. Rather, it is that such ties and obligations are taken on voluntarily rather than imposed by an illegitimate state.

Within Marxist thought, the idea of the Asiatic mode of production has also been used to criticise the nature of socialist systems. Umberto Melotti argues that the Chinese Communist Revolution

> in many respects fits the ancient pattern of periodic renewal of the Asiatic system . . . . The strong central power . . . has cleaned up the mess left by the half-century of semi-capitalistic anarchy spawned by imperialism . . . . Simultaneously, at the bottom of the pyramid, it has sponsored the formation of agricultural communes – the old village communities brought up to date . . . . [T]here still does not seem much possibility that China will finally be able to break out of the 'Asiatic' confines of the system and achieve that modern type of socialism, based on the recognition of the free development of each as the premise for the free development of all (Melotti 1977: 112–113).

John Rapp (1987) relates how the reform coalition around Deng Xiaoping protected themselves from attacks that they were 'taking the capitalist road' by using the concept of the Asiatic mode of production to criticise the Cultural Revolution as a 'feudal-fascist' episode. In 1980, Deng criticised officials for 'assuming the airs of a mandarin' and for 'being arbitrary and despotic' and said: 'From old China we inherited a strong tradition of feudal autocracy and a weak tradition of democratic legality' (quoted in Rapp 1987: 711). Joseph Fewsmith (1991: 41) also notes that

> although the CCP has continually criticized both 'feudalism' and 'capitalism', the emphasis in practice has been on expunging every manifestation of capitalism, thus leaving feudal influences to grow and develop. Thus, such intellectuals find the negative influences of feudalism strongly reflected in the practices of the CCP: over-concentration of power, rule by man rather than rule by law, one-man say, and the politicization of intellectual life.

The concept of the Asiatic mode of production was particularly useful for this critique, since it emphasised the way in which the absence of private property allowed despotic domination of society, and paved the way for reforms that emphasised material incentives and property rights. However, conservatives within the Communist Party fear a loss of social control resulting from reform policies, and intellectuals calling for political reform could find themselves cast as scapegoats whenever the policies of the reform coalition seem to 'lead to loss of state autonomy and social control' (Rapp 1987: 712). The political implications of the Asiatic mode analysis, of the representation of the State as despotic and impeding change, have led to its abandonment by reformers in favour of more technical justifications, particularly the dissociation between the market mechanism and capitalism, as will be shown below.

Xiaomei Chen (1992) has examined how positive evaluations of the West can be utilised as a critical counter-discourse promoting changes within China, as in the controversial 'River Elegy' television series broadcast in 1988. This series portrayed 'a dying and declining Orient' and contrasted it with an 'Occidental Other' which represented 'youthfulness, adventure, energy, power, technology, and modernity' (Chen 1992: 695). Writers holding this point of view 'see the "deep structure" of China's traditional culture as having formed an organic whole that is fundamentally antagonistic to the requisites of the modern world', and as being reproduced in the Communist regime, despite many surface changes (Fewsmith 1991: 42).

In the West, too, the view of the socialist nations as bound up with historical legacies of autocracy and pre-modern empires has been increasingly common,[5] as has been the view that the development of markets and secure property rights is the surest way of increasing political freedoms within these nations. Such conclusions, however, must be considered within the context of arguments that the 'East Asian economic miracles'[6] have been based upon national capitalisms that have utilised very different versions of markets and organisation in order to achieve rapid economic growth. From such a position, we must seriously entertain the possibility that the Market model is only a parochial Western version of the utilisation of market integration, and that other alternative market models may exist and may be more effective in certain circumstances. Should this be the case, the divergences from market perfection in China's reforms may not be economic weaknesses and dangers, may not be mere evidence of Oriental Despotism, but might actually be the source of strengths.

East Asian Development and Alternative Models

Much of the debate about economic development can be traced back to modernisation theories, and in the contours of the modern–traditional dichotomy we can see elements of the framework of Oriental Despotism. In the standard modernisation perspective, the amalgam of institutions characteristic of Euro-American societies always encourages progress towards economic prosperity, democracy and civil peace, and other forms of political, economic and societal organisation hinder development. Convergence with the patterns found in the West is conducive to modernisation, and inevitable should development be achieved, even if cultural lag could be identified in some areas.

In the Introduction, Carrier indicated that one of the objectives of this collection was to treat the Market model as a cultural artefact. One of the important changes of the late twentieth century is the rise of challenges to the conventional Western cultural representation of the Market, so that new varieties of market models are emerging, notably in Pacific Asia. These new models are distinct from counter-ideologies such as those of socialism, which reject the validity of the Market because of its long-term inadequacies or negative social and cultural outcomes. These new conceptions of markets accept the desirability of rapid economic growth, the need to limit government intervention in economic activity and the rational model of the individual. However, they challenge the idea that economic efficiency is based upon individuals seeking their self-interest.

There are two distinct alternative models. The first, associated particularly with Japan and South Korea but also apparent in the new managerial corporatism (Oi 1994) found in the collective sector in China, emphasises the need for individuals to identify their interests with those of a group, the avoidance of internal divisions and the acceptance of responsibility for subordinates by leaders (Tu, Hejtmanek and Wachman 1992). The second, associated particularly with Hong Kong, Taiwan and the overseas Chinese in Southeast Asia, emphasises network relationships between business associates, based upon trust and obligations, and has been referred to as *guanxi* capitalism. This model puts little emphasis upon collective solidarity beyond the family unit, but stresses widespread networks of alliances, cooperation and subcontracting, which integrate a wide variety of small, medium and large firms. Cooperation is generated and supported more by reciprocity than by careful delineation of obligations and rights through legal negotiations.

It has been argued that Confucian culture is particularly appropriate to modernisation without Western decadence. This argument is

> based on two main assertions. The one draws a grim picture of all the moral and social evils brought by industry, trade and technology to western societies and concludes that the modern world can only look to Chinese culture, mainly neoconfucianism, to find harmony and peace of mind. The other claims that, in East Asia, the Confucian tradition allows the four little dragons to 'avoid or reduce' the violent conflicts which the industrializing process has provoked in the West (*China News Analysis* 1994: 7).

Such arguments are particularly ironic, as Confucianism was widely seen as an obstacle to development in earlier modernisation theories. Now it is a 'cultural facilitator of growth' (Whyte 1994: 39). The 'new Confucians' argue that 'it is necessary to find the seeds of modernisation within Chinese tradition itself' and that 'unless China finds the sources of modernization within its own tradition, it will become detached from its "roots" and continue to face a "crisis of identity" ' (Fewsmith 1991: 41–42). Such Confucian capitalism 'can avoid the moral pitfalls of Western capitalist development' (Fewsmith 1991: 42; see also Huang and Wu 1994), and is credited with the unusual combination of 'rapid economic growth and high stability, extraordinary individual effort and persistent group effort', along with 'superior educational performance, low crime rates, high life expectancies, and an unusual degree of family stability' (Rozman 1991: 5).

The 'Confucian revival' or 'post-Confucianism' starts from 'the new-found power of Chinese societies within global capitalism' (Dirlik 1994: 341). These ideas endeavour to develop linkages between the values of capitalism and Confucianism, and as a result 'Confucianism has been rendered into a prime mover of capitalist development and has also found quite a sympathetic ear among First World ideologues who now look to a Confucian ethic to relieve the crisis of capitalism' (Dirlik 1994: 341). In this revaluation, the argument is made that the 'communitarian values of Confucianism may be more suitable to a contemporary managerial capitalism' than is the individualistic ethic of a prior entrepreneurial capitalism (Dirlik 1994: 354).

Raymond Lee (1994: 3) notes that while belief in modernity and progress is undergoing a serious crisis in the West, it appears to be 'enthusiastically promoted and celebrated' in the rapidly-developing Asian societies. Asian successes have led commentators to abandon defensive nationalisms and instead, 'the critique of Occidentalism under the sign of Asian/Third World modernization is unique because it is an attempt to appropriate Western technology and the model of rationality epitomizing modern Western civilization, while resisting in various ways the transformation of traditional values through technological enculturation' (Lee 1994: 4). In this construction, East Asian modernity is characterised by a 'bricolage of values bonded by an authoritarian ethos' (Lee 1994: 40). In this distinct form, the power of capitalism and markets is acknowledged. However, market actors are not self-interested individuals, but members of families, of localities and sometimes of religions (as in Malaysia) who incorporate a sense of social obligation into their economic activity. Following from this, state interventions are not inconsistent with capitalist development, since markets and individuals are not counterposed to governments and collectivities.

These Asian models share a considerable degree of overlap with academic ideas of social economics (Granovetter 1990; Mingione 1994) and flexible specialisation. Such models do not radically question the 'Market idea that market logic ought to predominate' and that this is revealed in 'the bottom line' (Carrier, this volume, Introduction). They simply argue that the reality of the world is that economic efficiency and competitive advantage in the global economy are not best achieved with self-interested individuals looking to the main chance, and supervisors and managers attempting to control and coordinate their activities. Rather, they are achieved through organisations, relationships and processes that recognise the compatibility between personal relationships built around trust and dynamic, effective enterprises and economies. Andrew Sayer and Richard Walker (1992: 148), for example, argue that developments in organisational technology, or the social relations of economic integration, have contributed significantly to the development of the forces of production, and that 'integration may be achieved with the help of such devices as authority, coercion, persuasion, moral stricture, reciprocity, planning, religious conviction, common language, national solidarity, and representative democracy' (Sayer and Walker 1992: 117).

Why are these ideas of social economies, particularly in the East Asian context, important? There have been proponents of such ideas since the Industrial Revolution, and they are quite reminiscent of ideas of 'moral economy' (Thompson 1966). However, in the West these ideas have commonly been presented as backward-looking efforts to hobble the market's dynamics that would reduce economic efficiency, or as utopian and unrealistic, given people's tendency to free-ride and rent-seek. However, proponents say that Asian Market models are not only feasible but have been part of the strategies that have allowed East Asia to catch up with the West in terms of economic growth and prosperity. It is now the West, with its bureaucratic corporations, poor communication, labour antagonism, lack of worker commitment, self-seeking managers and shareholders, and dysfunctional families producing poor educational levels and high crime rates, that is losing its competitive advantage. The market models deriving from Asia are not ignored by decision-makers in government and business, but instead are seen as sources of new economic and organisational strategies.

These models first gained public attention when the rapid development of Japan showed little evidence of convergence with the Western models (Dore 1973). The distinctiveness of post-war Japanese industrial organisation is almost universally accepted, but explaining these differences has been problematic (Peck and Miyamachi 1994). Western observers have often treated Japanese capitalism as

> a special case, distorted by the peculiarities of Japanese culture. But this is thoroughly ethnocentric, for if Japanese capital is shaped by its cultural contexts, then so too is American, British, etc. Once we recognize this, we can ask whether certain characteristics we had previously assumed to be normal, or intrinsic to capital as such, are really effects of parochial, national, or regional contexts (Sayer and Walker 1992: 164).

The rapid rise of the Asian Newly Industrialising Countries (NICs) soon made it clear that Japan was not an isolated, aberrant case, and these countries have become a critical battleground for the rival proponents of neo-liberalism and the developmental state (Killick 1994). It is clear that the neo-liberal argument that the success of the East Asian NICs springs from the free operation of market processes is incorrect. State interventions have been very much involved in their successes.[7] However, not just any state intervention will do, as the fate of import-substitution strategies indicates. The World Bank's position is that the secret of success lay in intervening in such a way that the net result was still 'to get the fundamentals right', and that when the policies strayed from the straight and narrow, the objectives were not met (World Bank 1993).

In contrast to the neo-liberals are the advocates of developmental states, which attempt 'systematically to restructure their economies by directly influencing investment decisions in targeted industries' (Deyo 1992: 298), although they may not directly own these industries. These advocates use the successes of the Asian NICs to support their criticisms of neo-liberal faith in market governance. For example, Alice Amsden (1990: 6–7) argues: 'In all late-industrializing countries – Japan, Korea, and Taiwan included – not only have governments failed to get relative prices right, they have deliberately got them "wrong", in order to stimulate investment and trade.' Proponents of the developmental state argue that late-developing economies can only succeed with the support of effective state intervention, and that the introduction of Free Market reforms on their own will only lead to chaos.

The conflict between the two positions can be resolved in part through attention to shifts in the world economy. A wide variety of scholars argue that 'there has been a paradigm shift from a Fordist growth model based on mass production, scale economies, and mass consumption to one oriented to flexible production, innovation, scope economies, innovation rents, and more rapidly changing and differentiated patterns of consumption' (Jessop 1993: 14–15). Within this context, the flexible firm 'survives through perpetual adaptability rather than perpetual cost reduction' (Lovering 1990: 161). The result is a tendency towards disintegration into divisions of labour which are widely distributed through space. This occurs because under a 'regime of flexible accumulation, internal economies necessarily decline and external economies proliferate' (1990: 161). That is, 'the costs of using the market decline relative to those of intrafirm transactions' (1990: 161).

In the case of East Asia, however, it has been argued that the division between market and hierarchical (or within-enterprise) organisation ignores a third set of alternatives, what has been called 'network governance' (Yeung 1995) or *guanxi* capitalism in the case of overseas Chinese firms. Enterprise groups, consisting of a mixture of vertical links between larger firms and smaller, subcontracting firms, and horizontal links between firms engaging in 'relational contracting between equals', involve ongoing interactions without formal relationships of control, and are very common in all East Asian economies (and rapidly developing in the West through 'strategic alliances') (Hamilton and Biggart 1992). Such networks are constituted and maintained through 'confidence, solidarity, trust mechanisms and trustworthy behaviour among actors' (Yeung 1995: 5).[8]

Representations of East Asian economies as distinct from those found in the West suggest that the division between civil society (along with its attendant civil liberties and human rights) and the state is not necessarily applicable (or efficient), dependent as it is upon Western preoccupations with individualism. Chun-chieh Huang and Kuang-ming Wu (1994) argue that Western political models are built upon principles inappropriate for Confucian societies, and that applying these models could lead to ecological and social disaster.

An Occidentalism that equates the West with individualism, albeit an individualism no longer celebrated but rather blamed for the causes of social decline, is becoming increasingly common. An excellent illustration can be found in comments from the 'top civil servant in the Singaporean foreign ministry'. Mr Mahbubani believes that 'American society is breaking down and falling apart' while Western Europe has 'socio-economic policies [which are] fundamentally untenable'. The problem in the West, as paraphrased by *The Economist*, derives from 'an excess of democracy and an overdose of freedom. An obsession with individual fulfilment has led to the breakdown of the family. An over-vigorous press has destroyed respect for institutions. Democratic politics are unable to produce the necessary responses' (*Economist* 1995 *a*: 34–35). Such comments could be dismissed as romantic nostalgia for the past, except for the economic successes of the Asian NICs. The argument is being made that avoiding the Market model can lead to greater economic efficiency. Bob Jessop (1993: 9) points out that the East Asian societies are now often taken as models for resolving the crisis of what he calls the 'Keynesian welfare state' in the West.

It seems, then, that the East Asian societies have a number of characteristics that make it difficult to categorise them in terms of the dichotomy contained in the Market model, that between free markets and state intervention. This difficulty is especially pronounced in the PRC, as I argue later in this chapter.

Transformation policies proposed for the post-socialist societies of Eastern Europe were based on this dichotomy, as manifest in the assumption that 'the reduction of state influence over the economy would automatically and quickly stimulate private sector recovery' as long as an appropriate 'regulatory and incentive framework' to support a market economy was put in place (Angresano 1994: 82). The need for 'Big Bangs' and 'shock therapy' is justified by fears of inefficiencies resulting from undesirable responses by firms and officials to market signals in the absence of private property rights. Anders Aslund (quoted in Nolan 1994: 3) makes this idea very clear: 'Common sense suggests that if you are sliding into a chasm, you should jump quickly to the other side . . . and not tread cautiously. There is no theory supporting a gradual switch of system.' Similarly, Jan Prybyla stated:

The sad chronicle of China's post-Mao attempt to introduce a modern economic system contains a useful lesson which others, notably the East Europeans, are taking to heart. The lesson is that to address the economic problem in a modern way in the context of a low calibre, inefficient, slothful, wasteful, cronified socialist system, one must go all the way to the market system, do it quickly, and not stop anywhere on the way (quoted in Nolan 1994: 5–6).

Here is the neo-classical argument that political distortions create market inefficiencies, and that the most radical reforms are those that are most likely to succeed. From this perspective, anything short of complete economic reform produces obstacles that distort efficient economic behaviour. These lead to rent-seeking, corruption and the preservation of 'soft-budget constraints' for state-sector enterprises, which impede the process of generating more efficient production and distribution systems.[9] Any economic successes in such countries are ascribed to the market-based reforms, and any weaknesses and problems are attributed to the incompleteness of these reforms.

On the other hand, some have argued that as economic governance by the state was demolished in Eastern Europe, 'market governance has not automatically sprung up to take its place . . .. The outcome has been, not a shift from state to market regulation, but an overwhelming deficit of regulation' (Lash and Urry 1994: 18). One point made by those who put forward this argument is that the efficient operation of markets is not based solely upon the absence of state intervention, but requires the appropriate social and political infrastructure.

Neo-classical analyses have been based upon a whole range of clearly unrealistic assumptions, including the assumption that market exchanges are enforceable without cost to the participants. There is an irony at the centre of the neo-classical model, which is that it assumes 'a world where a handshake is a handshake, in which individuals *irrationally* did not take advantage of each other' (Stiglitz 1993: 110). In other words, the model assumes that people characteristically *under-invest* in opportunism at the expense of their counterparts. Employees work hard when no one will notice and omit stealing when they could get away with it, business associates stick to their deals even when they might gain by breaking their word and so on. In general, 'the enforcement costs of a society without trust would be monumental' (Bowles and

Gintis 1993: 95). Consequently, a world populated by amoral economic agents would not be a more efficient one, because high levels of resources would have to be devoted to monitoring agreements and potentially desirable exchanges would not be undertaken. The 'under-socialised' firm in which everyone is 'out for number one' is likely to be as ineffective in the real world as is the 'over-socialised' firm where obligations to kin and other personal responsibilities outweigh competitive demands (Granovetter 1990).

These considerations suggest that the practical route to efficient economic relations and institutions will vary according to local conditions: social relations and cultural understandings and values are part of the raw material that can be drawn on to construct efficient firms. In the specific case of China, 'local conditions' include the fact that the concrete relations of production and distribution currently lie somewhere between state and market – at least, people can depend upon neither to provide a reliable and supportive framework within which to get on with business. Both have a pervasive influence on economic actors, but the construction of boundaries between state and market, and the subordination of certain types of activity to predominantly one or the other institution, is much less routinised and predictable than in the developed capitalist societies. Instead, actors selectively utilise and develop each, usually through personal claims (Smart 1993 *a*). The outcome varies dramatically, from unproductive rent-seeking to collusive manoeuvring to avoid the 'structural impediments' imposed by the central state. From a neo-classical point of view, all these processes are 'directly unproductive activity' that reduces the efficiency of an economy, and so should be minimised. The unproductive nature of 'graft and corruption' is taken for granted in such analyses, and the possibility that they may be part of the social and cultural infrastructure that underpins and makes possible market exchanges is never considered (Smart 1993 *a*; Smart and Smart 1991).

My argument, however, is that in certain concrete situations non-market patterns may be more efficient. Certain forms of rent-seeking may not be as unproductive as is suggested, if they help to reduce transaction costs. In particular, where the societal and legal infrastructures for market capitalism are incompletely developed, behaviours directed towards creating and capturing rents may make particularly important contributions to economic efficiency. The brokerage activities involved in rent-seeking may serve to constitute markets where none officially exist or where their efficacy is seriously compromised; and this seems to be the case in China. However, I am not arguing that the contribution to economic efficacy of personalised social relations will disappear once the institutions of the market are perfected. If Japan and the Asian NICs have been capable of drawing upon non-market social relations to create innovative and efficient economic patterns, there seems no reason why the same should not be the case in China. The travails of the former Soviet Union and Eastern Europe certainly do not generate much confidence in the competitive advantages generated by what Jeffrey Henderson and Richard Appelbaum (1992: 19) call 'market ideological political economies', where belief in the 'wisdom and benevolence of an invisible hand in a supposedly unfettered market' exists without 'the requisite conditions'.

The Market Reforms in China

There is extensive literature comparing plan and market and assessing the feasibility of market socialism, and I can not engage with it here. Instead, I want to use some of this literature as data for the consideration of the way in which the Market is represented by participants and observers of China's reforms. Then, I will consider the processes by which markets are constructed and operated on the ground in China.

One of the main issues I want to consider involves a distinction made by Carrier in the Introduction to this collection, the distinction between 'markets' and 'the Market model'. A basic feature of many market socialist strategies is the attempt to utilise markets as an economic mechanism that can produce some increases in efficiency, but without introducing (or keeping in close check) the broader implications of the Market model: capitalism and Western individualism and hedonism. The separability of markets as tools and the Market as bearer of societal transformation is central to these ideas; but the effort to maintain this separation has been subject to criticism and to a perception that partial market-based reforms, attempts to construct a 'half-way house' between market and plan, possess a dynamic of their own that invariably subverts other economic forms.

The liberation of China by the CCP in 1949 created a very poor socialist nation, one whose industry was in ruins and that was still fundamentally an agrarian economy.[10] Such a situation offered slim prospects for a rapid movement to a communist economy based on an end to scarcity. This led to a basic split within the Chinese leadership: should the medium-term goal of the CCP be to complete the transition to industrial capitalism that the former weak regimes had failed to accomplish, thereby laying the necessary productive foundation for a later transition to socialism? Or could the CCP mobilise the population to leapfrog capitalism and move rapidly into socialism? The concessions made initially to the 'national bourgeoisie' and the distribution of land to poor peasants who produced for their own subsistence and the markets were indications of the former strategy. However, the latter strategy, led by Mao Zedong, soon came to the fore in the expropriation of property from the national bourgeoisie, in the promotion of agricultural collectives and particularly in the Great Leap Forward launched in 1957. The Great Leap Forward incorporated all agriculture into large communes, with egalitarian distribution, and even attempted to eliminate domestic consumption through the creation of communal kitchens. Mao then succeeded in presenting those who argued for the necessity of markets and material incentives in developing the economy as 'taking the capitalist road'.

From this position, criticisms of the market 'centred on their promotion of attitudes of selfishness and profit-seeking, and their engendering of material inequalities. The market was considered to be the embodiment of capitalism and the antithesis of socialism' (Stockman 1992: 267). Norman Stockman (1992: 269) traces this attitude back to imperial China and the point of view of Confucian-trained scholar-officials, to whom 'marketing could easily offend against two of the highest social values: order and morality' (compare this with Kahn, this volume, Chap. 1). In other words: 'It is clear that traditional cultural orientations to marketing, especially on the part of the apparatus of authority, make available to modern Chinese communist leaders a rhetoric which justifies severe control and restriction of marketing activity' (Stockman 1992: 270).

The Great Leap Forward resulted in catastrophic famines with losses of tens of millions of lives. After this experience, the Maoist line was temporarily discredited and rural markets were reintroduced, after serious debate. In the view of radicals, rural markets are tied to profit-seeking and when left to their own course 'will inevitably spawn "spontaneous capitalism" ' (Solinger 1984: 267). The rightist perspective was that rural markets could be 'a component part of the socialist market under state direction', while the centrist position was that they were 'basically (but not fully) socialist', because the socialist transformation had eliminated capitalism from the market (1984: 267). The beginning of the Great Proletarian Cultural Revolution resulted in new attacks upon 'capitalist roaders' and the restriction of rural markets, private enterprise and material incentives for workers, until the 1978 economic reforms, since which time the scope of markets has progressively expanded.

From the perspective of this collection, the debates surrounding these changes addressed the question of whether markets inevitably lead to the Market. Are markets simply an economic mechanism that could have certain limited uses in the coordination of a socialist society in the early stages of development, or do they possess a dynamic that would tend to reproduce capitalism? Put in other words, these debates have come to centre upon the character of China's 'national economic identity' (Crane 1994). Do the changes represent 'socialism with Chinese characteristics', 'socialist modernisation', 'capitalist restoration' or gradual movement on the path to a market economy?

The events at Tiananmen Square in 1989 resulted in the slowing down of reform measures, but Deng's visit to South China and the Special Economic Zones in 1992 reignited China's economic transformation. Deng argued that

> a planned economy was not socialism – there was planning under capitalism too. A market economy was not capitalism – there was market regulation under socialism too. Planning and market regulation . . . were both means of controlling economic activity. Whether the emphasis was on planning or on market regulation was not the essential distinction between socialism and capitalism (quoted in Fukasaku and Wall 1994: 18).

The subsequent policy line was presented by General Secretary Jiang Zemin to the 14th National Congress of the CCP. He reported that

> the objective of the reform of the economic structure will be to establish a *socialist market economy* that will further liberate and expand the

productive forces. By establishing such an economic structure we mean to let market forces, under the macroeconomic control of the state, serve as the basic means of regulating the allocation of resources . . . . We should make use of pricing and competition to distribute resources to those enterprises that yield good economic returns (quoted in Fukasaku and Wall 1994: 18).

In this authoritative pronouncement, planning and markets are 'merely "economic measures" employed by socialist and capitalist countries alike, not truly distinguishing features of a national economy' (Crane 1994: 86). The economic meaning of socialism becomes the development of productive forces and the achievement of an ultimate common prosperity (1994: 86). The nature of the relations of production which permit such development are less consequential during the period of building socialism, as long as the Communist Party maintains control over the political sphere. In this process, markets can be allowed to expand whenever they prove to be more effective as an integrative economic mechanism.

The market reforms have been most extensive in the rural economy and the collective sector (locally controlled and with redistribution only to workers and the local community), rather than in the large cities and the state sector (publicly owned by provincial or national governments). While income redistributed from rural collectives had accounted for 66.3 per cent of rural household income in 1978, it had dropped to 8.4 per cent by 1985 (Nee and Su 1990: 4). However, the changes are not as dramatic as these figures suggest. For instance, Jean Oi (1994: 76) argues: 'Markets and hierarchies are not mutually exclusive in China's reform context. Instead of displacing the plan, in practice, even after ten years markets still must operate alongside centralized distribution and rationing for key inputs and commodities. What has emerged is a variety of alternatives to both plan and market.'

The adoption of market-based reforms continues to generate serious debate within China. While the leadership desires socialist modernisation in the form of increased economic efficiency, the ability to generate foreign currency through exports and the adoption of more sophisticated technology, there has been consistent concern with the social and cultural implications of the market-based reforms and the opening to the capitalist world economy. These 'side-effects' have been variously termed 'bourgeois liberalisation', 'sugar-coated bullets' and 'unhealthy tendencies' (Myers 1989). The trend within the leadership,

however, has been away from broad conceptualisations of the
Market and towards limited technical representations of the
market. Since the market is seen as something that can technically
be incorporated within a socialist political economy, and can be
compatible with planning, newer conceptions of the market
necessarily play down the idea that it is 'antithetical to socialism'
(Hsu 1985: 443–444).

On the other hand, there are extremely positive evaluations of
markets on the part of reformers, assumptions that the integration
of market mechanisms into China's economy will eradicate the
inefficiencies, loss of motivation and petty despotisms of the
existing system. These more positive evaluations bear on the
question of China's national economic identity, for they seem to
be related to the re-emergence of an alternative 'southern'
nationalist imagery. Edward Friedman describes how the dominant
nationalist narrative in China has been a Maoist anti-imperialist
one in which the CCP saved the nation by 'providing the correct
leadership that would mobilize patriotic Chinese, push imperialists out of China' and thereby permitted 'an independent China
to prosper with dignity'. This narrative treated the capitalism that
China had experienced as 'pure imperialism, a total evil made
up singularly of "aggression, plunder, national humiliation" '
(Friedman 1994: 67). In this northern 'anti-imperialist mythos,
China's choice was dictatorship or disintegration because only a
despotic centre could make China strong so foreign forces could
not invade and plunder the nation' (1994: 83). By the 1990s, much
of this narrative had been discredited, and one result was a new,
southern-oriented imagery, in which national success was

> identified with the market-oriented activities of southerners who
> joined with Chinese capital from diaspora Hong Kong, Macao, or
> Southeast Asia to produce world-competitive products that earned
> foreign exchange that could be invested in building a prosperous
> China. In the new narrative, northern peasants – a people whose
> culture fostered frugality and bravery, and permitted sacrifice and
> martyrdom for the national cause of independence from imperialist
> exploitation – were recategorized as backward, ignorant, super-
> stitious, insular, and static (Friedman 1994: 79).

On either side, the market is ascribed dramatic, almost magical
powers; but the sides differ upon whether these powers lead to
socialist modernisation and a quick path to prosperity and national

power or to the erosion of all that the CCP has struggled for. Michel Chossudovsky (1986: 131), for example, suggests that the restoration of the market mechanism in China is producing 'economic and social polarisation, industrial concentration and a tendency towards the technological subordination of Chinese industry to foreign capital'.

A debate has recently emerged among ethicists at Chinese universities. This debate accepts that moral standards have diminished, particularly with regard to corruption. The main cause of corruption is variously presented as 'the market economy, bourgeois liberalism or "extreme leftism" ' (*China News Analysis* 1994: 1). Some argue that the market economy can only develop at the expense of morality, whereas others argue that the

> commodity economy is not the corruption of morality, it rather provides the soil in which a new morality will grow. Today's moral decadence represents only the 'violent clash' between old and new at this time of transition when there is no ethical consensus and individuals vacillate between 'revived remnants of feudalism' and the 'extreme individualism of capitalism' (*China News Analysis* 1994: 5).

There are also serious concerns about the extent to which the reforms might loosen the Party's control on the population. Social control in contemporary China is bound up with processes of redistribution, particularly in the cities. When a significant private sector is created, a wide variety of mechanisms of control are lost. One question that is widely considered is whether a 'civil society' is being produced in China as a result (White 1993). Some argue that market reform 'would reduce the arena of party control and undermine the vested interests of cadres. Office-holding and patronage power would not be the only game in town. Impersonal market mechanisms would displace distribution of economic and social goods through personal connections' (Meaney 1989: 203). Such an outcome is not the only possibility, however. While it is true that market reform creates new ways to make money, access to these opportunities tends to be greater for party cadres. This is particularly the case where there is a hybrid economy in which 'those with official connections can benefit from disparities in prices, inside information, and access to goods' (Meaney 1989: 204). It is not clear, then, that market reforms will necessarily reduce the amount of control of the party-state. Other outcomes are also possible.

The result of the reforms has commonly been presented recently as neither a continuation of centralised hierarchical control nor a system of market-based integration, but one of local corporatism, where the ability of the central authorities to monitor and control local activities is limited, but 'private' entrepreneurial activity is closely linked with local government (Pearson 1994; Wank 1995). This is a characteristic, but far from universal, form taken by the township and village enterprises. These township and village enterprises have increased their share of industrial output from 10 to 40 per cent in fifteen years, employing 120 million workers (*Economist* 1995 *b*: S19).

The township and village enterprises, and the foreign-invested enterprises, are outside the centrally-planned sector; but the markets that they are involved with are far from pure. Instead, there are numerous narratives of the 'distortions' and 'impurities' of the markets that have emerged, narratives that focus particularly upon continuing regulatory obstacles and ubiquitous 'corruption' and 'rent-seeking'. In the next section, I turn to these narratives of markets in practice.

Impure Markets: Grassroots Economic Action

A persistent theme in discussions of China's reforms focuses on the 'impurity' of the actual markets that are operating there. These impurities take the form of government regulation and interference, and of corruption and rent-seeking. Such impurities share a great deal of similarity with the analyses offered by theorists of social economies. While, from a purist point of view, distortions diminish the efficacy of markets (for good or for bad), they may also provide a social and cultural infrastructure that actually facilitates economic effectiveness. Moreover, if markets are effective, this may result from the distortions as much as from the market mechanism itself. Oliver Williamson (1975) showed that opportunism between parties creates transaction costs that may result in a preference for hierarchy (firms) over market, but these costs are 'no more than a residual after the greatest dangers of exchange have been dampened by the heavy hand of the state' (Sayer and Walker 1992: 117).

It is a truism that market exchange can not provide its own conditions for existence, that non-market relations necessarily provide the grounding within which the exchanges take place. Normally, political institutions provide these. Jean-Philippe Platteau (1994) has recently criticised the neo-classical view that the crucial infrastructures necessary for the operation of the market mechanism are only private property rights, an appropriate legal framework, and fundamental liberties. He argues instead for the Weberian position that 'the market mechanism can function more or less effectively only if it is embedded into an appropriate social structure' and set of cultural values. An appropriate social structure, for Platteau, is 'one that solves the problem of the "market order" by ensuring low-cost enforcement of the rules of the "market game", among which honesty in economic dealings is particularly important' (Platteau 1994: 534). I would extend this argument further to suggest that in certain circumstances, 'an appropriate social structure' can substitute for absent or unreliable institutional underpinnings for a market order (Smart 1988). Although rules and guidelines for foreign investment and the operation of markets in China exist, they have tended to be underspecified, and have rarely been relied upon by Hong Kong investors in particular, while capitalist practices have consistently tested the limits of what is specifically legitimated by the central authority's rules.

Neo-classical economists emphasise that one of the dangers involved in partial marketisation is that rational economic action will become sidelined in pursuits of the rents that are available to those who have preferential access to non-market resources that are highly valued on the markets. The results of this include the corruption of officials who can provide access, the squandering of resources in the competition for such access and the transfer of the resources to brokers who can not directly utilise them, or to those who can not use them as effectively as others without access.

Corruption is seen as a particularly important market impurity, one that is almost invariably mentioned in discussions of China's reforms. A typical recent example is the comment that

> the surge of new money and the loss of ideological zeal caused by economic reform have damaged the [Chinese Communist] party from within. From bottom to top, the party is riddled with corruption. When Mr. Deng, fatally, encouraged party members to go into business, he may have failed to see that the business many of them could go into most easily was the trafficking of influence. A pragmatist

might argue that this is all to the good: a weak, corrupt, ideologically drained Communist Party is better than a strong, zealously Marxist one, because it allows more space in which wealth can be created . . .. But in reality, the price of Communist rule in China is much greater than the sum of bribes paid. So long as the Communist Party is above the law, there can be no true rule of law, and thus no guarantee of fairness and equity in business dealings, or security of property, or protection of human rights (*Economist* 1995 *b*: S6).

Corruption, then, is seen simultaneously to allow for and undermine market activity, creating space for wealth creation, while threatening the security of property and withholding guarantees of fairness and equity.

Given the double-edged character of corruption in China, I would suggest that the outcome might be indeterminate, that it might go either way depending upon circumstances. The perception of such practices will vary depending upon whether they are seen from the perspective of the Western Market model, where obstacles to the invisible hand create inefficiency, or the New Asian market model, where markets are valuable but must be kept in their place if they threaten to undermine the social relations and cultural values and commonalities that underpin competitive advantages. From the Western perspective, the solution is further extensions of markets, whereas from a post-Confucian perspective, corrupt activities are best tamed by channelling them into the confines of solidarity within a collectivity or the expectations of networks. Put more concretely, behaviours directed towards creating and capturing rents may make important contributions to economic efficiency in circumstances where the societal and legal infrastructure for market capitalism are incompletely developed. The brokerage activities involved in rent-seeking may serve to constitute markets where none officially exist, or where their efficacy is seriously compromised.

Conclusion

The arguments I have presented should suggest a rich terrain for the investigation of ideas about and practices in the Market, although this chapter has only scratched the surface. Representations of the Market are present in the reports of officials in the World Bank and the Chinese government, in the negotiations of

Hong Kong investors and local officials, in criticisms of the deterioration of societal morals and in hopes for the end of disruptive political campaigns and petty despotisms. But the market that is being constructed on the ground, as China undergoes one of the most dramatic and perhaps least understood transformations of contemporary history, is far from consisting of the elements that Carrier identifies with the Market model.

On the ground, whether in Hong Kong-run factories in Guangdong or in the township and village enterprises of the Chinese interior, we do not have economic transactions taking place for impersonal reasons of economic efficiency and 'the bottom line' between autonomous, independent and self-reliant individuals. In a context where there is little trust in the availability of impartial third-party guarantors of economic transactions and justifiable fear of the potential for opportunistic action on all sides, engaging in impersonal market-based transactions would be neither rational nor economically effective. Instead, the representative of *Homo oeconomicus* who engaged in a short-term calculus of impersonal self-advantage or who relied upon the conformity of contracting parties to the details of carefully negotiated agreements would be likely to offend his or her counterparts and encourage their opportunism, or to waste considerable resources and time preparing contracts that have little efficacy. It seems to be partly because of these departures from the neo-classical prescriptions, rather than simply despite them, that Hong Kong and other overseas Chinese investors have so far been so much more effective at investing in China. Such outcomes are not surprising from the perspective of some of the analysts of regimes of flexible specialisation that I have described, nor would they surprise social economists like Mark Granovetter.

Certain representations of the Market model, and its implementation in 'modernising' a socialist or post-socialist economy, assume that the paramount task is to put in place the institutions, property rights and other infrastructural underpinnings of a market economy, and to do so as quickly as possible. Once this has happened, the market mechanism will operate automatically to produce efficient results and to help construct an economy that will be capable of competing in the world market on the basis of its competitive advantages. From this point of view, the success of China in producing exports of manufactures and other goods and in increasing its productivity and prosperity compared to Eastern Europe, is a temporary aberration that will inevitably be undermined if the market reforms are not continually extended.

Paul Bowles and Xiao-yuan Dong (1994: 51), by contrast, offer a view that focuses on the achievement of innovation and highlights 'the role of an active local state as a centrally important feature of China's reform programme'. They admit that in some cases an extension of the market would be desirable, but argue that this 'should not be done at the expense of reducing the state's developmental capacity' (1994: 65). This argument is quite consistent with Bob Jessop's (1993: 18) thesis that the primary concern of governments in an era of post-Fordism is to promote innovation and structural competitiveness. It is arguable that in a period of rapid transformation of the fundamental ground-rules of a political economy, attempting to design a rational system of rules and institutions and attempting to impose them from the top is doomed to the same failures that are claimed to be inevitable for a command economy of central planning (Stark 1994). A chaotic system that seems to be characterised by corrupt, self-serving local officials making questionable deals with local and foreign entrepreneurs without clear-cut rules and guidelines may, paradoxically, be more consistent with the need to innovate and produce locally effective solutions, as long as such localities are characterised by 'hard-budget constraints' that require them to compete on wider markets and provided that rent-seeking can somehow be avoided or kept below a dangerous level.[11]

It is clear that China is different from the West; but we can not thereby dismiss as insignificant the lack of fit between the Market model and the actual practices of constructing markets and market-oriented enterprises in China. The reason for this is that if the Market model were to describe the most effective economic mechanism for coordinating economies, as the textbooks and policy prescriptions suggest, then any divergence from the path of marketisation should decrease economic efficiency and economic growth. While there are still many sceptics saying that China is just piling up future problems through its 'half-way house' style of reform, fifteen years of growth that is among the highest recorded in history must surely suggest to those willing to look at economic performance rather than rhetoric that something other than the efficiency of the Market model has been involved in this transformation. After all, if all the improvements could be ascribed to the Market, every divergence should have generated drag and inefficiency, and we should expect moderate performance at best, not output in the ranks of the 'East Asian miracles'.

My task here has not been to identify the factors that have made China's transformation possible, but rather to examine sceptically the Market model and set the policy prescriptions and grassroots practices within the context of Western and Chinese representations of the Market. Thus I have not offered a solution to the puzzle of why China has been so successful in the last fifteen years; I have only asserted strongly that there is indeed a puzzle here, one that would seem to offer some important clues to how economies actually operate. Those who can solve that puzzle may be able to combine economic growth with the preservation of elements that exist outside the Market realm, although it should be remembered that the non-economic can be despotic and oppressive, as well as solidary and supportive. China suggests that there are indeed alternatives available to us, and that the Market rhetoric may, if implemented, erode some of the potential sources of competitive advantage.

Notes

1. Much could be made of the irony of the biggest success story of the last two decades in the capitalist world economy being a communist country that is preserving its Leninist autocracy. This chapter can not deal with the details of how this apparently paradoxical situation has been accomplished, but will concentrate on its ramifications for discussions of markets and the Market model.
2. Jean-Louis Rocca (1992: 413) notes that 'corruption has become an indispensable means of operation' for private entrepreneurs in China, and suggests the need for a distinction between 'predatory' and 'creative' corruption, the latter being a 'means of renewing society and a vehicle of modernization' (1992: 415). The definition of corruption, and the boundary between bribes and gifts, is a complicated question that is obviously related to this chapter's theme. However, as I have dealt with the question

at length elsewhere (Smart 1993 *a*), here it will only be considered in passing and where relevant.

3. It is clear from a great deal of work, including the chapters in
   this volume, that this conception of market relations does not
   accurately reflect the reality of market relationships. Some of
   these issues will be dealt with below.

4. These distinctions are also closely related to those made by Max
   Weber between feudalism and prebendalism, where the latter
   refers to a system 'in which land is allocated to state officials,
   not as heritable property, but as a right to extract tribute from
   the peasantry' (Turner 1978: 50).

5. Andrew and Rapp (1994: 1237) refer to 'the recent trend of
   Chinese and Western scholarship that views the Chinese
   Leninist regime as a restoration of traditional imperial struc-
   tures.'

6. Cumings (1993: 30) notes the ubiquity of the trope of 'miracle'
   in discussions of East Asian and Pacific Rim economies.

7. However, the differences between the four 'tigers' are often
   conveniently glossed on both sides, and the more free-market
   approach of Hong Kong is receiving increasing attention (see
   Choi 1994).

8. The distinction between network governance and market-based
   interactions between firms is subtle. In practice, market
   transactions between firms in the West often become long-
   standing patterns of 'relational contracting' that are usually not
   discarded easily, despite the availability of lower-priced
   alternatives. Network governance simply takes these patterns
   further, and makes them explicitly recognised rather than
   implicitly constituted characteristics of inter-firm relations.
   The strong growth of 'strategic alliances' among Western
   transnational corporations, usually drawing upon Japanese
   experiences, suggests the emergence of such explicit patterns.
   Among Overseas Chinese businesses such networks are often
   informal, though explicitly recognised, and based on the kinship
   and personal ties of the founders of the firms.

9. The terminologies of 'rent-seeking' and 'soft-budget constraints'
   signal important debates in political economy that I can not
   deal with in the space available here. The rent-seeking literature
   has attempted to extend neo-classical economic analysis into
   the realm of politics, and sees most government interventions
   as producing 'rents' or revenues resulting from privileged

access to some resource, the proceeds of which are largely dissipated through competition for access to them, resulting in waste. For a critique of these ideas in the context of China, see Smart (1993 *b*) and Smart and Smart (1993). The contrast between 'soft-budget' and 'hard-budget' constraints is based upon the work of János Kornai (1986), who argued that enterprises in socialist economies do not share hard-budget constraints with their capitalist counterparts, since bankruptcy is politically unfeasible and troubled firms will always be bailed out. These circumstances lead to very different versions of economically rational action, and help to explain the poorer economic performance of socialist economies, particularly once the possibilities of extensive (mobilising new resources) as opposed to intensive (increasing factor productivity) growth are exhausted.

10. The following account is necessarily very schematic and does not begin to touch upon the complexities of the PRC's history. The intention is simply to provide some of the outlines that are most relevant to understanding the issues at stake in representations of the market.

11. This sentence raises a large number of complex issues that can not be dealt with in detail here. The potential positive dimensions of corruption and rent-seeking are dealt with in Smart (1993 *b*), while the issue of local innovation is examined at some length in Smart (1994).

References

Abrahamian, Ervand 1974. Oriental Despotism: The Case of Qajar Iran. *International Journal of Middle East Studies* 5: 3–31.

Amsden, Alice H. 1990. Third World Industrialization: 'Global Fordism' or a New Model? *New Left Review* 182: 5–31.

Anderson, Perry 1974. *Lineages of the Absolutist State*. London: Verso.

Andrew, Anita M., and John A. Rapp 1994. Review of Zhengyuan Fu, *Autocratic Tradition and Chinese Politics*. *Journal of Asian Studies* 53: 1237–1239.

Angresano, James 1994. Institutional Change in Bulgaria: A Socioeconomic Approach. *Journal of Socio-Economics* 23: 79–100.

Antoniadis-Bibicon, Helene 1977. Byzantium and the Asiatic Mode of Production. *Economy and Society* 6: 347–376.

Bailey, Anne M. 1981. The Renewed Discussions on the Concept of the Asiatic Mode of Production. Pp. 89–107 in Joel Kahn and Josep Llobera (eds), *The Anthropology of Pre-Capitalist Societies*. Houndmills, Hants: Macmillan.

Bottomore, Tom (ed.) 1983. *A Dictionary of Marxist Thought*. Cambridge, Mass.: Harvard University Press.

Bowles, Paul, and Xiao-yuan Dong 1994. Current Successes and Future Challenges in China's Economic Reforms. *New Left Review* 208: 49–76.

Bowles, Samuel, and Herbert Gintis 1993. The Revenge of Homo Economicus: Contested Exchange and the Revival of Political Economy. *Journal of Economic Perspectives* 7: 83–102.

Carrier, James G. 1992 *a*. Occidentalism: The World Turned Upside-Down. *American Ethnologist* 19: 195–212.

Carrier, James G. 1992 *b*. Emerging Alienation in Production: A Maussian History. *Man* 27: 539–558.

Chen, Xiaomei 1992. Occidentalism as Counterdiscourse: 'He Shang' in Post-Mao China. *Critical Inquiry* 18: 686–712.

China News Analysis 1994. The Market Economy and Morality. *China News Analysis* (1 May): 1–10.

Choi, Alex 1994. Beyond Market and State: A Study of Hong Kong's Industrial Transformation. *Studies in Political Economy* 45: 28–65.

Chossudovsky, Michel 1986. *Towards Capitalist Restoration?* Houndmills, Hants: Macmillan.

Crane, George T. 1994. 'Special Things in Special Ways': National Economic Identity and China's Special Economic Zones. *The Australian Journal of Chinese Affairs* 32: 71–92.

Cumings, Bruce 1993. Rimspeak; Or, the Discourse of the 'Pacific Rim'. Pp. 29–47 in Arif Dirlik (ed.), *What Is in a Rim?* Boulder, Col.: Westview Press.

Deyo, Frederic C. 1992. The Political Economy of Social Policy Formation. Pp. 288–306 in Richard Appelbaum and Jeffrey Henderson (eds), *States and Development in the Asian Pacific Rim*. Newbury Park, NJ: Sage.

Dirlik, Arif 1994. The Postcolonial Aura: Third World Criticism in the Age of Global Capitalism. *Critical Inquiry* 20: 328–356.

Dore, Ronald 1973. *British Factory, Japanese Factory*. Berkeley: University of California Press.

Duara, Prasenjit 1993. Bifurcating Linear History: Nation and Histories in China and India. *Positions* 1: 779–804.

Economist 1995 *a*. The Scourge of the West. *The Economist* (22 April): 34–35.

Economist 1995 *b*. A Vacancy Awaits: A Survey of China. *The Economist* (18 March): S 1–S 22.

Fewsmith, Joseph 1991. The Dengist Reforms in Historical Perspective. Pp. 23–52 in Brantly Womack (ed.), *Contemporary Chinese Politics in Historical Perspective*. Cambridge: Cambridge University Press.

Friedman, Edward 1994. Reconstructing China's National Identity: A Southern Alternative to Mao-Era Anti-Imperialist Nationalism. *Journal of Asian Studies* 53: 67–91.

Fukasaku, Kiichiro, and David Wall 1994. *China's Long March to an Open Economy*. Paris: OECD.

Gellner, Ernest 1994. *Conditions of Liberty: Civil Society and its Rivals*. New York: Allen Lane.

Granovetter, Mark 1990. The Old and the New Economic Sociology. Pp. 3–49 in Roger Friedland and A. F. Robertson (eds), *Beyond the Marketplace*. New York: Aldine de Gruyter.

Hamilton, Gary, and Nicole W. Biggart 1992. Market, Culture and Authority: A Comparative Analysis of Management and Organization in the Far East. Pp. 181–221 in Mark Granovetter and Richard Swedberg (eds), *The Sociology of Economic Life*. Boulder, Col.: Westview Press.

Henderson, Jeffrey, and Richard Appelbaum 1992. Situating the State in the East Asian Development Process. Pp. 1–26 in R. Appelbaum and J. Henderson (eds), *States and Development in the Asian Pacific Rim*. Newbury Park, NJ: Sage.

Hsu, Robert C. 1985. Conceptions of the Market in post Mao China. *Modern China* 11: 436–460.

Huang, Chun-chieh, and Kuang-ming Wu 1994. Taiwan and the Confucian Aspiration: Toward the Twenty-First Century. Pp. 69–87 in Stevan Harrell and Chun-chieh Huang (eds), *Cultural Change in Postwar Taiwan*. Boulder, Col.: Westview Press.

Jessop, Bob 1993. Towards a Schumpeterian Workfare State? *Studies in Political Economy* 40: 7–39.

Killick, Tony 1994. East Asian Miracles and Development Ideology. *Development Policy Review* 12: 69–79.

Kornai, János 1986. *Contradictions and Dilemmas: Studies on the Socialist Economy and Society*. Cambridge, Mass.: MIT Press.

Lash, Scott, and John Urry 1994. *Economies of Signs and Space.* London: Sage.

Lee, Raymond L. M. 1994. Modernization, Postmodernism and the Third World. *Current Sociology* 42 (2): 1–63.

Lovering, John 1990. Fordism's Unknown Successor: A Comment on Scott's Theory of Flexible Accumulation. *International Journal of Urban and Regional Research* 14 (1): 159–174.

Mauss, Marcel 1990. *The Gift.* London: Routledge.

Meaney, Constance S. 1989. Market Reform in a Leninist System. *Studies in Comparative Communism* 22: 203–220.

Melotti, Umberto 1977. *Marx and the Third World.* London: Macmillan.

Mingione, Enzo 1994. Life Strategies and Social Economies in the Postfordist Age. *International Journal of Urban and Regional Research* 18: 24–45.

Myers, J. 1989. Modernization and 'Unhealthy Tendencies'. *Comparative Politics* 21: 193–213.

Nee, Victor, and Sijin Su 1990. Institutional Change and Economic Growth in China. *Journal of Asian Studies* 49: 3–25.

Nolan, Peter 1994. Introduction: The Chinese Puzzle. Pp. 1–20 in Qimiao Fan and P. Nolan (eds), *China's Economic Reforms.* New York: St Martin's Press.

Oi, Jean C. 1994. Rational Choices and Attainment of Wealth and Power in the Countryside. Pp. 64–79 in David Goodman and Beverly Hooper (eds), *China's Quiet Revolution.* New York: Longman Cheshire.

Pearson, Margaret M. 1994. The Janus Face of Business Associations in China: Socialist Corporatism in Foreign Enterprises. *The Australian Journal of Chinese Affairs* 31: 25–48.

Peck, Jamie, and Yoshihiro Miyamachi 1994. Regulating Japan? Regulation Theory versus the Japanese Experience. *Environment and Planning D* 12: 639–674.

Platteau, Jean-Philippe 1994. Beyond the Market Stage where Real Societies Exist: Part I. *The Journal of Development Studies* 30: 533–577.

Polanyi, Karl 1957. *The Great Transformation.* Boston: Beacon Press.

Rapp, John A. 1987. The Fate of Marxist Democrats in Leninist Party States: China's Debate on the Asiatic Mode of Production. *Theory and Society* 16: 709–740.

Rocca, Jean-Louis 1992. Corruption and its Shadow: An Anthropological View of Corruption in China. *China Quarterly* 130: 402–416.

Rozman, Gilbert 1991. The East Asian Region in Comparative Perspective. Pp. 3–42 in G. Rozman (ed.), *The East Asian Region.* Princeton: Princeton University Press.

Said, Edward W. 1978. *Orientalism.* New York: Vintage Books.

Sayer, Andrew, and Richard Walker 1992. *The New Social Economy: Reworking the Division of Labor.* Cambridge, Mass.: Blackwell.

Smart, Alan 1988. The Informal Regulation of Illegal Economic Activities: Comparisons between the Squatter Property Market and Organised Crime. *International Journal of the Sociology of Law* 16: 91–101.

Smart, Alan 1993 *a*. Gifts, Bribes and *Guanxi*: A Reconsideration of Bourdieu's Social Capital. *Cultural Anthropology* 8: 388–408.

Smart, Alan 1993 *b*. The Political Economy of Rent-Seeking in a Chinese Factory Town. *Anthropology of Work Review* 14 (2–3): 15–19.

Smart, Alan 1994. Economic Transformation in China: Comparisons with the Post-Socialist Economies. Presented at the American Anthropological Association annual meeting, Atlanta, Georgia.

Smart, Josephine, and Alan Smart 1991. Personal Relations and Divergent Economies: A Case Study of Hong Kong Investment in South China. *International Journal of Urban and Regional Research* 15: 216–233.

Smart, Josephine, and Alan Smart 1993. Obligation and Control: Employment of Kin in Capitalist Labour Management in China. *Critique of Anthropology* 13: 7–31.

Solinger, Dorothy S. 1984. *Chinese Business under Socialism.* Berkeley: University of California Press.

Stark, David 1994. Path Dependence and Privatization Strategies in East Central Europe. Pp. 63–100 in János Kovacs (ed.), *Transition to Capitalism?* New Brunswick, NJ: Transaction Publishers.

Stiglitz, Joseph 1993. Post Walrasian and Post Marxian Economics. *Journal of Economic Perspectives* 7: 109–114.

Stockman, Norman 1992. Market, Plan and Structured Social Inequality in China. Pp. 260–276 in Roy Dilley (ed.), *Contesting Markets: Analyses of Ideology, Discourse and Practice.* Edinburgh: Edinburgh University Press.

Thompson, E. P. 1966. *The Making of the English Working Class*. New York: Vintage Books.

Tu, Weiming, Milan Hejtmanek and Alan Wachman 1992. *The Confucian World Observed*. Honolulu: The East–West Center.

Turner, Bryan S. 1978. *Marx and the End of Orientalism*. London: George Allen & Unwin.

Turner, Bryan S. 1981. *For Weber*. Boston: Routledge & Kegan Paul.

Wank, David 1995. Private Business, Bureaucracy, and Political Alliance in a Chinese City. *The Australian Journal of Chinese Affairs* 33: 55–74.

White, Gordon 1993. Prospects for Civil Society in China. *The Australian Journal of Chinese Affairs* 29: 63–88.

Whyte, Martin K. 1994. Review of 'The East Asian Region'. *Contemporary Sociology* 23 (1): 39–40.

Williamson, Oliver E. 1975. *Markets and Hierarchies*. New York: The Free Press.

Wittfogel, Karl A. 1957. *Oriental Despotism*. New Haven: Yale University Press.

Wolf, Eric R. 1982. *Europe and the People Without History*. Berkeley: University of California Press.

Womack, Brantly 1991. In Search of Democracy: Public Authority and Popular Power in China. Pp. 53–89 in B. Womack (ed.), *Contemporary Chinese Politics in Historical Perspective*. Cambridge: Cambridge University Press.

World Bank 1993. *The East Asian Miracle*. Oxford: Oxford University Press.

Yeung, Henry Wai-chung 1995. Business Networks and Transnational Operations: A Study of Hong Kong Firms in the ASEAN Region. Presented at the Institute of British Geographers meeting, January, 1995.

Chapter 5

Democracy under the Influence: Cost–Benefit Analysis in the United States

Carol A. MacLennan

We're looking at the legislative equivalent of a drive-by shooting.

> Representative Ron Wyden (Democrat, Oregon), in reference to
> the House version (H.R.9) of regulatory reform.

S. 343 will eviscerate – if not repeal – those [environmental, health and safety] laws by making it impossible for agencies that are assigned the task of implementing those laws to perform their jobs. In our view, it would be far more forthright and less wasteful of taxpayer dollars if the bill simply said: 'No more rules.'

> D. Vladeck from Public Citizen, before Congressional committee,
> 8 March 1995, in reference to the Senate version of the regulatory
> reform bill proposed under the 'Contract With America'.

The 'Contract With America' probably will be history by the time you read this. You may never have heard about if you do not live in the US. It is an agreement that the Republicans in Congress claim to have made with the American public in 1994, which came to encompass specific legislation that could radically alter the practice of American governance. How radical? One piece of it, legislation that Republicans called the 'Job Enhancement Act', would require changes in business regulation for safety, health and the environment that seriously challenge democratic practice and threaten the ability of citizens to be involved in the political process beyond the act of voting.

How could such a big threat be in one piece of legislation? Easy. Turn all criteria for making public decisions on the environment and consumer and worker health and safety into market-based tests. Make it so that in order for the government to limit citizen and worker exposure to toxic substances, for instance, it had to *prove* that the cheaper solution was to limit exposure rather than to endure it. This is a market-based test and, although a crude example, it is called 'cost–benefit analysis'.

The Contract with America puts the Market first in government decision-making by requiring that stringent cost–benefit tests be applied to all regulatory decisions. Before this, the Market was not the *primary* criterion on which decisions were made to clean up polluted air, protect workers from asbestos or require airbags in passenger vehicles. The Job Enhancement Act has yet to be passed. But if it is, it will cause a radical change.

The economist's tool of cost–benefit analysis was never intended to change the way the US does business in the regulatory sphere. But, over time, it has. Originally intended to shed light on only one aspect of the economic impact of regulation, it now characterises the regulatory reform movement. A close study of the implementation of cost–benefit analysis as a decision-making tool reveals the story of how the Market has entered into the democratic process and transformed it. That study is the purpose of this chapter.

Market values have become, to use Laura Nader's (1994) phrase, a 'controlling process', a way of thinking that has come to dominate the day-to-day bureaucracy of regulation. Hidden, but powerful, the Market values embedded in cost–benefit analysis have reordered regulatory thinking, with some significant and costly consequences. In particular, the intrusion of Market values into regulation lessens democracy in the US. The dominance of the cost–benefit framework reflects important changes in political power that threaten the citizen's right to be involved in setting regulations. The most important political result of increased use of this seemingly benign tool is the closing of doors to debates over public health and the environment to all but the most educated, sophisticated expert.

In the Free Market era that spawned the Contract with America, it is a good time to look specifically at how the Market has come to be synonymous with responsible government. This story of the growing power of cost–benefit analysis tells a deeper tale about change in American political culture and the place of the Market in it.

This chapter has four sections that describe various elements of the significance of that change. First is a description of the basic principles of cost–benefit analysis, along with a short history of its use in the US government. Here it becomes apparent how Market values can easily permeate and dominate government decision-making. The second section provides a context: the historical interplay between notions of the Market and regulatory practices in the US. This provides a backdrop for understanding how the politics of regulation threaten the values of public space and democratic governance in the US, the topic of section three. The fourth section brings us back to cost–benefit analysis. It is a detailed political history of exactly how the cost–benefit paradigm has come to represent the idea of the Market and, as a result, has effectively depoliticised regulatory politics.

Cost–Benefit Analysis

Cost–benefit analysis compares the monetary benefits and costs of government actions. The analyst first enumerates tangible and intangible benefits and costs, and assigns a monetary value to them. The analyst then compares the dollar value of costs and benefits. For a proposed regulation, a cost–benefit test requires that the value of benefits must outweigh the costs to society, in practice represented by costs to private industry.

The cost of regulation, particularly upon industry, is more easily determined in money terms than is public benefit. This is especially true in environmental protection and in health and safety policies, which often intend to protect values that have no standard market prices attached to them. This imbalance between the character of economic costs and societal benefits of a given regulatory action – say, protection of diverse species – means that cost–benefit analysis amounts to comparing apples and oranges.

It is most difficult to monetise benefits that are not typically market commodities – beauty, health, safety. A value can legitimately be attached to health protection, in the form of medical expenses and lost wages, and this is how it is generally done. But such an exercise uses the most narrow definition of health, and typically does not account for major quality-of-life considerations.

Indeed, the benefit side of such analysis has become a complicated and rigorous exercise devoted to monetising things that might otherwise have only scientific, cultural, moral or aesthetic value. Things that Americans may never before have considered to be market goods are assigned a market price. Reduced to monetary equivalents in the cost–benefit analysis, the value of social and cultural life is narrowed in scope and constricted in meaning in order to calculate its dollar price. The final result may be dollar estimates on things like the scenic view at the Grand Canyon or people's willingness to risk their lives or health through exposure to dioxin.

This sort of reduction to monetary terms is at the core of many regulatory changes over the last two decades. The public debate is, of course, waged in the language of industrial costs and public benefits. But more significant is how monetisation, the language of the Market, has become a controlling process, how the translation of societal values into Market terms has changed the very *way* we regulate and, importantly, *what* we regulate. This is the subject of this chapter.

Because of the wide variation of methods employed to determine the worth of benefits, experts can legitimately come up with widely varying numbers. For example, in the 1970s the National Highway Traffic Safety Administration set the value of a life at $200,000 for the purpose of assessing the cost of automotive fatalities. The White House Office of Science Policy set it at $140,000 (Rhoads 1980: 172 *n* 3). These values were largely calculated on the basis of lost wages discounted over time, the discounted earnings method. Assumptions in discounting created the difference between the two figures. When automotive fatalities are aggregated, these different figures led to widely different statements of the benefits of saving lives.[1] The Occupational Safety and Health Administration utilised a completely different method for calculating the cost of lost lives and injuries due to workplace hazards: how much is a worker willing to pay to avoid a particular hazard – the 'willingness-to-pay' method.

Cost–benefit analysis poses practical problems as well. Benefit estimation must be justified by scientific research. This is expensive, and obliges government agencies to spend their money on the task of satisfying the demands of the cost–benefit exercise, leaving less for research to determine new regulatory initiatives. This cost introduces an implicit cost–benefit calculation into regulatory planning, one that amounts to a form of Market censorship at the earliest stages of defining a problem and its solution. If it appears that benefit estimation will require new research, which is expensive, an agency may avoid a regulatory solution altogether (Moore 1995).

Use of cost–benefit analysis dates back to the large public works projects of the 1930s, particularly those of the Army Corps of Engineers. The Flood Control Act of 1936 brought cost–benefit analysis into government practice. The large public works projects of the Depression created concern over their impact, so Congress required that the benefits of the projects should outweigh the costs. Cost–benefit analysis was to be conducted when a project was being formulated and it, along with the project proposal, was submitted to Congress for approval. At that time, the cost to government was the issue. Cost–benefit analysis was used to check government expenditure, ensuring that the benefits to society for large public works made the huge expense worthwhile. As a result, cost–benefit analysis became common practice in the Army Corps of Engineers, the Tennessee Valley Authority, the Bureau of Reclamation of the Department of the Interior, and the Soil and Conservation Service. For nearly two decades, the use of cost–benefit analysis differed from agency to agency. In the 1950s, however, the Bureau of the Budget attempted to reconcile the different methods utilised to assess costs and benefits.

Gradually cost–benefit analyses were done for other construction and engineering projects in the military, transportation, and urban renewal. In the 1960s, it was applied beyond physical infrastructure to include social spending in health, welfare and education (Heimann *et al.* 1990: 553–563). However, in the 1970s cost–benefit was turned on its head.

Congress established new regulatory powers in the 1960s and 1970s to protect consumers, public health, the environment and workers from the negative consequences of rapid industrial and technological change. Opponents of these initiatives successfully utilised cost–benefit analysis to deter or rescind government requirements for health, safety and environmental protection. They did so by redefining the pertinent costs, expanding them to include the cost of government action to industry. No longer a tool to check government spending on large projects, it is now used to limit government action for public health and environment improvements. With this change it came to privilege the private property rights of industry over public goals of citizen protection and corporate responsibility to the community. Once a management tool for public funds, it is now a Market tool. To analyse these political trends, we must examine how Market values have affected the evolving practice of regulation in the US.

The Context: Regulation and the Market

Today, when one enters the market, one enters the realm of global corporate power. Although the Market may symbolise the exchange of goods among many small producers and consumers in the country, that era is long past. Now global corporations seek to shape markets in ways that dramatically affect consumer choice and many spheres of life outside commerce. Further, the globalisation of markets for both commodities and labour has unleashed a powerful set of forces that affect all people, no matter how remote or distant from one another, linking them into a vast network of societies experiencing industrial and technological change at an increasing rate.

In this type of economic and social environment, national public values of health, safety, environmental protection and equity have become subordinate to the dominance of the global market's 'bottom line'. In the era of the North American Free Trade Agreement and the General Agreement on Trade and Tariffs, the US is caught in the squeeze of global economic competition, and corporate values of efficiency, profitability and property increasingly dominate public space. Unlike Europe's more protectionist stand, more respectful of workers and environmental concerns, the US has chosen to drop trade barriers, thus propelling its corporations into a world market that demands lower costs of production. As political figures on both the right (Patrick Buchanan) and the left (Ralph Nader) point out, this creates corporate incentives to hire low-priced labour abroad and to push for government deregulation of consumer and environmental protection.

The recent history of regulation in the US reflects these changes in the global economy. It is in the context of this history that the powerful rise of cost–benefit analysis as a Market tool to limit government action in public health and environmental protection begins to make sense. To see how this is so, it is worth going back to the origin of American regulation in the Populist and Progressive eras.

The decades around 1900 saw the rapid spread of industrialism in the US, and with it came the darker side of the free market economy, in the form of unfair trade practices, tainted food and unsafe drugs. The regulatory state emerged from this period, as citizens, workers and politicians sought to control business behaviour in the public interest. Beginning with the Sherman Anti-Trust Act of 1893 and for eight decades thereafter, numerous federal laws sought to regulate business activity in the interest of fair trade and consumer protection.

Two types of regulation, economic and social, have evolved over these decades of legislation. Economic regulation concerns the terms of entry into and conditions of operation of particular industries. Agencies such as the Interstate Commerce Commission and the Federal Trade Commission set regulatory standards that fall into this category. On the other hand, social regulation creates standards for specific types of activities or imposes controls that limit the effects of these activities (Salamon 1981). Generally, social regulation addresses an industry's technological product or its manufacturing process. Agencies such as the Food and Drug Administration and Environmental Protection Agency administer the laws typical of social regulation, such as the Food, Drug, and Cosmetic Act, the Clean Water Act and the Clean Air Act.

It is important to recognise the distinctive nature of social regulation. Technological issues are at stake. Some of the most important new laws, such as the Clean Air Act, require many industries to rethink the technological design of their manu-facturing process – an expensive proposition. This is very different from economic regulation, which is characterised by rate-setting, route-awards, licensing, all of which are industry-specific and entail only limited costs. Further, economic regulation often helps rationalise business operations, thus reducing costs in the long run. Social regulation, however, is function-specific and potentially costly. It seeks technological remedies to meet goals of consumer, environmental, and worker protection. As such, it crosses over industry lines and often demands technological innovation ('technology-forcing') to meet social, not business, goals.

This technology-forcing character of social regulation has important political implications. In distinction from the case of economic regulation, where market-based practices are controlled, social regulation is usually concerned with industrial technology. The Motor Vehicle Safety Act of 1966 shifted the focus of highway safety away from driver behaviour and to vehicle design. The Consumer Product Safety Act of 1972 directed attention to the effects on purchasers of millions of products. The 1972 Clean Water Act required industrial and municipal facilities to move toward technology-based pollution controls. This shift of regulatory attention to industrial technology threatens the perceived property rights of US corporations more directly than does economic regulation, and corporations reacted. For example, because of the staunch, and politically successful, opposition by automobile manufacturers, it took nearly twenty years to implement the regulation requiring airbags in all passenger vehicles. The airbag came to symbolise the stand of industry against the new social regulation (MacLennan 1988 *a*: 233–250). Regulation of technology generally benefits the environment, workers and consumers, but not industry, at least in the short run.

Traditionally, US technological design, development and production occurs in the private sector, where market, not public, rules dominate. Yet, technology's effects are socialised, are often felt outside the marketplace. Some of these are very complex. For instance, acid rain is the product of certain kinds of industrial activity. You can measure the effect of acid rain in market terms as the loss of harvestable timber or the decline of a fishery. However, it is impossible to measure the significance of some of the known secondary effects of acid rain, such as the loss of species or soil erosion, in market terms without trivialising them. Thus, social regulation operates in a complex social, economic and political field: technologies under the control of private industry have social effects that demand societal solutions, which makes them the responsibility of government.

This complexity can be analysed from two different perspectives. One stresses incommensurability, the incommensurability of money and health or money and nature. How can one put a price on a social value without violating the nature of what is being lost? From this perspective, it is impossible to monetise social values. The other perspective sees the problem as one of externalities that can be easily resolved through market mechanisms. These consequences should be monetised and calculated in the original price or cost of the technology. If this is impossible because of the inability to anticipate consequences, then those who are adversely affected should be compensated. From a Market perspective, then, the socialising of technological consequences has no political dimension. Externalities are incorporated in pricing or paid for in compensation. The problem becomes one of how the market can best accomplish this.

This perspective is, in fact, deeply embedded in regulatory law. In the US, regulation is predicated upon market failure. That is, it is when markets do not meet the social standards expected of them, that government is authorised to create some means to correct this failure. Traditionally, market failure has been the justification of economic regulation. For instance, the Sherman Anti-Trust Act sought to regulate monopolies and oligopolies because they hindered the free market. Market failure is also a requirement for initiating social regulation. However, its use is more problematic, because the failure that must be proved is a form of social harm caused by business practices, rather than the failure of a free market to operate. Except in the case of documented fatalities that are linked to specific activities, social harm is more typically characterised by long-term illness or gradual environmental degradation, which is almost invisible except in the aggregate. Because of the absence of documented individual cases, proving market failure is inevitably linked to science; but regulatory science is inexact to say the least. Questions of uncertainty abound, as attempts to link cause and effect lead to multiple answers. Hence, the public debate over the cancer-causing effects of food additives, for instance, is often reduced to irresolvable questions of scientific proof (Jasanoff 1990).

A history of regulatory practice in the US illustrates the political problems that I have said accompany social regulation. Before the 1960s, regulatory initiatives were primarily of the economic type. The focus of the nation's regulatory energy was upon banking, securities, airline travel, trucking, utilities and communications. Some attention was devoted to food and drug safety, but this was when unsafe products threatened the economic viability of the meat and drug industries. The rationalisation of trade and business practices through standard-setting generally benefited the large companies and the regulated industries. Over time, a loose consensus emerged among citizens, businesses and politicians, acknowledging the right of government to intervene in the market (Kolko 1963; Weinstein 1968).

The consensus fell apart when Congress passed several pieces of social regulation in the 1960s and 1970s, reflecting initiatives in consumer and worker health and safety, and in environmental protection. Rather than regulating markets, these acts set health and safety standards and established new federal programmes, the Environmental Protection Agency, the Occupational Safety and Health Administration, the Consumer Product Safety Commission, the National Highway Traffic Safety Administration. Technology-forcing regulations were expensive. The clean air standards of the Environmental Protection Agency and the fuel economy standards of the National Highway Traffic Safety Administration cost money to meet. As America entered a recession in 1975 and again in 1979, the global marketplace began to put its mark on business decision-making, and firms decided they were too expensive. By 1980 the business community organised to convince government and citizens that deregulation was in the public interest.

Organisations such as the Chamber of Commerce, the Business Roundtable and the National Association of Manufacturers claimed that the new regulatory laws had created a runaway government. During the Carter administration a regulatory reform movement gained strength. With large sectors of the business community pressing for elimination of costly new standards, Carter and his economic advisers began a regulatory reform programme. However, this focused primarily upon economic, rather than social, regulation, especially of airlines, banking, savings and loans, and communications.

Ronald Reagan won the election in 1980 partly on a platform of deregulation. After taking office he quickly launched an attack on environmental, health and safety laws, and the business community shifted its deregulation initiative almost exclusively to social regulation. The more expensive, technology-forcing regulations became targets for business appeal to citizens for widespread deregulation.

One of the most visible examples was the campaign to stop the Occupational Safety and Health Administration from requiring new manufacturing processes in the textile industry, protecting workers from brown lung disease. The National Cotton Council, an industrial association, told Americans in an advertising campaign: 'Over-regulation could cost your family a home of your own. You want a home of your own where your children can play in a yard. And not in the street. But you might not be able to afford it. Because of over-regulation' (Green, Waitzman and Nader 1981:

Appendix A). Thus began what became conventional wisdom, that regulation hurts the economy and therefore hurts all of us in our pursuit of the American dream. In retrospect, we can see how global economic pressures on corporations to cut their costs continually helped fuel the vehemence with which industries such as textiles fought hard to roll back health and safety regulations.

It was at this point that the economist's tool of cost–benefit analysis burst into everyday political rhetoric. It became reasonable to tally-up the cost of regulations for industries that were struggling in the recession of the early 1980s. This practice was criticised only by a few citizens active in environmental, labour and consumer organisations. It was easy to calculate increased production costs to industry for new regulations. But regulators had an almost impossible task in estimating the costs to society for *not* regulating in comparable terms.

Consumer advocates Mark Green, Norman Waitzman and Ralph Nader were among the first to identify this shift in corporate thinking. They warned that cost–benefit analysis, the core of the Reagan regulatory reform programme, served to legitimate the business campaign for deregulation and that it reflected the corporate definition of health, safety and the environment as market commodities. They provided a counter-position that later became a central argument against the use of the cost–benefit paradigm. Health, safety and the environment are values that can not be assigned a monetary value in the way that one can assign such a value to a commodity like a bicycle or house. In fact, '[h]ealth, safety, and environmental protection . . . are prerequisites for full appreciation and enjoyment of all "economic goods". Sacrificing them for short-term production is like using the walls of one's house for firewood on an wintry night' (Green, Waitzman and Nader 1981: 10). Their protests went largely unheard in the White House and in Congress. Instead, cost–benefit analysis became institutionalised, gradually incorporating Market values into the regulatory process.

Only in the 1990s have citizens begun to accept the fact that the societal values embedded in social regulation can not always be treated as monetised commodities, and that the values of health, safety and a secure environment are not necessarily business values. However, this fifteen-year gap between the early warnings about cost–benefit analysis and the current awareness of its limitations has been costly.

The Loss of Public Space

Civic values have always occupied space in American political culture, sometimes along with Market values, sometimes alone. When legislators and regulators identified and sought to correct market failures in the regulatory reforms around 1900, they created public spaces in which values of consumer protection, health and safety were, ideally, to supersede Market values of property and profit. Decades later, Congress included values of beauty, ecological balance and community preservation in the public space of regulation.

It was during this later period, beginning in the 1960s, that regulatory protection for citizens and communities was most clearly and deliberately established. It began in 1966 when Congress addressed the problem of highway death and automotive safety. In passing the Motor Vehicle Safety Act, it provided the new Department of Transportation with a simple social mandate: reduce death and injury on the nation's roads and highways. The public health goal was unambiguous. Even in 1970, with the Occupational Safety and Health Act, Congress's caveat that standards be 'feasible' did not significantly weaken the more powerfully stated 'right' to safe and healthy working conditions. Market values clearly were subordinated to concerns about public health.

As I have noted, however, since the middle of the 1970s regulatory actions have been increasingly subjected to a critical review based on how they affect corporate rights of property and profit. The health-based standards that marked the Motor Vehicle Safety Act rapidly became replaced by cost-based standards. This shift reflects the internalisation of Market values in the bureaucracy, from the earliest stages of regulatory science to the later stages of final rule-making. It also signals the loss of a public space.

This loss was to be expected. The Market has always lurked in the background of American political culture. In the first decades of the regulatory state the Market maintained a different sort of presence than it does today. It was less obtrusive, it did not invade the public space of regulation. Instead, it had a different role, to make public bureaucracies operate more efficiently.

Business values of efficiency and organisation have been applied to governance for over a century, having long been touted as good devices for making government work better. Beginning with political reform after the Civil War, good government became synonymous with the use of business management principles. This attitude prevailed well into the 1960s through the use of Presidential Task Forces dedicated to making government administration more efficient in monetary terms. Task Force recommendations usually called for cost-cutting, greater productivity and smaller bureaucracies (MacLennan 1988 *b*).

The incorporation of business values into government management during the early industrial period coincided with the rise of a large national bureaucracy. Where political action had focused on the courts and on the national political parties, by the end of the nineteenth century it had shifted to a newly centralised bureaucracy. The development of a civil administration, a more organised army and a bureaucracy for business regulation created a new form of governance by 1920. And the Market had a decided role to play (Skowronek 1982). Business values became the management tools of that national centre. From President Taft's Commission on Economy and Efficiency to President Clinton's Task Force on Reinventing Government, principles of economy and efficiency have been central to managing and streamlining the federal bureaucracy.

Regulatory law, legitimated by market failure, had secured a small public space of action that remained relatively free of Market intrusion until the 1970s. At that point, the Market, which had been in the background, burst into the regulatory sector to dominate and direct the once-public values of consumer and environmental protection. The precipitating set of events was the regulatory legislation of the 1960s and 1970s. Its citizen- and environment-oriented values directly challenged those of the Market.

The loss of public space in the regulatory sphere was facilitated by two factors. First, the legal basis of regulatory policy is tenuous at best. The regulation of industry in the interests of citizens is predicated upon what Peter Montague (1996) calls the 'prove harm philosophy', where only documented harm creates a regulatory jurisdiction. Thus, regulatory law is reactive, implemented in response to specific public problems, like unsafe cars, dirty water and air and pesticides toxic to humans. Furthermore, regulatory strategy must be constructed within the paradigm of market failure. If cotton dust kills textile workers and industry fails to remedy the problem, then government can propose new standards to cut down cotton dust in factory air. The new era of social regulation may have privileged health protection over property, but only in circumstances in which technological harm had been identified and proved, and in which regulatory strategies were successfully implemented and enforced. This system, based on the prove harm philosophy, makes it difficult to regulate industries in order to prevent harm before very much of it occurs, as would be typical of good public health programmes.

The second factor facilitating the loss of public space is what Charles Lindbloom (1982) calls the 'prison' or punishing effect of the Market. When government policies directly challenge its dominance, the Market indirectly imprisons government through a punishing effect of layoffs, business declines and plant closings. Since America's democracy is capitalist, such punishing business actions can cripple political society and drive it toward crisis. For the punishment to work, Americans must accept business decisions to close factories, relocate plants overseas and fire large numbers of employees. Typically they accept these decisions, because American culture, more than European, stresses individualism and autonomy. That is, when business fights government regulation, it is perceived as acting morally. Firms are publicly supported in their right to remain independent from 'intrusive' government regulation. So, when business is especially articulate in making a case for deregulation, the appeal to a moral autonomy and freedom from constraint falls on sympathetic ears.

Corporations produced such appeals in response to the new social regulations that challenged corporate control of technology and allocation of industrial costs. They organised successful campaigns against particular regulations as well as regulation in general, such as the National Cotton Council's campaign against the proposed cotton dust standard. Electric utilities were no less dramatic in their cries that clean air standards required expensive alterations to coal-fired power plants that would cripple the industry and send electricity bills sky-rocketing. More concretely, in 1979 the Chrysler Corporation told the White House that if it had to conform to standards on fuel economy, an average by 1985 of 27.5 miles per gallon, it would close the one remaining automotive plant in Detroit, throwing a large black workforce into unemployment in a city already hit hard by recession.

Standards for clean air, cotton dust and fuel economy all required expensive technological change to meet new societal criteria for health and conservation. However, in all these cases the government gave manufacturers several years to phase in the necessary technological changes. Firms resisted these, even when meeting standards was not expensive, as in the case of the airbag. The strength of the resistance and the success it achieved suggest that more than just economic factors were at work. A culture that supports the moral autonomy of business was important as well.

The public space for regulation shrank considerably after the 1980 election of President Ronald Reagan. The story of how this happened is best told by returning to our study of cost–benefit analysis, how it came to represent the power of the Market, and the types of political changes it signified in democratic governance.

The Lessening of Democracy

How did the relatively obscure economist's tool of cost–benefit analysis become such an important factor in increasing Market dominance in democratic government? This tale must be told in two parts. First, there is the story of the growth in power of the President's Office of Management and the Budget (OMB) over regulatory matters. A direct challenge to Congress and to the independence of executive agencies in implementing public law, the OMB's ability to represent corporate interests against regulatory standards began in the Johnson administration. Gradually, the OMB has moved from its Congressionally-mandated role as a manager of the Executive branch to one of effectively setting regulatory standards, a responsibility Congress explicitly delegates only to regulatory agencies.

Second, there is the related story of how cost–benefit analysis effectively rendered regulatory politics 'citizen-proof'. Illustrating a point made in the Introduction to this collection, cost–benefit terminology became the language of currency in every debate over whether or not to regulate. As a result of this, mastery of it became a criterion for those seeking to be involved in the participatory process required for each new regulation – a criterion that most citizens can not meet. The use of cost–benefit analysis also alters the formal and informal process by which regulations are made, so that citizens who *do* try to participate are virtually shut out. The net effect of both the increased power of the OMB and the use of cost–benefit analysis has been to lessen public participation in regulatory politics, rendering American government that much less democratic.

The Rise of the OMB

The OMB began in 1921 as a small office in the White House whose purpose was to review Executive branch budgets for the President. It continued in this manner for several decades, reviewing budgets but with little power to direct the budget process of executive agencies. This changed in the 1960s, and by the 1980s the OMB was a powerful agency that directed regulation and research, as well as budgets.

The expansion of government after the Second World War brought efforts by Presidents to gain more control over the complex organisation of the Executive branch. Strategies for increased oversight by the White House were motivated by an interest in better management and organisation. In 1965, President Johnson issued an Executive Order implementing an analytical budget process, called the Planning-Programing-Budget System, in order to centralise planning. The rules of budget planning, once set individually within each executive agency, were now uniformly established by the OMB. This procedure was modified and replaced by President Nixon's Management by Objectives system, which brought White House staff further into agency budget planning and decision-making. Jimmy Carter's Zero-Based Budgeting was the last of these initiatives. Once a process whereby agencies submitted their annual budgets to the OMB for financial review, the setting of budgets became a management planning tool as a result of these changes, all of which served to centralise budget preparation and control in the White House.

Furthermore, President Nixon and his successors sought to bring regulatory rule-making under White House control as well. In a direct response to the expansion of federal powers brought about by the growth of social regulation, Nixon established the Quality of Life Review Process, to allay industry concerns about costly environmental regulations. It was designed to establish the review, by the OMB, of regulations in executive agencies such as the Environmental Protection Agency. However, this reform never took root because, under the Budget Act of 1920, the OMB had the authority to review budget decisions but not regulations. At the Environmental Protection Agency, for instance, the formal authority to issue regulations lay with the agency administrator. The OMB could not, under the Quality of Life Review Process, intervene in this process without raising serious legal questions. The proposed review process, however, did have an impact upon the Environmental Protection Agency, the agency it was designed to restrain.

The review process that did emerge allowed the OMB to organise an inter-agency review of all proposed and final regulatory rules prior to their being formally announced by publication in the Federal Register. While not affecting the final decision, the review process allowed for comment on the impact of rules by executive agencies. The review process also changed rule-making inside the Environmental Protection Agency. The agency established internal reviews and began informal consultation with industry, in order to head off controversy at the formal inter-agency review stage (Eads and Fix 1984: 46–50). Anticipating criticism of the costs of regulation inevitably changed the internal intellectual framework for regulatory planning. New regulatory initiatives that, at first glance, appeared costly were avoided. This quietly but effectively raised the threshold of evidence required for agency action against a potential technological hazard.

Gradually the OMB employed budget and management strategies that enabled White House review of regulations; but the office was still cognisant of legal barriers. By 1981, Reagan's OMB developed a regulatory review programme that greatly resembled Nixon's original Quality of Life Review Process. These changes between 1970 and 1980 were gradual and almost invisible to the public; but where Nixon's OMB officers were unable to intervene in and alter agency rule-making, Reagan's staff were able to review and virtually veto impending regulations by demonstrating the burden of regulatory costs on industry. Regulatory review had become institutionalised, and cost–benefit analysis provided the preferred criterion for review.

The process began under President Ford, when the OMB issued a requirement that all significant regulations and rules issued by the Executive branch must be reviewed for their 'inflationary impact' upon the economy. With this requirement, regulatory review was extended for the first time beyond the OMB to other executive organisations. The Council on Wage and Price Stability began to issue analyses of the economic consequences of proposed regulations, which were filed during the public comment period for each major regulation. Generally, the regulatory review process was becoming more professional, extending to other social regulation agencies and occurring more regularly. George Eads and Michael Fix note that although controversy surrounded the new environmental, health and safety, and consumer protection regulations, 'most members of the Ford administration accepted the underlying principle that such regulation was socially desirable. The object of the administration thus was to achieve the goals of such regulation, but to achieve them as efficiently and as inexpensively as possible' (Eads and Fix 1984: 53–54).

The basic philosophy of socially-based standards remained intact; but further development of cost-based research also occurred, and continued with President Carter: Ford's 'inflation impact' Executive Order remained in place, and the Council on Wage and Price Stability continued to issue its analyses of proposed rules. In addition, Carter's Council of Economic Advisors proposed broadening the requirement for regulatory review beyond questions of inflationary impact to include a consideration of the cost-effectiveness of proposed regulations. Carter issued an Executive Order requiring that rule-making agencies submit an economic impact statement for major proposed regulations. In spite of these changes, the legislative authority to issue regulations, like the timetable of public comment required under the Administrative Procedures Act, remained secure.

The economic impact statement introduced under Carter's presidency included a new definition of what types of cost were important in the cost analysis for major rules. However, there was no requirement that a cost-effectiveness test be met. The effect of Carter's reforms was, then, the continued refinement and application of the already existing tools used to analyse the cost of regulatory proposals (Eads and Fix 1984: 54–67). As a part of this, regulatory analysis was broadened to include several components: the specification of alternative regulatory strategies; the economic consequences of different strategies, including cost–benefit analysis; justifications for the chosen alternative. As long as proposed regulations were not required to meet a cost test, however, the impact on agency life was restricted to the policy offices, which had to prepare the regulatory analysis. Other sectors of the regulatory agency – research, consumer education, enforcement – remained relatively free from OMB scrutiny on items other than budget matters.

These changes in the regulatory review process did not eliminate discontent. The cotton dust standard, the Department of Interior's strip-mining regulations and the Environmental Protection Agency's ozone standard were bitterly protested against during the Carter presidency. Further, senior economic advisers in the White House and members of industry agreed that substantial sections in the Clean Air Act, the Occupational Safety and Health Act and the Food and Drug Act's Delaney Clause needed revision. In each of these acts, the law prohibited the use of cost criteria in setting standards. Interestingly, reform of these laws was not proposed outright. Instead, several bills were introduced to reform regulatory procedure, essentially by turning the various Executive Orders for regulatory review into law. They failed (Eads and Fix 1984: 80–85).

By the end of the Carter Administration in 1980, the regulatory reform movement was in full force. Ronald Reagan campaigned on a platform of regulatory relief, the idea that regulations needed to be reduced, not just analysed and debated more carefully. By this time, the primary mechanism for regulatory reform had become procedural, because there was no support in Congress for substantial reform of the law. The various Executive Order review strategies had effectively given the OMB powers over the final stages of agency rule-making by requiring consideration of cost. Reagan capitalised on this strategy by further enhancing the OMB's oversight powers. This created an office with little public accountability that regulated the regulators.

On 22 January 1981, just a few days after taking office, Reagan established a highly-publicised Task Force on Regulatory Relief. Its purpose was to review all major regulatory proposals by Executive branch agencies, and to assess Executive branch regulations already in existence 'especially those that are burdensome to the national economy or to key industrial sectors' (Eads and Fix 1984: 109). Within three weeks, two other features of the regulatory relief programme were established by Executive Order: centralisation of regulatory oversight powers in a new OMB office, the Office of Information and Regulatory Affairs; and a requirement that, except in cases explicitly prohibited by law, proposed regulations had to meet a cost–benefit test.

The Task Force on Regulatory Relief, headed by George Bush, immediately began scrutinising proposed health, safety and environmental regulations and reviewing those already enacted. Cost–benefit data and analyses were critical to keeping or eliminating regulations. As a result of this review, two of the most thoroughly researched and debated safety and health standards were considered for possible elimination, the airbag rule and the cotton dust standard.

The airbag rule, ready to be implemented in 1982, was re-evaluated, a cost–benefit study was completed, and the rule was rescinded in October 1981. The National Highway Traffic Safety Administration had first proposed this rule in 1969, had analysed the technology thoroughly, and had withstood several challenges to the rule from automotive manufacturers. During this time, public pressure for the standard increased, technological issues were resolved, and substantial research was completed comparing the abilities of airbag and seatbelt systems to reduce injuries in crashes. As a result of a case brought by the insurance industry, the Supreme Court ordered the National Highway Traffic Safety Administration to re-evaluate its abandonment of the proposed airbag standard. It did so, and the standard finally became law in 1984, with initial introduction of airbags during the 1986 model year (Bollier and Claybrook 1986; Marshaw and Harfst 1990; Tolchin 1984).

The cotton dust standard, enacted in June 1978, was recalled by Reagan's Occupational Safety and Health Administration after review by the Task Force on Regulatory Relief. The textile industry had won a review before the Supreme Court in 1981, arguing that the standard should be submitted to a cost–benefit test. Textile manufacturers argued that the health criterion should not have been decisive in evaluating the proposed standard. In a parallel move, the Occupational Safety and Health Administration asked the Court to suspend the review it had granted at the urging of the textile industry, and instead send the regulation back to the agency for cost–benefit assessment. The Court denied this request and ruled on the industry's case. In an important decision for regulatory reform, the Court upheld the cotton dust standard, arguing that the Occupational Safety and Health Act clearly specified that 'threat to worker health' was the primary criterion for regulation, not cost–benefit analysis (Claybrook 1984: 83–84; Noble 1986). This prevented the White House from requiring cost-benefit tests of regulations in cases where the enabling legislation explicitly specifies health, safety or other criteria.

Because of the high public profile of the Task Force on Regulatory Relief, public interest organisations and unions were successful in alerting citizens about the proposals for numerous reconsiderations and suspensions of regulations. This limited the success of the task force. However, the rearguard action of citizen and worker organisations created a singular focus on preventing regulatory rollbacks, rather than upon future initiatives. This, coupled with the more quiet actions of OMB and the new Reagan Executive Order 12,291, created a climate in which Market values became more deeply imbedded in the regulatory decision process. A look at the significance of OMB's new Office of Information and Regulatory Affairs and at the substantial place of cost–benefit analysis in that Executive Order will help show how this happened.

When Reagan established the Office of Information and Regulatory Affairs in the OMB, he centralised executive regulatory oversight in an unprecedented way. The OMB is relatively free from public scrutiny, and over the years had developed a quiet system of influencing agency budgets. The traditional budget negotiations between agencies and the White House, while not open to the public, would eventually become the subject of Congressional questioning once the President submitted the budget for discussion. In the regulatory sphere, however, no such check on interference by the OMB in regulatory authority existed. How did this happen?

Reagan's Executive Order 12,291 authorised the OMB only to review cost–benefit analyses of regulatory agencies, not to generate them. OMB staff have seen this primarily as quality control. However, this oversight function has diminished the regulatory authority of other executive agencies. The OMB has the power to persuade because it acts with the authority of the President and negotiates with the heads of agencies who are appointed by the President. The OMB can threaten to delay a regulatory proposal or can put pressure on an agency head to accept the OMB's view. It can also apply pressure through budgeting, to its 'persuasive' advantage (Heimann *et al.* 1990: 599 *n* 342). An additional effect of Reagan's centralisation of regulatory oversight under the Office of Information and Regulatory Affairs was that the public analysis of proposed regulation by the Council on Wage and Price Stability ceased. In fact, the council itself was eliminated. The council's documents at least had allowed the public access to Executive branch comments on pending regulations during the public comment period (Eads and Fix 1984: 108–110; Heimann *et al.* 1990: 595–601). Now the comments would be private and oral.

Executive Order 12,291, issued on 17 February 1981, is known as the 'cost–benefit' order. Less well known is the fact that it also gave the OMB broad regulatory authority. All major regulations,[2] prior to final issuance, had to pass through OMB review twice. Further, under this order the OMB acquired the authority to question any agency determination that a particular rule was major. The first review of the regulatory analysis (written by the agency) occurred before the agency even submitted a preliminary notice to the Federal Register (the Notice of Proposed Rulemaking). If the OMB found the analysis weak, it could delay the preliminary notice until its questions were answered satisfactorily.

The second review occurred thirty days before the rule was to be issued. If the OMB objected to the final regulatory analysis, it could hold up the publication of the final notice of the regulation in the Federal Register. In doing so, it violated the spirit of the Administrative Procedures Act, which specifies deadlines for publication of final rules in the Federal Register. Further violating the spirit of the act, Reagan's Executive Order did not require record-keeping of the communications between the OMB and the agencies during these reviews (Eads and Fix 1984: 110–112).

The heart of Executive Order 12,291, the cost–benefit analysis requirement, obliged agencies to satisfy the OMB that the net benefits to society of a proposed rule outweigh the net costs. Agencies were required to take three factors into account when establishing benefits and costs: the national economy, industries affected by the regulation and regulatory activities by other agencies. Essentially, the burden of proof was on the agency to show that a regulation was cost-effective. This reversed the previous practice, which placed the burden of proof on the OMB. All of these requirements were 'subject to existing law', because of the Supreme Court ruling on cotton dust (Eads and Fix 1984: 109; Moore 1995).

Reagan's Executive Order remained in place for twelve years, until President Clinton replaced it with Executive Order 12,866 in 1993. The Office of Information and Regulatory Affairs continued in Clinton's OMB, but requirements for regulatory analyses were altered, as regulatory objectives now had to be based upon 'public need'. In considering public need, however, agencies are to justify the cost of regulations on the basis of expected benefits (Moore 1995). Even though Clinton weakened the power of cost–benefit analysis in the development of regulation, the twelve years of Reagan and Bush policies had the effect of instituting cost–benefit analysis as a part of agency practice and outlook, and the continuing stress on cost criteria meant that Market values remain very much a part of daily life in the federal regulatory bureaucracy. Cost–benefit analysis, now internalised, influences regulations without a requirement that it do so.

Citizen-Proof Regulation

The logic and practice of cost–benefit analysis have significant implications for democracy, enshrining Market values more thoroughly than might be suggested by Lindbloom's prison effect, and altering democratic practice. This is because cost–benefit analysis makes government procedures less equitable and government agencies less accountable.

Cost–benefit analysis affects the procedure of decision-making because it limits the criteria on which decisions are to be based to only those that can be monetised. This introduces the Market as a silent actor in the process of governance. When social values like health, safety and beauty become social benefits under cost–benefit analysis, they come to be commodities. They are subsumed by the logic of the marketplace, which defines things in terms of what people will buy and sell them for rather than in terms of their intrinsic worth and meaning. Additionally, it forces us to equate aspects of our lives that we care about to conventional economic goods. Thus, the application of cost–benefit analysis changes the outcome of a regulatory decision because it forces the conceptual transformation of social values into commodities.

Further, cost–benefit analysis can easily put citizens at a disadvantage. We trade easily in the language of values, but not so easily the economic language of cost–benefit analysis. Many citizens and their organisations are concerned with issues that are not part of the market, and they expect that their demands for things like health protection or environmental safety will be considered as important as, or in some cases more important than, their costs to businesses or taxpayers. This does not mean that such citizens are profligate, for they expect government to search for the most reasonable and effective way to correct problems. Concerns for non-Market values and efficient government are not incompatible. Even radical critics of cost–benefit analysis acknowledge its use in evaluating public gains and losses in government spending (Campen 1986).[3]

Yet making cost–benefit analysis the *sole* test for public action places the Market above and beyond politics, a self-evident and natural truth that is no longer a legitimate topic of political debate. This sanctification of the Market in regulatory practice has meant, moreover, that government is hindered in its ability to constrain the Market through regulation of its technologies and industries.

The implementation of cost–benefit analysis has not weakened democratic government only by restricting the terms and values that underlie policy. In addition, it has led to a restriction of citizen participation in regulatory decisions. Participation rights had been strengthened during the era of social regulation as citizens sought standing in the courts, access to information and enforcement of environmental impact statements on public projects. These rights were laid out originally in the Administrative Procedure Act of 1946 and strengthened by the Freedom of Information Act, the Government in the Sunshine Act and the Federal Advisory Committee Act. These laws ensure that citizens have access to the same information that government analysts use when considering regulations, that government meetings are open to the public, and that the professional, scientific and citizen advisory groups that aid in regulatory planning and review are equitably selected and operate in the open. In addition to these general acts, specific laws provide extra public access to information in specific circumstances, allowing organised groups to press for new regulatory initiatives where government has neglected to act.

Access to information and the ability to participate in policy formulation were undercut by the implementation of cost–benefit analysis. The Administrative Procedure Act established a formal process that ensures that impending rules are published in the Federal Register, that adequate time is available for public comment, that agencies respond to comments and that the final rules take account of the public input. The informal rule-making process, however, is just as important for citizens. Long before the preliminary publication of a proposed regulation in the Federal

Register, an agency conducts research and begins to identify potential problems such as workplace hazards, environmental pollution or drug safety. Laws such as the Freedom of Information Act and Advisory Committee Act enable interested individuals and organisations to monitor the informal process, probably the most critical phase in rule-making. Citizen groups have an interest in how a possible area of regulation is initially identified and subsequently defined, as does the industry that is to be affected. Theoretically, it is the responsibility of agency scientists and professionals to consider the data, the interests of numerous parties and the demands of the law in writing a new regulation. Citizen rights in this informal process are embedded in two expectations: that market factors are only one among many considerations for regulatory strategies, and that civil servants are independent of political and commercial influence. These expectations are reinforced by professional codes of conduct and by civil service regulations.

With the growing power of the OMB and the use of cost–benefit analysis, however, citizen rights of access, information and participation were weakened. For instance, established policy had been that all written comments and documentation of the regulatory process were open to the public after the proposed regulation was first published in the Federal Register. Moreover, White House comments on proposed rules had been filed during the normal comment period by the Council on Wage and Price Stability. Under Reagan's Executive Order 12,291, however, discussions between the OMB and the pertinent regulatory agency were never public, and often they were not written down, even though these negotiations frequently lead to substantial changes in the proposed regulations. These discussions are important also because they can act as a channel for the expression of commercial interests to the regulatory agency – an expression that can now remain secret not only because discussions between the OMB and regulatory agencies are secret but also because informal communication between the OMB and commercial organisations is not required to be a matter of public record (Morrison 1986: 1067; Rosenberg 1981).

Furthermore, under the Executive Order the agencies submit their regulatory analyses *before* the proposed regulation is first published. These types of changes made it very difficult for citizens to determine which parties influenced the consideration of new regulations. Finally, reviews of draft rules by the OMB have delayed the issuing of final rules considerably. By requiring a regulatory analysis before the publication of the proposed regulation, the OMB could delay the notice with a long period of questions and answers. By requiring the final regulatory analysis 30 days before the final rule was issued, the OMB could delay the final implementation by months. It is true that Executive Order 12,291 requires the OMB to respond to a draft rule within sixty days. However, it appears that the OMB frequently violated this rule. In 1985 the average response to rules from the Environmental Protection Agency was 75 days, and from the Occupational Safety and Health Administration it was 173 days (Heimann *et al.* 1990: 599 *n* 353).

Conclusions

As these instances show, the implementation of cost–benefit analysis through an OMB with expanded power has weakened the procedural guarantees afforded citizens by existing legislation. At its most basic, it supplants procedures based on open government and accountability with those based upon Market logic. Democracy suffers as the scope of decision-making narrows to an agenda that easily satisfies economic standards of value.

From the point of view of the anarcho-capitalists (discussed in Brown, this volume, Chap. 2), this trend toward government based on the Market model is positive. Essentially, the strict application of monetised principles to government actions reduces regulatory constraints upon the Market. Through the reduction of social values to economic terms in public decisions, an 'anti-state state' begins to emerge. Contradictory as this may sound, the anti-state state is increasingly possible as the Market model intrudes upon the democratic practice of tolerating widely different, non-Market definitions of value in the public sphere, and hence corrodes the ideal of collectivity embodied in the democratic state.

On the other hand, most academic political analysts are ambivalent about the intrusion of the Market model into the public sphere. They do not worry about the use of cost–benefit analysis as such, which they see as one of a number of tools that are useful in formulating policy. Instead, they lament the politicisation of science and regulation that cost–benefit analysis and OMB practices have brought to environmental, health and safety policy (Eads and Fix 1984; Salamon 1981). From their point of view, the problem is not the Market model, but it is its application by a politicised agency, the OMB. They worry about undue influence of special interests under the guise of Presidential power through the OMB.

In fact, just the opposite is happening. From the citizen's point of view, this decision strategy has *depoliticised* regulation. Fixed standards of how to value health and the environment are derived from the Market, and as they are implemented they remove the most important aspects of regulatory policy from political debate. Participation in regulatory decisions becomes the domain of the experts who can most easily manipulate the language and economics of cost–benefit analysis. In this way, the authority of the Market comes to supersede that of the citizenry. Democratic influence is increasingly barred from two of the most important sources of power that affect American life: technology and the global corporation.

As the 104th Congress comes to a close in 1996, the Contract with America flounders. The likelihood of new laws that require all regulatory decisions to meet cost–benefit tests, thus extending the Reagan Executive Order, is small. But the ease with which these laws passed the House with minimal opposition, swept past public review with limited hearings and national discussion, and came close to passage in the Senate with only a few modifications, speaks of the institutionalisation of Market values in US regulatory policy and practice. At the very end of the 104th Congress a cost–benefit mandate was added to the Safe Drinking Water Act Amendments of 1996. Virtually the only significant environment and health bill of the Congress, the amendments now require a cost–benefit analysis for each new drinking water regulation to determine whether the benefits justify the costs. The Environmental Protection Agency still has the authority to use the previous test of affordable technology to make a final decision on a standard, so the cost–benefit test is not to be the sole criterion. However, the Drinking Water Amendments represent the first step in the new approach to cost–benefit tests. Very probably, then, the debate in the next Congress will not be about *whether* to legislate cost–benefit analysis, but about *under what conditions* to do so.

Notes

1. It is worth noting here that, particularly in the case of automotive technology, civil damages awarded to victims of industry negligence have served to monetise 'pain and suffering', which is one of the most elusive costs borne by the injured and their families. It is interesting that these large awards are not based upon the types of calculations typical in administrative calculations of the costs of injuries. Rather, they are based upon a jury's definition of the consequences over time of damages and harm. Sometimes these awards are significantly higher than the calculations used in cost–benefit analysis for the same pain and suffering.
2. 'Major' traditionally meant regulations that would have an impact on the economy of over $100 million annually. The redefinition of major regulations to include costs of $50 million in recent proposed legislation has become a major issue.
3. James Campen (1986) makes the interesting argument that cost–benefit analysis is most useful to liberal, not conservative, politicians. Developed originally as a tool to legitimate cost-effective government action when markets fail to meet social needs, it is designed specifically to work when markets fail, and thus can be a tool of an expansionist state.

References

Bollier, David, and Joan Claybrook 1986. *Freedom from Harm: The Civilizing Influence of Health, Safety, and Environmental Regulations*. New York: The Democracy Project and Public Citizen.

Campen, James 1986. *Benefit, Cost, and Beyond: The Political Economy of Benefit–Cost Analysis*. Cambridge, Mass.: Ballinger Publishing Co.

Claybrook, Joan 1984. *Retreat from Safety*. Washington, DC: Public Citizen.

Eads, George, and Michael Fix 1984. *Relief or Reform: Reagan's Regulatory Dilemma*. Washington, DC: The Urban Institute Press.

Green, Mark, Norman Waitzman and Ralph Nader 1981. *Business War on the Law*. Washington, DC: The Corporate Accountability Research Group.

Heimann, Christopher, *et al.* 1990. Project: The Impact of Cost Benefit Analysis on Federal Administrative Law. *Administrative Law Review* 42: 547–654.

Jasanoff, Sheila 1990. *The Fifth Branch: Science Advisors as Policy Makers*. Cambridge, Mass.: Harvard University Press.

Kolko, Gabriel 1963. *The Triumph of Conservatism*. New York: The Free Press.

Lindbloom, Charles 1982. The Market as Prison. *Journal of Politics* 44: 324–336.

MacLennan, Carol 1988 *a*. From Accident to Crash: The Auto Industry and the Politics of Injury. *Medical Anthropology Quarterly* 2: 233–250.

MacLennan, Carol 1988 *b*. The Democratic Administration of Government. Pp. 49–78 in Marc Levine *et al.* (eds), *The State and Democracy: Revitalizing America's Government*. New York: Routledge.

Marshaw, Jerry, and David Harfst 1990. *The Struggle for Auto Safety.* Cambridge, Mass.: Harvard University Press.

Montague, Peter 1996. Shifting the Burden of Proof. *Rachel's Environment and Health Weekly* (491, 26 April). Electronic publication. Annapolis, Md: Environment Research Foundation.

Moore, John L. 1995. *Cost–Benefit Analysis: Issues in its Use in Regulation.* Report #95-760 ENR. June. Washington, DC: Congressional Research Service.

Morrison, Alan B. 1986. OMB Interference with Agency Rule-making: The Wrong Way to Write a Regulation. *Harvard Law Review* 99: 1059–1074.

Nader, Laura 1994. Controlling Processes. *Kroeber Anthropological Society Papers* 77 (special issue: *Controlling Processes*): 1–11.

Noble, Charles 1986. *Liberalism at Work: The Rise and Fall of OSHA.* Philadelphia: Temple University Press.

Rhoads, Stephen E. (ed.) 1980. *Valuing Life: Public Policy Dilemmas.* Boulder, Col.: Westview Press.

Rosenberg, Morton 1981. Presidential Control of Agency Rule-making under Executive Order 12,291. *Michigan Law Review* 80: 193–247.

Salamon, Lester M. 1981. Federal Regulation: A New Agenda for Presidential Power. Pp. 147–173 in Hugh Helco and Lester M. Salamon (eds), *The Illusion of Presidential Government*. Boulder, Col.: Westview Press and the National Academy of Public Administration.

Skowronek, Stephen 1982. *Building the New American State: The Expansion of National Administrative Capacities, 1877–1920*. New York: Cambridge University Press.

Tolchin, Susan 1984. Airbags and Regulatory Delay. *Issues in Science and Technology* 1 (1): 66–83.

Weinstein, James 1968. *The Corporate Ideal in the Liberal State, 1900–1918*. Boston: Beacon Press.

Chapter 6

Markets, Transaction Costs, Economists and Social Anthropologists

Malcolm Chapman and Peter J. Buckley

In 1937 Ronald Coase published a short article called 'The Nature of the Firm'. In it he asked a brilliantly obvious question that had not been asked before: 'Why do firms exist?' Why, that is, are some transactions organised through a market (buying and selling between organisations or between individuals), and others organised through a hierarchy (giving and taking orders, as in a company or university)? Why is it not feasible to have all transactions organised through a market? Or, conversely, why is the world not one big firm?

Imagine, as Coase suggested, a production process involving several stages. Say that we are making a widget, which requires a bolt and a sheet of metal to be fitted together. Three people are needed. One makes the bolt on a lathe. A second cuts out the metal sheet. A third joins the two together. That is our production process (never mind the iron mines, the steel-makers, the accountants, marketers and distributors). We expect to find this production process going on in a small metal-bashing company – call it MetalCo plc. But what is it about the process that requires the three people to work for the same company? Why could not worker 1 make his bolts on his own lathe (this is a male-dominated industry), and worker 2 cut up his own metal sheets, and both of them (independently) sell their production to worker 3, who would fasten them together and sell the finished product? All three would be independent economic units, coordinating their activities through a market. In the fully assumption-protected world of neo-classical economics there are conditions of perfect competition, perfect knowledge, frictionless transactions and rational behaviour, and under these conditions there is no reason why the three workers should not coordinate their production through a market. In the real world, however, such conditions do not hold. Neo-classical economics has various explanations why this so (market concentration and power, variable efficiency, ease of entry and exit); Coase added another set of 'market imperfections' to this list, which can be summed up in the phrase 'transaction costs'.[1]

Coase's work lay little noticed for several decades. It was rediscovered in the 1970s, and was rapidly grown into something called 'the new institutional economics'.[2] This has come to dominate the economic analysis of organisations, and an octo-genarian Coase received a belated Nobel prize for his work. Delacroix has recently argued that 'the conceptual rigour that transaction costs theorists bring to bear . . . is great enough . . . for contending schools of thought to appear on the verge of extinction' (Delacroix 1993: 106). The first works in the broadly Coasian tradition that were published in the 1970s became major works in themselves, and have been widely cited in subsequent discussion (see particularly Buckley and Casson 1976; Williamson 1975). In 1991 Oliver Williamson, perhaps the best-known of the transaction cost economists, made the yeasty claim that 'the 1990s is the decade when the new science of organization will come of age' (William-son 1991: 91, referring back to Williamson 1990). 'Organisation' can mean a great deal, extending into the most informal and temporary arrangements; the claim for a 'science of organisation' is not very far from being a claim to a unified social science, which will subsume social anthropology as well as all the other players (see also Williamson 1993: 455). We are dealing here with big works, and with big claims.

What are transaction costs? We can go back to our three workers to get some idea. Worker 3 needs reliable supplies of adequate quality at a decent price. He has to monitor workers 1 and 2, to make sure that their quality is right. He has to engage in price negotiations with them and needs to make sure that he is possessed of all the necessary information to stop them from cheating him by overcharging. He must worry that either of his suppliers (they are his sole suppliers, remember) will suddenly hold him to ransom – charge five times the normal rate, knowing that he has no other source of supply and (in the short term at least) no option but to pay the rate demanded. Similar (sometimes reciprocal) issues arise also for workers 1 and 2.

The costs of dealing with all these (and other) problems (costs of information search, of opportunistic betrayal, of monitoring performance, of negotiation, of managing relationships, of loss of proprietary knowledge) are 'transaction costs'. They do not enter explicitly into a company's balance sheet or profit and loss account, but they are nevertheless reckoned to amount to a considerable fraction of the costs of doing business – estimates as high as 40 per cent have been made (for reasoned estimates of this order, see Wallis and North 1986; Welch 1993).

The alternative to organising the work of our three workers through a market is to bring them together. Perhaps worker 3 forms a company, MetalCo plc, and takes the two others on as employees (or partners, or worker-shareholders, or whatever). They can now coordinate their activities through a 'hierarchy' rather than through a 'market' (the terms of this opposition have been popularised by Williamson 1975). If worker 3 is worried about the quality of work produced by worker 1, he can threaten him with dismissal or send him on a management training course. Worker 1 may dream of making more money by selling his output to another assembly organisation, but this option is contractually closed to him. There are no more price problems, either, apart from negotiations about wages. The three workers in MetalCo plc can start to *trust* one another, within their own particular institutional constraints, without worrying about abrupt changes (apart from dismissal or resignation). Moreover, they no longer need to spend large amounts of time (time = money) gathering necessarily inadequate data about one another. They are no longer troubled by some of the major issues arising from *bounded rationality* and *opportunism* (these terms are a central part of Williamson's influential analysis).[3]

The central argument of transaction cost theory is a simple one, which echoes a basic tenet of the Market model: organisations will choose whichever transaction costs are lower. If it is cheaper to make your own widgets than it is to buy them, then make them; and vice versa (assuming that production costs are equal in both cases). Everything that a company does is subject to considerations of this kind. Because transaction costs affect decisions about what a company should do for itself or acquire in a market, the boundary of any and every company is a specific solution, however *ad hoc* it may be, to transaction cost problems. The term 'internalisation' is often used by academics in this area: a company may at any time decide to 'internalise' within itself an activity that it previously acquired through a market. The term 'internalisation', although frequently used, only captures one half of the possibilities, in that any transaction cost theory of this kind is not only about 'internalisation', but also about 'externalisation'. Companies not only grow on transaction cost grounds; they also contract, transform themselves and experiment continually with their configurations. The financial pages of the newspapers are full of the news of acquisitions, mergers and divestments, with transaction cost issues behind them.

Some of the clearest and most intuitively appealing of transaction cost arguments arise in the activities of multinational corporations. Take the case of a company that has very valuable assets in knowledge, in technical expertise. It wishes to maximise its rents on these assets. One way to do this is through a market – to sell the knowledge for its full market rate (i.e., taking account of the net present value of all future income streams in all relevant markets arising from the exploitation of the knowledge). However, knowledge is difficult to price. The buyer does not know the value until the knowledge is revealed. However, once the knowledge is revealed the buyer no longer needs to pay, since he has the knowledge already. In these circumstances, sellers will not disclose sufficient to allow the knowledge to be properly priced, and buyers will not pay the full price, since they remain in doubt of its value. The market fails to price the assets at their true value. In these circumstances, the company wishing to operate in foreign markets is less likely to choose market-like solutions (licensing, for example), and more likely to choose to carry out the activity itself, and expand its own operations. This is perhaps the most robust of all explanations for the existence of multinational companies in knowledge-intensive industries (see Buckley and Casson 1976).

In the spirit of Williamson's grand claims for transaction cost economics, this chapter will raise some grand questions about it and about the set of assumptions on which it rests. These questions spring ultimately from the assertion by its advocates that transaction cost economics is an objective and predictive science of human behaviour. This assertion sits uneasily next to some of the conclusions that social anthropologists have reached about the dangers inherent in any effort to pursue such a science. While this chapter confronts anthropology with economics, the points that emerge apply as well to the Market model that is the theme of this collection. This is because transaction cost economics reflects that model's assumptions about market actors rationally pursuing the lowest cost, which is to say, their own best material advantage. As will become apparent, costs are tricky things, no less so for firms in transaction cost analysis than for actors in the Market model.

Some Problems with Transaction Cost Economics

There are plenty of problems with the transaction cost approach, and we can discuss only some of these (very briefly).[4] Before doing so, however, it is important to stress again that, although the theory faces problems, it is also extremely powerful. It has become perhaps the major orthodoxy in the minds of those who discuss 'organisations', a general term that includes most of the institutions in which people are involved in the modern world. It is, moreover, only a rather thoughtless academic-institutional bias that confines transaction cost economists to the 'modern' world. There is no real reason, as far as can be seen, why they should not take their analyses into the kinds of societies and institutions that anthropologists have traditionally studied, and colonise the entire range of human 'organisations' or 'corporations', as the term was used by the anthropologist M. G. Smith (1974).

In academic economics, from which transaction cost thinking has emerged, it is most criticised for being strong on theory but weak on empirical verification. To put this in another way, it has generated some strong ideas with large explanatory power, but any theory deriving from these has been difficult to prove empirically, in the hypothetico-deductive manner that prevails in this domain. Williamson concedes this criticism (1993: 456 *n* 25), while noting that empirical work in the area is growing fast. Scepticism about such empirical work has been voiced by various authors (see Buckley and Chapman 1995).

There is also ambiguity within the theory about whether it is predictive (allowing economists to predict what will happen) and prescriptive (telling managers what they should do next), or whether it is a *post hoc* means of understanding past and existing states of affairs. This ambiguity is a characteristic of neo-classical economics in general, although it is perhaps particularly noticeable in the transaction cost area. Most commentators (implicitly or explicitly) treat the theory as if it were predictive and prescriptive. There are good reasons for being sceptical of this, however, and any attitude towards the theory must depend crucially upon this issue. It is unclear at the moment how the matter will settle, and there is reason to be deeply sceptical of the grander claims.

The decisions that a company makes concerning its configuration are, within transaction cost analysis, conceived as a choice between 'firm' (or 'hierarchy') and 'market'. The two are considered to be polar opposites. A further criticism of the typical transaction cost analysis arises from this. Richardson (1972) pointed out some time ago that most business transactions take place in a space which is, in its characteristics, somewhere between the two formal extremes of market and firm (see also the discussion of Dore and Granovetter in the Introduction to this volume). The extremes are not the only possibilities, with an existential waste-land between them; on the contrary, they are the theoretical extremes of a continuum, where most of reality lies somewhere towards the middle, either more or less market-like or firm-like, but almost always with elements of both. The market is conceived as the domain of selfish optimisation, of rationality, of antagonism, of arm's-length dealing; the firm is conceived as the domain of cooperation and trust.

In reality, as Richardson (1972) notes (implicitly chiding economists for not caring quite enough about reality), most inter-firm relationships, which might be expected to display market characteristics, have about them aspects of relationship, trust, consideration, friendship, loyalty, commitment and so on. That is the empirical situation, and it complicates transaction cost analyses to perhaps an impossible degree. Transaction cost analysis typically proceeds by making simplifying assumptions, and one of these is that a clear conceptual distinction can be made between market and hierarchy (or between market and organisation, or whatever opposition is locally appropriate). If the terms of this opposition are hopelessly muddled, then sorting out the transaction cost issues begins to look very much more difficult. That is not to say that such issues are absent, but rather that any determinate, predictive or prescriptive analysis begins to look very unlikely. A production manager contemplating a change of supplier might also be contemplating a change of golfing partner (just to keep to simple possibilities). What is transaction cost economics going to do with that?

The point to draw from Richardson is a simple one, but important. The context in which people make decisions is so muddled that the basic assumptions that transaction cost economics has to make if it is to be a predictive science may be unjustified and even unjustifiable. And if this is true for transaction cost economics, it may also be true for the neo-classical economics on which it is based. To justify this point, it is necessary to consider the scientific claims associated with transaction cost economics.

Transaction Cost Economics and Social Anthropology

Williamson considers that a 'science of organisations' is in the making. Put very bluntly, his programme derives from Herbert Simon's work of the 1940s (see Simon 1957 *a*), given rigour from the ideas of Coase (1937). He puts his own work, in terms of its stage of development and its aspirations to formalisation, in parallel with the work of Gary S. Becker (1976), whose emphasis is on optimisation. He also puts it alongside what he calls the 'rational choice' approach to sociology, and cites here, as fellow-travellers, James Coleman (1990), Siegwart Lindenberg (1990) and Michael Hechter (1987). He also cites parallel and cognate works in law and politics (see Williamson 1993: 454–455). The agenda is a full one, and at the end there is, at least in potential, not very much left uncolonised. Social anthropologists might feel that they had an interest here, if only in self-defence. English scholars are also working to something like the same agenda. The economist Mark Casson (1991) has recently produced a book called *The Economics of Business Culture*, in which he takes transaction cost and game-theory arguments well into territory that social anthropologists might feel was their own.

It is no accident, either, that the branch of anthropology that most appeals to Williamson and to Casson, and to which both have referred (Casson pers. comm.; Williamson 1993: 459), is the sociobiology deriving from neo-Darwinian arguments, as popularised by Richard Dawkins (1976). There is a clear affinity between the selfishness of the gene and the rational optimisation of neo-classical economics, although it is arguable whether this affinity between the two fields is anything more than a vague metaphor. Dawkins and some of his followers are making attempts to move their arguments beyond biogenetics into the understanding of human institutions, and this approach seems generally to be welcomed by economists of an optimising and game-theoretic bent.

It seems possible that the first anthropological response to these economic arguments will be a sort of weary *déjà vu*. The meeting of social anthropology and economics has been exhaustively discussed, after all, within the context of the formalist–substantivist debate of a previous generation. Most of the criticisms of formal economics that were made within the course of this debate, particularly by one of its originators, Karl Polanyi, still stand. We could re-publish one of Polanyi's essays critical of the individualistic rationality that formalists presuppose, and feel that it was still entirely relevant (and better written than we could manage). Nothing much has moved. As far as memory serves, the protagonists in this debate did not stop because the issues had been resolved one way or the other. Rather, the academic public got bored with the same old disagreements, and the two subjects, economics and social anthropology, drifted back into their own academic and institutional enclaves. For a time, indeed (certainly for our generation, doing a first degree in England in the early 1970s), the entire economics debate within anthropology came to seem rather old-fashioned, replaced as it was by concerns with structuralism, symbolism, classification, meaning and the like. There is, presumably, a generation of social anthropologists for whom the formalist–substantivist debate is part of the archaeology of the subject (to be kept on the shelf next to Morgan and Maine) rather than a living feature. This makes it possible, of course, that the debate will be fashionably rediscovered. (Perhaps as a result of this volume?)

In any event, the major changes within post-war anthropology make it little disposed, in general, to pay attention to the kind of economic arguments discussed above. We have said that Williamson's endeavour of the 1990s is the linear development of a scientific ambition (the scientific study of organisations) that was first expressed in the 1940s by Simon. This is still the land, if you like, of unreconstructed positivist modernism.

British social anthropology had its own modernist and scientific ambitions. Radcliffe-Brown (1968 [1952]) and Malinowski (1944) both, in their different ways, imagined that they were constructing a 'science of society' from within social anthropology. It is perhaps worth noting that for Radcliffe-Brown and Malinowski, these statements of intent, although they were roughly contemporary with that of Simon in the field of organisation studies, were made towards the end of their academic lives and quickly came to seem outdated. Simon's statement came near the start of his academic work, and is best seen as part of the great wave of social-scientific positivism which occurred in the United States in the immediate post-war period. In subject after subject (and the management disciplines are exemplary here), new scientific programmes were announced.

British social anthropology (and to a degree American), although influenced by this post-war enthusiasm for scientific formalisation, was not within it. On the contrary, the scientific ambitions of Radcliffe-Brown foundered when rigorously confronted with the problem of whose category-definitions should be privileged, those of the observer or those of the observed: a series of intellectual assaults on the scientific ambition of social anthropology began in the 1960s, and still in some ways continue (Ardener 1989 *b*: Chap. 1; Leach 1961; Needham 1962). These assaults appear to apply to the scientific ambitions of transaction cost economics.

Simon began the chase for science in 1945, and speculated that within a couple of decades his work would seem out of date (Simon 1957 *a*: ix). It does not, however, and the trajectory that he sighted is still being followed, by Williamson and others. The programmatic statements made by Radcliffe-Brown and Malinowski now appear, by contrast, either outmoded or eccentric. British social anthropology moved (as one formulation has it) from 'function' to 'meaning' in the 1960s and 1970s (Ardener 1989 *b*: Chap. 1; Pocock 1961). This, in local understanding, put it intellectually in advance of those subjects that had not made this break.

Some suggestion that this was a correct perception can be found in the slow spread of similar ideas into adjoining subjects. Gibson Burrell and Gareth Morgan (1979) a decade or so later argued the case for a similar shift in paradigms in organisation studies (see also Czarniawska-Joerges 1992). Donald McCloskey (1986, 1990) has done a beautiful, if still rather isolated, job from within economics itself. Nak Boyacigiller and Nancy J. Adler (1991) have made a belated programmatic statement relevant to the entirety of management studies. There is an abundance of other examples. Some of the arguments have been first experienced, in subjects unfamiliar with them, as 'post-modernism', with all the attendant confusions, and the breathless rediscovery and bowdlerisation of long-established anthropological positions. This is not the place for a discussion of post-modernity, but it is important to urge (does it need urging among social anthropologists?) that one of the main arguments arising from post-modernity – the incantatory 'separation of the signifier from the signified' – is either an anthropological commonplace, or a serious misunderstanding of Saussure.[5] In either case, the issue is an important one for social anthropology, when it steps into interdisciplinary argument in the way this chapter does.

One might readily conclude from all this, at least from within social anthropology, that transaction cost economics in the 1990s – scientific, rationalist, positivist, aspiring to determinate explanations, imposing observer categories, measuring and predicting, following an agenda written in the 1940s – was simply a hopelessly outmoded form of discourse, against which all the necessary arguments had already been made. The great army of workers in the field, however, in economics, transaction cost economics, game theory, rational-choice sociology (not to mention positivist sociology and behavioural social psychology), do not seem to have noticed that the rug has been pulled from under them. If anthropologists are kings of the castle, it is a castle most other people have never heard of. Perhaps you need to spend some time entirely outside social anthropology in order to be convinced of the truth of this.

The Management of Cooperative Strategies

To consider the adequacy of neo-classical economists' scientific programme, it is worth discussing a research project we are undertaking. This project is especially useful for seeing what happens to transaction cost theory when research into transaction cost issues incorporates anthropological ideas and sentiments.

We have spent two and a half years carrying out a research project in which a great deal of information relevant to these issues has been gathered. The project has involved study of a small number of companies in pharmaceuticals and scientific instruments. The project was designed in the first place by Peter Buckley, the economist, and some of its terms of reference are evidence of this. Companies have been studied longitudinally over the duration of the project: in the academic context of business economics, this means that they have been studied over time. Anthropologists would hardly be surprised by this, but it is a fact that most studies in the area have been synchronic, based on interviews or questionnaires conducted only once, over a sample whose size is often dictated by the requirements of statistical analysis software, particularly SPSS.

The original plan was to conduct repeated structured interviews, with a fairly determinate research agenda and more or less closed questions. At Malcolm Chapman's suggestion, we moved instead to repeated in-depth unstructured interviews with managers. This has allowed the development of the conversations, reflections, asides and confidences that anthropologists expect from their work, but that have, in their richness and relevance, surprised the economist in the research team. Although the interviews have been unstructured, attention has been directed nevertheless to corporate management of the relationship with entities at the boundaries of the company (and so implicitly to the question of the internalisation and externalisation of activities). The interviews allow us to track decisions through their life: through the period of gestation, through the decisions themselves, through retrospective consideration. This is not anthropological fieldwork, but in the academic context it is a significant move in that direction. Furthermore, the period of research has been one of upheaval in the pharmaceutical industry, with various powerful contrary trends at work. There has been a great deal of opportunity to observe managers in the process of coping with transaction cost issues, as the corporate configurations around them underwent, or threatened to undergo, radical change.

We have seen that transaction cost economics purports to provide a determinant, predictive theory to explain choices between market and hierarchy. It purports to be a *science* that explains these choices in terms of a calculus of costs of different alternatives. Moreover, for it to be a science these costs have to be determinable and even numerical. Were they not, were the costs matters of interpretation and judgement to be argued over and debated by the actors involved, then the analyst-oriented model of transaction cost economics would have to yield at least some ground to an actor-oriented approach.

In our research we have come across no case whatsoever in which managers involved in decisions had access to, or had personally generated for their own purposes, anything like a numerically-justified assessment of transaction cost issues. This is not to say that the managers involved were making ill-considered or unjustified decisions. Far from it; they were prepared to engage in long and thoughtful justifications of their activities and decisions. They always considered that they had valuable insight into the industry around them, which informed their decisions in a positive manner. They were, almost without exception, unaware of the existence of the theoretical discourse of transaction cost economics, but they were necessarily engaged in decisions where transaction cost issues were paramount, and their discussions of these issues were often sophisticated. In terms of a distinction raised in the Introduction to the volume, they were clearly being reasonable, but in no case were they being rational, because enumeration was never brought to the issues.

Costs and prices were, of course, often discussed in numerical terms, but not transaction costs. What was enumerated was the familiar elements of business economics: cost of goods in, price of goods out, costs of production, overheads, cost of capital, opportunity costs within the company, and the like. A manager, for example, discussing the issue of whether to make or buy a component, in a situation where both were possible options, would discuss the relative costs of in-house production versus the external price. This is the classic 'make or buy' decision, and it seems on the face of it that we could get easy access to reliable comparative figures. Even here, however, the enumeration was less straightforward than it might appear. Although managerial discourse of comparison was often numerical and arithmetic, there was often ambiguity. Companies and managers varied very much in the zeal and conscientiousness of their attempts to put comparative figures to their own production costs and to the alternative costs of buying-in. Some flew their buses entirely by feel (thereby avoiding the very real costs of search and calculation). Some went into exhaustive detail, attempting to wring the truth out of the figures, and taking real intellectual pleasure in doing so.

We are referring here, remember, to the more obviously 'objective' of costs in industry, not to transaction costs as such (if indeed there is an 'as such'). Several interesting features emerged that raise questions about a model that presupposes an objective numerical calculus.

To begin with, attempts at calculation and cost-comparison often turned out to have a rather interesting history that does not really accord with the ever-optimising manager of transaction cost economics. It has often been observed that companies, or the management of companies, tend to leave things alone if everything seems to be going well. This is really opting for a quiet life, rather than rational optimising. However, as long as the company turns a decent profit economists can pretend that something approximating to rational optimising is going on. It is often only when threat appears that management starts to react (and sometimes this is too late: the literature of strategic management is full of dire threats concerning what will happen to companies that are 'reactive', not 'proactive'). Certainly, in most of the cases that we explored, some upheaval or threat often provoked the first attempt at documentation or a renewed and more determined assault upon an old problem: perhaps a new manager came in, anxious to do better than the old one, or the company started running at a loss, or technical changes that could not be ignored began to intrude into established ways of doing things.

Moreover, once the attempt at calculation began, various things could happen. Sometimes, one pass over the figures was considered enough. This was particularly true where the figures confirmed what management wanted to hear. One managing director who used outside consultancy reports said: 'If they don't say what we want, we simply commission another report.' Sometimes, however, the calculations were done and redone internally, with various political and technical interventions. One odyssey of invention showed the complexities of such a process. It began as an attempt to justify an expenditure on a new manufacturing investment. This went through several revisions, with various new considerations taken into account at each stage, and with strikingly different results revealed. Then the calculations got sucked into a debate about whether head office was treating the branch fairly, whether corporate overheads were being properly distributed, whether ideologues in head office were deaf to rational debate and so on.

The subject of costing is very complex, and as investigators we were frankly not always able to appreciate the subtleties that one or another manager would bring to the problem. It was clear, however, that by the time the process reached a conclusion any notion of simple and unambiguous measurement had been left far behind. And what was the nature of the conclusion? Something had to be done, a decision had to be made, at some stage. There was no evident guarantee, however, that the process of revision had reached a final or optimal conclusion. On the contrary, all the evidence suggested that if the subject were revisited, new issues and perspectives would arise. We, as well as the managers, also faced the problem that technical innovations in the analysis of costs were continually floating across the corporate psyche, blown by waves of fashion in management consultancies and business schools. Even without all the internal complexities, there was no right way to do things. (See the discussion of pension fund managers in the Introduction to this volume.) Even in relation to strictly internal costs, then, there was never any assurance that unambiguous figures existed, and hence never any assurance that objective, numerical rationality could be applied to the problem.

In relation to external costs, the prices offered by suppliers were often unambiguous enough, but here we rapidly entered the realm of transaction costs. Company B might well be able to supply a component cheaper than Company A could make it for itself, but concerned managers in Company A worried about reliability of supply, more particularly because the component was crucial to their products and could not be easily acquired elsewhere. There were functional differences in attitude here that find no ready place in the transaction cost model. Production managers, who were the ones that got shouted out if production was halted, were typically more concerned about security of supply than financial managers, who saw a cost saving without its associated transaction costs. In comparing internal and external costs of performing the same activity, then, there were some exceedingly complex social and rhetorical activities and judgements being made. These seem amenable to an interpretative approach based on actors' per-spectives, while the formal simplicity of the 'make or buy' decision, to be decided on comparison of internal costs and external prices, appears to be of only very limited analytical use.

The value of an interpretative approach is apparent in two companies that we studied, where production managers created quite explicit propaganda statistics designed to ensure that production continued in their units. They were from engineering and technical backgrounds – they liked machines and they liked making things. On both cost and transaction cost grounds, there was no reason for them to continue to produce their own supplies, and on corporate strategic grounds the environment was turning against them. The margins of error and ignorance about costs and control, however, made it possible for them to make the case that they wanted in such a way that their views could not be formally challenged.

Similarly, we found that companies had a moral life in the imaginations of those that worked within them that was in many respects independent of cost considerations. Some major and unresolved debates about how shareholder value is generated start to intrude at this stage. For a long time, companies grew and incorporated new activities, often without serious consideration and rarely with any thought of giving up old activities as new ones were taken on. Only within the last ten years has it become possible to think that a company might best deliver value by effectively destroying itself through de-merger. ICI's struggle to bring itself to this point marked a major change in corporate attitudes to this problem. After all, many companies had grown into their great range of activities through high-tech consultancy talk about synergies, and growth of virtually any kind had been perceived to be a virtue. The idea that making a company *smaller* might be a good thing, or that making several small companies out of one big one might be better for shareholders, was a radical about-face, and many polysyllabic words had to be eaten. The difficulty that major corporations have found, in bringing themselves to confront this problem, is a demonstration of the seemingly non-rational attachment that managers come to have for their companies.

It is perhaps no idle metaphor to say that companies have identities, just as do clans or countries. They are part of actors' classifications of the universe. As such, they partake of the qualities of classification in general. Managers invest moral virtue in the integrity of the classification with which they are familiar. Threats to it, and anomalies within it, generate sentiments straight out of *Purity and Danger* (Douglas 1966). In various cases that we studied, it was quite easy to see that, on transaction cost grounds, the company had no particular reason for existing. There was almost no spontaneous managerial realisation of this, however, and on the rare occasions when we tried to suggest it, we evoked either suspicion or lack of comprehension. The *survival* of the company, as a definitional unit within more or less its current boundaries, was always considered important, and this survival attracted far more understanding and knowledge than any cost issues, particularly transaction cost issues, that might lie behind survival.

Profit was always understood to be a *sine qua non* of corporate survival, but scarcely anybody we interviewed was prepared to pursue profit at the *cost* of corporate survival. In this context, issues of cost clearly come secondary to what an anthropologist might like to think of as symbolic features. This needs further consideration, and there is not much literature to help, in spite of the fact that much attention is devoted in managerial literature to analysing corporations. In the context of symbolic anthropology, however, it may be that the company is an irreducible feature of the modern world, not readily comparable with anything else but itself.

Even in areas where costs might be expected to be explicit and unambiguous, we found that there were many complicating features. These difficulties did not stop managers generating figures. Some of them were real number-junkies, who lived lives in which the tight specification of products and the tight monitoring of production quality were cardinal virtues. Nevertheless, the clarity of comparison that simple economic optimising requires was often only dimly perceptible.

We have looked at classic 'costs', and found that even here numbers were motivated and wound around with other factors. When we move more specifically into the realm of transaction costs, further complications arise. Two such complications, not commonly acknowledged in the transaction cost literature, might particularly be noted. Firstly, production costs and transaction costs are often difficult to separate, both empirically and theoretically. Secondly, transaction costs are heterogeneous and contradictory; by attempting to minimise one transaction cost (say, the cost of information search) you may increase another (say, the cost of opportunistic betrayal).

In relation to the difficulty of separating production and transaction costs, we might note that managers frequently discussed problems in their relationships with other companies. For many of them, this was a subject that set them talking for as long as we had energy to listen and take notes. Many of the issues that they raised concerned what an economist would call 'transaction costs'. These were issues like reliability of supply, trust, control, motivation and the like. These were never discussed in the numerical terms necessary for computationally rational decisions, but were subject to a parallel discourse, one whose terms were verbal rather than numerical and that was suited to reasonable decisions. The mechanisms of decision were construed in terms of things like 'judgement', 'gut-feeling', 'intuition', 'experience', 'knowledge'. This has proved true for a wide range of transaction cost problems. Managers, if offered the idea that there might exist an *objective* answer to the problems they faced, typically laughed. 'Everybody knows the world is not like that!', or words to that effect, was a common riposte. Even in discussion of a simple 'make or buy' decision, the comparison of numbers (internal costs and external prices) was accompanied by a kind of counterpoint of words and judgements.

In many cases, decisions were made primarily on judgemental grounds, as verbally expressed, without any attempt at invoking numerical or mathematical arguments. In others, the mathematical comparisons were outlined, but the reliability or relevance of the numbers was determined by other means: 'They're the cheapest, sure, but how do we know they'll still be producing in six months' time?', 'I can't deal with them, I don't know why; it's just something about the set-up', 'Some of these guys are cowboys, with a production outfit in the garage; all right for some things, but not when it matters', and so on. We have found no case where a decision was made on mathematical or computational grounds alone, without the intervention of complex judgements of the kind suggested. There are many cases, by contrast, where numbers were virtually ignored, overridden by questions of trust, loyalty, familiarity and the like.

This, although not altogether surprising, has some major implications for our outlook upon research in these areas. We need to go back again to the ambitions of transaction cost economics, and of economics in general. It is well known that economics, as a discipline, has made 'rationality' into a central assumption. The central idea of micro-economics is a perfect market (whose characteristics can be detailed) within which buyers and sellers (people) have perfect knowledge and behave with total rationality. Reality is approached as a set of deviations from this analytically simple state. It is also well known that this assumption of rationality is the feature that most offends non-economists. 'How can your analyses be useful', they ask the economists, 'when we know that most of the time people behave irrationally, and not rationally as your theory supposes?' ('Got you there', they think.) Economists have met these criticisms by combining the core assumption of individual optimisation with 'various sets of specific assumptions adapted to different fields of application' (Buckley and Chapman 1993: 1035). This enables economists to meet challenges from outsiders and the 'sheer diversity of the specific assumptions that can be accommodated gives the theory enormous "survival value" ' (1993: 1037).

In the perfect market of the neo-classical economist's imagination, economic analysis can not be faulted. Where reality approximates to this perfect market, then economic analysis has great power. Various aspects of reality have been accommodated to economic analysis as 'market imperfections' or 'market distortions' (see the discussion of these in the Introduction to this volume). Transaction cost analysis represents another step in this direction. A non-economist might well feel that representing reality as a distortion of a non-existent and purely hypothetical perfection was logically absurd; but one can scarcely deny the power of much economic analysis conducted from this point of view.

Within neo-classical economics, the firm tended to be treated as a 'black box', with inputs and outputs, represented by a graph called a 'production function'. The new institutional economics has transformed this, and made the internal structure of the firm, the 'structure of governance', also an issue that economics can approach. At the same time, it aspires to render theoretically accessible not just the choice between markets and hierarchies, but also the empirical jumble that lies between: alliances, joint ventures, long-term relationships, trusting partnerships, friendships, informal patterns of reciprocal obligation and so on. It is trespassing further and further, that is, into areas that anthropology might consider its own. There is very little that might be called 'the anthropology of the firm'; but if there were, it would be feeling seriously challenged by transaction cost economics.

Perhaps we could put the problem like this: Transaction cost economics is emerging out of traditional areas of economic analysis, with a powerful mensurational, calculative and scientific theory, and attacking areas that anthropologists would not consider to be amenable to such methods. Most anthropologists might be able to ignore this, and carry on as normal. (Those working jointly within both frameworks, however, can not.) Anthropologists, on the basis of their own arguments in the 1960s and 1970s, have disallowed in many of their domains the sort of positivist analysis used in neo-classical economics. With the appearance of transaction cost economics, the arguments against positivism seem to need rehearsing once again.

Various areas of contention seem potentially profitable. Though presented separately, these all revolve around the difference between an analyst-centred scientific approach and an actor-centred interpretative approach.

Firstly, the general question of empirical material arises. Transaction cost economics has tended to be long on theory and short on empirical verification. There is scope for a contribution here, and it is just such a contribution that we have been trying to make in the research project referred to above. In a world of optimisation and calculativeness, we need to know what it is that people are optimising, and how they are calculating it.[6] This leads on, however, to the more profound issue of category definition: who defines the categories of optimisation and calculation, the observer or the observed? Social anthropology has made a conspicuous and successful virtue of looking at categories and classifications from the point of view of those living within them. Economics in most of its guises, by contrast, imposes magisterial observer-defined categories upon the data (see, for example, the very different approaches taken to the idea of 'trust' in Davis 1992 and Williamson 1993). If anthropology was right in giving privilege to native definitions, then it seems likely that transaction cost economics will be interestingly vulnerable to arguments relating to this.

Secondly, an argument concerning mensuration arises. As we have described, our research thus far indicates that managers have little or no sense of the existence of an objective and measurable set of transaction costs to which they could refer in the course of their decisions. On the contrary, the transaction costs that are *really there*, in the sense that they determine the outcome, are those transaction costs *that are perceived by the managers who make the decisions*. Within economics, perception of reality has tended to be perceived as a marginal problem. Social anthropologists, by contrast, have long been content with the notion that *all* reality is, in important senses, perceived reality, that the world we live in is socially constructed and that the material is subordinate to the cognitive. In terms of our research project, 'real' transaction costs and 'perceived' transaction costs are the same thing, for the perceived costs are the ones that really shape actions. Social anthropologists have a handle on conceptual issues of this kind – something that is largely lacking in economics. 'Definition' and 'measurement' become, as Ardener (1989 *b*) noted, conceptually intertwined in the lived world-structures of the social actors themselves.

Thirdly, there are important issues arising from problems of prediction and foreknowledge. Transaction cost economics is ambiguous about whether it is a theory predicting futures and providing prescriptions for action, or is a theory offering some quite robust interpretations of things that have already occurred. While it is clear that some have made powerful claims for its predictive and prescriptive role, it is hard to see how it can be more than retrospective, even if powerfully so. McCloskey (1990), in relation to prediction within economics, has asked economists what he calls 'the American question': 'If you're so smart, why ain't you rich?'; if you know what future states of the world are going to be, why don't you bet on them? The same question could profitably be asked of transaction cost economists, and the answer would probably be rather feeble. If this is so (one would need more space to establish this), then the theoretical power of transaction cost economics, as opposed to an interpretative analysis, looks rather less striking. Anthropology, moreover, has provided some interesting work about interpretations of the past that appear to generate retrospective prophecy, and about prophetic situations (see, for example, Ardener 1989 *a*; Tonkin, McDonald and Chapman 1989). These, too, might start to look relevant.

Conclusions

Williamson, who is to blame for much of the above, has allowed arguments based upon *optimising* and *economising* to be extended from the arena of the *market* (transparent, arm's-length, contract-based) to the arena of the *hierarchy* (to, that is, intra- and inter-corporate activities). At least, that is the claim. It is not just markets that are market-like, in that people optimise their outcomes using rational decision-making processes; hierarchies are also market-like and calculative, although the calculus is slightly different.

Economists use ideas of rationality and optimisation. Their models, formally perfect, often define the real world as altogether out of bounds. Thus, we have seen above that information about real-world decisions is complex and heterogeneous, and certainly not amenable to computation in any normally accepted sense, which includes the sense contained in the notion of economic rationality and optimisation. One might be tempted, on the basis of this study of practical decision-making, to agree with Amitai Etzioni when he writes:

> Rather than arguing with, adapting, or modifying the rationalist model, we should heed a large body of social science evidence pointing to a radically different model of decision making. In this model, most choices are made on the basis of emotions (e.g. impulse) or values (e.g. taboos); they are not the product of deliberation. And when deliberation does occur, it is often far from extensive, let alone complete (Etzioni 1993: 1068).

While it is easy to sympathise with this perspective, it may not get us very far. Thoroughgoing economising, of the kind proposed by Williamson (1993), and earlier by Becker (1976), can optimise on sentiments derived from emotions, and on values derived from taboos. The tautology at the heart of the analysis remains undisturbed. Moreover, the opposition between 'rationality' and 'emotion' may not be a useful one. It does, however, have a uselessly seductive quality: many people think that they dislike markets, because markets are the realm of optimisation and calculation, which are respectively perceived as selfish and cold-hearted characteristics. Opposed to this 'market', are emotions, community, commitment and generosity – warm-blooded humanity.[7] The political utility of this metaphor is clear enough, even if the oppositions are rather flabby.

Our objections to transaction cost economics take a slightly different form. What interests us is its failure to come to determinate optimising analyses, empirically based, coupled with its ability to disguise that failure, and the institutional success that it has therefore enjoyed. This success is so great that Williamson can perceive transaction cost economics as a colonising move from the heartland of neo-classical economics. The strengths of economics, recognised in the analysis of markets, will now allow it to take over the analysis of human institutions of every degree of formality.

However, there is another way of interpreting the relationship between economics and those institutions. The discussion above showed that the data that transaction cost analysis would need if it were to approach the desired computational apotheosis are not available, and this is not because the data are difficult to get hold of, but because they do not exist and in any determinant form can not exist. Local perceptions, local structures of knowledge, specific understandings, native definitions of reality, linguistic and discursive construals of reality, world-structures – all these take the place, in empirical reality, of the idealised computation and mensuration of economic analysis. In contrast to Etzioni, they are not 'emotional'; they are often calculative and comparative. They are not, however, even in potential, open to determinate computation on the basis of any single theory. In the empirical domain of transaction costs, it appears that the computation that economically rational analysis requires is not possible. It is absolutely necessary, in this area, to take a broader and more interpretative view of a non-rational but clearly reasonable human practice than economists have traditionally done. In this sense, Etzioni's statement at least points in the right general direction. However, if an interpretative approach is established in transaction cost economics, then it will provide a basis for making the same arguments in neo-classical economics entire. Thus, while Williamson sees transaction cost economics as a bridge across which economists, with their big ideas, can march across into other subjects, social anthropologists may pass them, marching across the bridge in the opposite direction.

Notes

1. Adam Smith explained why workers should specialise, and different stages of the production process should be given to different individuals – he invoked economies of scale, of skill and learning, and the like. It is not surprising that our three workers should *specialise* in different parts of the production process, rather than each carrying out all three tasks. Specialisation is not the issue. There remains the possibility that the three workers could be specialised *and* independent. They need one another, but could satisfy their needs through a market, as we all do when we go out to buy our vegetables.
2. The 'old' institutional economics was based upon the work of John Commons in the 1920s, which did not survive the competition of other branches of economics, particularly Keynesian

and neo-classical forms (see Commons 1934; Kitch 1983).

3. 'Bounded rationality' is an idea introduced by Herbert Simon (see 1957 *b*, 1959, 1965), whose work has been influential in what is often called 'the behavioural theory of the firm'. A social anthropologist would find much to quarrel with in the idea of 'bounded rationality', and in the idea of a 'behavioural theory' of any kind. There is no space to pursue these issues here, but it is perhaps worth noting that there are probably about 183 times more people in world academia working within 'bounded rationality' and 'behavioural theory' structures than there are social anthropologists to quarrel with them.

4. The problem with transaction cost economics that is simplest to state springs from the fact that it is an elaboration of neo-classical economics. As such, it is potentially vulnerable to all the range of criticisms of neo-classical economics that have come from the Austrian school (Hayek 1949; Menger 1871; Mises 1935 [1920]; Schumpeter 1934; for a recent summary, see Kirzner 1992). Members of the Austrian school stress emergent patterns, partial knowledge, chance and discovery as central principles, rather than the complete knowledge and rationality and the perfect competition that lie at the heart of neo-classical economics. An Austrian school criticism of transaction cost economics in its dominant form might therefore be expected. There is no reason why an Austrian transaction cost economics should not appear, although it would be very different from Williamson's version.

5. For a *good* account of Saussure, see Ardener (1989 *b*: Chap. 1). For Derrida as the source of the misunderstanding of Saussure that lies at the centre of so much post-modern presentation, see the critical account in Ellis (1989).

6. One could argue that what people think does not matter, that regardless how they are reached some decisions are more optimal than others. This touches on a point made below. Here, however, it is important to remember that such an argument excludes the possibility that transaction cost economics can be normative and predictive of individual decisions, restricting it instead to the retrospective explanation of outcomes and the resulting commercial and economic structures.

7. This contrast between market and sentiment is a popular one (Carrier 1992; Schneider 1980), and even appears in academic economics (England 1993).

References

Ardener, Edwin 1989 *a*. Vestiges of Creation. Pp. 22–33 in Elizabeth Tonkin, Maryon McDonald and Malcolm Chapman (eds), *History and Ethnicity*. London: Routledge.

Ardener, Edwin 1989 *b*. *The Voice of Prophecy and Other Essays by E. W. Ardener*. Ed. Malcolm Chapman. Oxford: Blackwell.

Becker, Gary S. 1976. *The Economic Approach to Human Behavior*. Chicago: University of Chicago Press.

Boyacigiller, Nak, and Nancy A. Adler 1991. The Parochial Dinosaur: Organisational Science in a Global Context. *Academy of Management Review* 16: 262–290.

Buckley, Peter, and Mark Casson 1976. *The Future of the Multinational Enterprise*. London: Macmillan.

Buckley, Peter, and Malcolm Chapman 1993. Economics as an Imperialist Social Science. *Human Relations* 46: 1035–1052.

Buckley, Peter, and Malcolm Chapman 1995. The Perception and Measurement of Transaction Cost. Presented at the Academy of International Business annual conference, Seoul, Korea.

Burrell, Gibson, and Gareth Morgan 1979. *Sociological Paradigms and Organisational Analysis, Elements of the Sociology of Corporate Life*. London: Heinemann.

Carrier, James G. 1992. Occidentalism: The World Turned Upside-Down. *American Ethnologist* 19: 195–212.

Casson, Mark 1991. *The Economics of Business Culture*. Oxford: Clarendon.

Coase, Ronald 1937. The Nature of the Firm. *Economica* 4 (n.s.): 386–405.

Coleman, James 1990. *Foundations of Social Theory*. Cambridge, Mass.: Harvard University Press.

Commons, John 1934. *Institutional Economics: Its Place in Political Economy*. New York: Macmillan.

Czarniawska-Joerges, Barbara 1992. *Exploring Complex Organizations: A Cultural Perspective*. London: Sage.

Davis, John 1992. *Exchange*. Buckingham: Open University Press.

Dawkins, Richard 1976. *The Selfish Gene*. Oxford: Oxford University Press.

Delacroix, Jacques 1993. The European Subsidiaries of American Multinationals: An Exercise in Econological Analysis. Pp. 105–135 in Sumantra Ghoshal and D. Eleanor Westney (eds),

Organization Theory and the Multinational Corporation. London: Macmillan.

Douglas, Mary 1966. *Purity and Danger*. Harmondsworth: Penguin.

Ellis, John M. 1989. *Against Deconstruction*. Princeton: Princeton University Press.

England, Paula 1993. The Separative Self: Androcentric Bias in Neoclassical Assumptions. Pp. 37–53 in Marianne A. Ferber and Julie A. Nelson (eds), *Beyond Economic Man: Feminist Theory and Economics*. Chicago: University of Chicago Press.

Etzioni, Amitai 1993. Normative–Affective Choices. *Human Relations* 46: 1053–1069.

Hayek, Frederik 1949. *Individualism and Economic Order*. London: Routledge & Kegan Paul.

Hechter, Michael 1987. *Principles of Group Solidarity*. Berkeley: University of California Press.

Kirzner, Israel 1992. *The Meaning of Market Process*. London: Routledge.

Kitch, Edmund W. 1983. The Fire of Truth: A Remembrance of Law and Economics at Chicago, 1932–1970. *Journal of Law and Economics* 26: 163–234.

Leach, Edmund 1961. *Rethinking Anthropology*. London: Athlone Press.

Lindenberg, Siegwart 1990. Homo Socio-Oeconomicus: The Emergence of a General Model of Man in the Social Sciences. *Journal of Institutional and Theoretical Economics* 146: 727–748.

McCloskey, Donald 1986. *The Rhetoric of Economics*. Brighton: Wheatsheaf.

McCloskey, Donald 1990. *If You're so Smart*. Chicago: University of Chicago Press.

Malinowski, Bronislaw 1944. *A Scientific Theory of Culture and Other Essays*. Chapel Hill: University of North Carolina Press.

Menger, Carl 1871. *Grundsatze der Volkswirtschaftlehre*. Vienna: Braumuller. (Translated as *Principles of Economics*. New York: New York University Press, 1981.)

von Mises, Ludwig 1935 (1920). Economic Calculation in the Socialist Commonwealth. Pp. 87–130 in Frederik Hayek (ed.), *Collectivist Economic Planning*. London: Routledge & Kegan Paul.

Needham, Rodney 1962. *Structure and Sentiment*. Chicago: University of Chicago Press.

Pocock, David 1961. *Social Anthropology*. London: Sheed and Ward.

Radcliffe-Brown, A. R. 1968 (1952). *Structure and Function in Primitive Society*. Oxford: Oxford University Press.

Richardson, B. 1972. The Organization of Industry. *Economic Journal* 82: 883–896.

Schneider, David 1980. *American Kinship: A Cultural Account*. Second edition. Chicago: University of Chicago Press.

Schumpeter, Joseph 1934. *The Theory of Economic Development*. Cambridge, Mass.: Harvard University Press.

Simon, Herbert 1957 *a* (1945). *Administrative Behavior*. Second edition. New York: Macmillan.

Simon, Herbert 1957 *b*. *Models of Man*. New York: John Wiley.

Simon, Herbert 1959. Theories of Decision Making in Economics and Behavioral Science. *American Economic Review* 49: 253–283.

Simon, Herbert 1965. The New Science of Management Decision. Pp. 53–111 in *The Shape of Automation for Men and Management*. New York: Harper and Row.

Smith, M. G. 1974. *Corporations and Society*. London: Duckworth.

Tonkin, Elizabeth, Maryon McDonald and Malcolm Chapman (eds) 1989. *History and Ethnicity*. London: Routledge.

Wallis, John Joseph, and Douglass C. North 1986. Measuring the Transaction Sector in the American Economy 1870–1970. Pp. 95–161 in Stanley L. Engerman and Robert E. Gallman (eds), *Long Term Factors in American Economic Growth*. Chicago: University of Chicago Press.

Welch, Lawrence S. 1993. Outward Licensing by Australian Companies. Pp. 64–90 in Peter J. Buckley and Pervez N. Ghauri (eds), *The Internationalisation of the Firm*. London: Academic Press.

Williamson, Oliver E. 1975. *Markets and Hierarchies: Analysis and Antitrust Implications*. New York: Macmillan.

Williamson, Oliver E. 1990. Chester Barnard and the Incipient Science of Organization. Pp. 172–206 in O. E. Williamson (ed.), *Organization Theory: From Chester Barnard to the Present and Beyond*. New York: Oxford University Press.

Williamson, Oliver E. 1991. Strategizing, Economizing, and Economic Organization. *Strategic Management Journal* 12: 75–94.

Williamson, Oliver E. 1993. Calculativeness, Trust, and Economic Organization. *Journal of Law and Economics* 36: 453–486.

Afterword

William Roseberry

This book, which takes as its critical object a central concept and model of economic discourse, is written by anthropologists. Readers familiar with anthropological writing on economics and the market might have expected a rather different kind of book than the one they have just read. Most anthropologists writing on these issues have offered a preliminary, simple definition of 'the market' or 'the economy', and then turned to primitive or non-Western societies, where they found the definition inadequate for the processes and relations they wished to understand. Commonly they then move toward a consideration of economic processes in non-capitalist situations that seems to reject their original definition of the market while simultaneously accepting, even reaffirming, its basic assumptions. They accomplish this impressive feat with the use of oppositional models: market vs. non-market societies, Western vs. non-Western, commodity vs. gift exchange and so on. Behind this apparently critical facade, the basic categories of economic thought remain unexamined. They work in their time and place (and a rather long time and a huge place this is), but not, say, in 'Melanesia'. Let us call this time-worn anthropological approach a retrospective or oppositional (in the sense that it depends on oppositional and dichotomous models) stance.

In contrast, the essays in this book take 'the market' and 'the West' as their central problem. That is, while anthropological thinking on the market has generally taken a retrospective or oppositional stance closely related to the expressivists discussed by Kahn, most of the contributors to the book turn their critical energies toward modern, Western, capitalist situations – the self-understanding of Paul Hawken, California mail-order niche marketer in relation to the economic man envisioned by Adam

Smith; anarcho-capitalists as a strain of anti-state economic ideology in the United States; the growing infusion of cost–benefit analysis in government policy in the United States; or the complex social and interpersonal calculus followed by managers at industrial firms.

The only two essays that deal with non-Western situations, moreover, do not fit within the tradition of retrospective or oppositional critique. Smart looks at present-day China to explore a situation of state-controlled market development *without* the freedom of actors the Market model presumes. Kahn moves from twentieth-century US (or US–German–Australian) representations of Latin American processes to nineteenth-century German thought that was anti-Market, yet both modern and Western, and then turns to twentieth-century Islamic economic thought, especially in Malaysia, and its complex relationship with an earlier German expressivism. The essay undercuts a retrospective or oppositional critique, or at least any simple appropriation of anthropological 'others' as critical counterpoints to the capitalist West, by showing a whole series of social, intellectual and political mediations between the two; that is, a process by which the anthropological other has been constructed as a critical object within Western thought.

It might be useful to begin with this Western dimension of the critical traditions that have challenged the Market model, and the one-sided way in which they have been appropriated by anthropologists. Put simply, the retrospective oppositions used by scholars like Marx, Weber or Polanyi were designed to illuminate certain features of the capitalist West, to denaturalise the apparently natural and historicise the apparently universal. But the principal objects of their analyses remained Western and capitalist, and the authors devoted the bulk of their attention to a detailed analysis of the dynamics and inner workings of capitalist societies. Their retrospective exercises helped them to establish the inadequacy of any simple model of the market for understanding those societies and the importance of an analysis of the social structuring of economic relations. Having established these basic points, they turned toward the examination of the processes of social structuring themselves.

This is especially clear in the case of Marx, whose most detailed and accomplished analysis was of capitalist development in England and whose statements on pre-capitalist societies, while suggestive, were sketchy at best. His clear aim was that of denaturalising the central relations of capitalism, to show that the opposition between capital on one hand and free labour on another was the result of a particular history (in, for example, Marx 1964, 1977: Part 8).

Weber devoted rather more attention to the comparative historical examination of world civilisations, and when he turned to the analysis of the historical development of capitalism in Europe, in the *General Economic History*, the account of pre-capitalist European forms was richly detailed and based on deep historical knowledge. But he also had recourse, throughout his work, to a broad and vague concept of 'tradition', which he used in critical counterpoint to capitalism and the practice of instrumental rationality.

Polanyi, of course, was the author who was to have the most direct and extensive influence on anthropological thinking about the market, and the development of a retrospective critique of our 'obsolete market mentality'. Brief reflection on his work, and its selective appropriation by anthropologists, might help us situate and appreciate the contribution of this book. It is well known that Polanyi placed the self-regulating market in historical opposition to earlier modes of economic provisioning and transaction. Having criticised our market mentality and popular attempts to universalise relatively recent economic relations and processes, he set out to construct a body of concepts that might be adequate for non-market societies. He began:

> The outstanding discovery of recent historical and anthropological research is that man's economy, as a rule, is submerged in his social relationships. He does not act so as to safeguard his individual interest in the possession of material goods; he acts so as to safeguard his social standing, his social claims, his social assets. He values material goods only insofar as they serve this end. Neither the process of production nor that of distribution is linked to specific economic interests attached to the possession of goods; but every single step in that process is geared to a number of social interests which eventually ensure that the required step be taken. These interests will be very different in a small hunting or fishing community from those in a vast despotic society, but in either case the economic system will be run on non-economic motives (Polanyi 1968: 7).

Polanyi then concentrated on what he saw as the two great principles on which non-market economic activities might be socially organised, reciprocity and redistribution, each of which was in turn associated with distinct institutional patterns, symmetry and centricity.

This attempt to turn an oppositional critique into a set of positive concepts for the analysis of non-Western and non-capitalist societies, combined with Polanyi's active collaboration with anthropologists and historians at Columbia University on the analysis of non-capitalist forms of trade and marketing (Polanyi, Arensberg and Pearson 1957), provided inspiration and a conceptual repertoire for anthropological attempts to consider non-capitalist, and decidedly non-market, economics.

In doing so, however, the intellectual stakes were changed. Instead of using the retrospective opposition to establish a critical counterpoint and move toward a richer social analysis of the West, they used the oppositions, and concepts that could be derived from them, as if they could be unproblematically applied to a range of non-Western or non-capitalist societies. The problems with such exercises are now apparent: they perpetuate a historical and conceptual divide between West and East, or West and non-West, that homogenises both ends of the polar opposition, creating unrecognisable conceptual monstrosities; they ignore the centuries-long economic, social and political relations crossing that conceptual divide through which each of the postulated ends has been constituted; and they ignore the intellectual lines of critique, counter-critique and social construction that also cross the conceptual divide (Carrier 1994, 1995; Kahn 1993; O'Brien and Roseberry 1991; Roseberry 1988, 1989).

What has been less frequently noted or remembered by anthropologists, however, is that Polanyi, like Marx and Weber, focused his critical energies on the West itself. Having pointed toward earlier principles and institutional patterns, he devoted most of *The Great Transformation* (1957) to an examination of the history of the self-regulating market in the West, especially England. And one of his principal conclusions was that this market, central model and metaphor for capitalist society, had a fleeting existence in the nineteenth century, but that its birth was attended by an active state and that its own imperfections (see the Introduction for an important comment on 'imperfections') gave way to new forms of state regulation and social embeddedness by the end of the nineteenth century.

The central aim of these invocations of a non-market or non-capitalist past was not at all unlike the aim of this book: as Carrier expresses it in the Introduction, 'making this central concept [here, the Market] seem strange'. This is precisely what Weber attempted in *The Protestant Ethic* (1958) when he presented the practical, and apparently quite sensible, wisdom of Benjamin Franklin on the equation of time and money and suggested that for most people living in most times and places Franklin's advice would have been bizarre. It was also his aim as he played off the concept of 'freedom' in his delineation of the characteristics of capitalism. In the *General Economic History*, he defined capitalism as a system based on rational capital accounting and suggested that the development of rational accounting required not just a new 'spirit' but the creation of a whole institutional complex that would include 'the appropriation of all physical means of production – land, apparatus, machinery, tools, etc. as disposable property of autonomous private industrial enterprises'; 'freedom of the market'; 'rational technology, . . . which implies mechanization'; 'calculable law'; 'free labour', that is the presence of persons 'who are not only legally in the position, but are also economically compelled, to sell their labour on the market'; and 'the commercialization of economic life' (Weber 1981: 276–277).

It is worth considering the importance of such words as 'free', 'disposable' and 'calculable' in Weber's account and the (here implicit) contrast with situations in which fundamental elements of economic life are *un*free, *non*-disposable or *non*-calculable. Freedom, here, means that labour, goods and resources have been freed from interpersonal or communal claims and obligations, that land, for example, is not considered a collective resource that members of the collectivity may use, because of their membership in the group, to secure a livelihood; that goods are not considered shareable items within some circle of kin or community and saleable commodities outside that circle. For rational accounting to be effective, all such goods and resources had to be treated as subject to account, calculable in terms of quantifiable measures of benefit and cost.

Indeed, when Weber wrote of the spirit of capitalism he did not refer to the spirit of enterprise or the search for profits. He pointed out that such spirit and search have been common in many types of society, though they were generally applied outside some social and cultural boundary. That is, while the search for advantage and profit was not acceptable within the circle of kin and community, it was acceptable and expected outside the circle. In Weber's view, what distinguished the capitalist spirit was the taming of that search for profits and the dissolution of the boundary. That is, within the circle, social claims to shareable goods and resources were dissolved, and the exchange of goods and resources was subject to a single, quantifiable form of accounting. Outside the circle, the emphasis was no longer on the highest possible profit or, in other language, the quick buck or easy killing, but on the long-term profitability of the enterprise. This required that exchanges be recursive and that costs (and profits) be calculable and predictable (Weber 1981: 355–356). The rational spirit Weber described was not that of the maximiser but that of the instrumentalist, and thus the reduction of all considerations to a cold calculability, the ability to list them on a ledger sheet.

The freeing of land, labour, capital, and other goods and resources for this singular kind of accountability is the result of a complex social history. It requires a kind of social and economic flattening, one that purges land, labour or goods of social content. Theorists like Polanyi were referring to that history when they stressed the 'fictional' nature of commodities like land or labour. Much anthropological and historical work on capitalism has concentrated on the social and cultural processes, relations and problems associated with the development of capitalism in formerly non-capitalist milieux, the freeing of labour from land, of resources from the claims of community and kin, the blurring of boundaries between those inside and those outside a community where values other than those that can be registered on a balance sheet might be taken into account.

In order to appreciate the value of Weber's or Polanyi's discussion, one need not construct a rigid boundary between capitalism, in which economic relations are seen to be disembedded from social institutions, and non-capitalism, in which economic relations are seen to be socially embedded, or propose that the socially meaningful exchange of gifts prevails on one side of that divide while the cold world of commodities prevails on the other. As I have already suggested, such polar oppositions, and the attempt to analyse non-capitalist societies with concepts derived from them, are extremely problematic. But the attempt to render the Market strange, and the use of past and other forms of economic and social relation to do so, remains essential for any critical discussion of the meanings of the Market.

The multiple meanings of 'freedom', treated as an unproblematic moral value in Market discourse and a centre-piece of anti-state discourse of the anarcho-capitalists, can be usefully discussed through an exercise such as Weber's. Similarly, the complex relation between state formation and the development of the market is illuminated by such investigations. Weber saw the modern, rational state as crucial for creating the kind of free calculability that made capitalism possible, and Polanyi stressed the intimate role of the English state in the creation of the self-regulating market. Neither would have been surprised by, but both would have been interested in, the market development Smart describes in China.

Engagements with past and other societies are also useful in puncturing perversely naive statements such as Margaret Thatcher's claim, quoted in the Introduction: 'There is no such thing as society.' (I note in passing that it is a distressing pleasure to find such a coincidence between neo-conservative and post-modernist thought.) Consider, here, a comment E. P. Thompson made in his conclusion to a useful collection on family and inheritance in Europe from the Middle Ages through the early modern period. Noting that many of the contributions had discussed inheritance practices and strategies and the devolution of property as if 'property' were an unproblematic category, a 'thing' as it were, he suggested that the land and other goods that were passed from generation to generation in past times were encumbered by a whole range of social and interpersonal claims and obligations, and that these claims and obligations constituted a kind of grid:

> The farmer, confronted with a dozen scattered strips in different lands, and with prescribed stints in the commons, did not (one supposes) feel fiercely that he *owned* this land, that it was *his*. What he inherited was a place within the hierarchy of use-rights; the right to send his beasts, with a follower, down the lane-sides, to tether his horse in the sykes or on the baulks, the right to unloose his stock for Lammas grazing, or for the cottager the right to glean and to get away with some timber-foraging and casual grazing. All this made up into a delicate agrarian equilibrium. It depended not only upon the inherited right but also upon the inherited grid of customs and controls within which that right was exercised. This customary grid was as intrinsic to inheritance as the grid of banking and of the stock exchange is to the inheritance of money. Indeed one could say that the beneficiary inherited both his right *and* the grid within which it was effectual:

hence he must inherit a certain kind of social or communal psychology of ownership: the property not of his family but of his-family-within-the-commune (Thompson 1976: 337).

There is plenty in Thompson's argument that could lead simply to a romantic nostalgia, but notice the analogy he used when he introduced the idea of a grid: it was 'as intrinsic to inheritance as the grid of banking and of the stock exchange is to the inheritance of money'. He brought us back to the present, and to the market. And while the grid-like aspects he points to are aspects of the market, it requires little extension to contend that free, self-serving individuals operating in a world of market transactions also, *necessarily*, work within a grid 'of customs and controls', and that the grid structures, in important ways, both the individuals and their transactions.

One value of comparative and historical work on capitalism and the market is that it can sharpen our analytical focus on the present. This is a move anthropologists have less frequently made, but it is a central feature of this book. When Mr Smith meets Mr Hawken, we find, among other things, a social grid, or a range of social grids, in which entrepreneurs might act. When the owners of Hannah Anderson met the forces of market competition, the social grid with which they conducted business was challenged and the owners 'disciplined', as the language of the Market would have it. They, in turn, applied new (in Market terms, old) forms of discipline to their workers. Part of what makes this story something other than just another tale of market forces at work is the consideration of the grids in which such forces operate. And it draws our attention back to good Mr Hawken, who in one sense is operating against Market forces but in another sense has found a particular (and particularly lucrative and growing) market niche.

Considerations of freedom, both in the discourse of anarcho-capitalists and in the complex social and ideological load the word bears, or of the state are other areas where anthropologists have important roles to play. Smart's essay makes a necessary move by looking at the conjunction of market development with the action of a strong state in China, and there remains much to be done on the presence and role of the state within the grid of the market in, say, the United States.

Similarly, Chapman and Buckley's study of transaction costs in pharmaceutical and precision instrument firms draws our attention to a social and cultural grid within firms. In reading essays such as this, one is necessarily reminded of Polanyi's observation and its relevance for capitalist and Western situations: 'Man's economy, as a rule, is submerged in his social relationships. He does not act so as to safeguard his individual interest in the possession of material goods; he acts so as to safeguard his social standing, his social claims, his social assets.'

To the extent that anthropologists and historians have limited the application of this insight to pre-capitalist or non-market situations, they have accepted Market ideology for recognisably market situations at face value. They therefore have no critical intellectual tools with which to argue against the bizarre and frightening fantasies and politics of the anarcho-capitalists or policy-makers who wish to reduce social and political questions to a cost–benefit calculus.

The value of this book is that it does not respect the historical divide between a socially and culturally embedded non-market economy and a non-social, transaction-based market economy. By insisting that we examine the manifold ways in which market transactions are socially, culturally and politically embedded, the essays in this book clear new ground for critical anthropological work.

References

Carrier, James G. 1994. *Gifts and Commodities: Exchange and Western Capitalism since 1700*. London: Routledge.

Carrier, James G. (ed.) 1995. *Occidentalism: Images of the West*. Oxford: Clarendon Press.

Kahn, Joel 1993. *Constituting the Minangkabau: Peasants, Culture and Modernity in Colonial Indonesia*. Oxford: Berg.

Marx, Karl 1964 (1858). *Pre-Capitalist Economic Formations*. New York: International Publishers.

Marx, Karl 1977 (1867). *Capital*, Vol. 1. New York: Vintage Press.

O'Brien, Jay, and William Roseberry (eds) 1991. *Golden Ages, Dark Ages: Imagining the Past in Anthropology and History*. Berkeley: University of California Press.

Polanyi, Karl 1957. *The Great Transformation: The Political and Economic Origins of our Time*. Boston: Beacon Press.

Polanyi, Karl 1968. *Primitive, Archaic, and Modern Economies: Essays By Polanyi.* Ed. George Dalton. Boston: Beacon Press.

Polanyi, Karl, Conrad M. Arensberg and Harry W. Pearson (eds) 1957. *Trade and Market in the Early Empires.* Glencoe, Ill.: The Free Press.

Roseberry, William 1988. Domestic Modes, Domesticated Models. *Journal of Historical Sociology* 1: 423–430.

Roseberry, William 1989. The Construction of Natural Economy. Pp. 197–232 in W. Roseberry, *Anthropologies and Histories: Essays in Culture, History, and Political Economy.* New Brunswick, NJ: Rutgers University Press.

Thompson, E. P. 1976. The Grid of Inheritance: A Comment. Pp. 328–360 in Jack Goody, Joan Thirsk and E. P. Thompson (eds), *Family and Inheritance: Rural Society in Western Europe 1200–1800.* Cambridge: Cambridge University Press.

Weber, Max 1958. *The Protestant Ethic and the Spirit of Capitalism.* New York: Charles Scribner's Sons.

Weber, Max 1981. *General Economic History.* New Brunswick, NJ: Transaction Books.

Contributors

Susan Love Brown is assistant professor of anthropology at Florida Atlantic University in Boca Raton. She received her doctorate from the University of California, San Diego. Her areas of interest are political and psychological anthropology, with areal interests in the Caribbean and the United States. She is currently working on the baby-boom generation and American culture.

Peter J. Buckley is Professor of International Business, Department of Business and Economic Studies, University of Leeds, where he is director of the Centre for International Business. He has published extensively on multinational enterprises and international business, including *Foreign Direct Investment and Multinational Enterprises* (London, Macmillan, 1995), and two books written with Mark Casson, *The Future of the Multinational Enterprise* (London, Macmillan, 1976) and *The Economic Theory of the Multinational Enterprise* (London, Macmillan, 1985). He has just completed, with Malcolm Chapman, an ESRC-funded research project, 'The Management of Cooperative Strategies'.

James G. Carrier teaches anthropology at the University of Durham. He has done fieldwork in Papua New Guinea and historical research on exchange and circulation in Western societies. His most recent books are *Gifts and Commodities: Exchange and Western Capitalism since 1700* (London, Routledge, 1994) and *Occidentalism: Images of the West* (Oxford, Clarendon Press, 1995).

Malcolm Chapman teaches international business in the Centre for International Business, University of Leeds. Trained as an anthropologist, he worked closely with the late Edwin Ardener (a volume of whose papers he edited after Ardener's death in 1987). His fieldwork was in Scotland and Brittany, and this gave rise to various publications, including *The Gaelic Vision in Scottish Culture*

(London, Croom Helm, 1978), and *The Celts – the Construction of a Myth* London: (Macmillan, 1992). He subsequently took an MBA from the University of Bradford, and since 1989 he has been working to bring social anthropology into various aspects of business and management studies.

Joel S. Kahn is Professor in the School of Sociology and Anthropology at La Trobe University in Melbourne. He has taught previously at University College London and Monash University, and carried out fieldwork in Indonesia and Malaysia. His most recent books are *Constituting the Minangkabau: Peasants, Culture and Modernity in Colonial Indonesia* (Oxford, Berg, 1993) and *Culture, Multiculture, Postculture* (London, Sage, 1995).

Carol A. MacLennan is an associate professor of anthropology at Michigan Technological University. She worked for six years in fuel economy and auto safety research for the US Department of Transportation. She has published articles on automotive regulation and democratic participation, and co-authored, with Mark Levine and others, *The State and Democracy: Revitalizing America's Government* (New York, Routledge, 1988).

William Roseberry is Professor of Anthropology in the Graduate Faculty of the New School for Social Research in New York. He is the author of *Coffee and Capitalism in the Venezuelan Andes* (Austin, Texas, 1983) and *Anthropologies and Histories* (New Brunswick, Rutgers, 1989), and co-editor of *Golden Ages, Dark Ages: Imagining the Past in Anthropology and History* (Los Angeles, California, 1991) and *Coffee, Society, and Power in Latin America* (Baltimore, Johns Hopkins, 1995).

Alan Smart is an associate professor of anthropology at the University of Calgary and has been conducting field research in Hong Kong and China since 1982. He is the author of *Making Room: Squatter Clearance in Hong Kong* (Hong Kong: Centre of Asian Studies, 1992) and numerous articles in journals such as *Cultural Anthropology, Critique of Anthropology, International Journal of Urban and Regional Research* and *International Journal of the Sociology of Law*.

Index

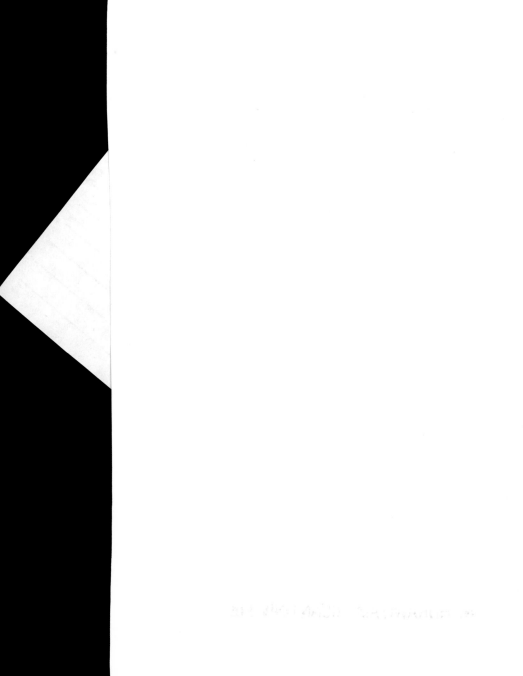

DEMCO, INC. 38-2931